CLASSIC *f*M

JOHN SUCHET

TCHAIKOVSKY

THE MAN REVEALED

First published 2018 by
Elliott and Thompson Limited
27 John Street, London WC1N 2BX
www.eandtbooks.com

ISBN: 978-1-78396-383-6

9 8 7 6 5 4 3 2 1

A catalogue record for this book is available from the British Library.

Designed by James Collins

Printed and bound in Italy by Printer Trento

MIX
Paper from
responsible sources
FSC® C015829

For my Dad, for making me learn the piano at the age of nine.

For my Mum, who let me buy a Tchaikovsky
biography at the age of seventeen.

For my darling wife Nula, who was with me every step of the way.

'If I am in a normal state of mind, I can say that I am composing
every minute of the day, whatever the circumstances. Sometimes I
observe with curiosity that unbroken labour which . . . goes on in
that region of my head which is given over to music. Sometimes
this is some preparatory work . . . while on another occasion a
completely new independent musical idea appears and I try to retain
it in my memory. Whence all this comes is an impenetrable secret.'[1]

Tchaikovsky

CONTENTS

TCHAIKOVSKY FAMILY TREE

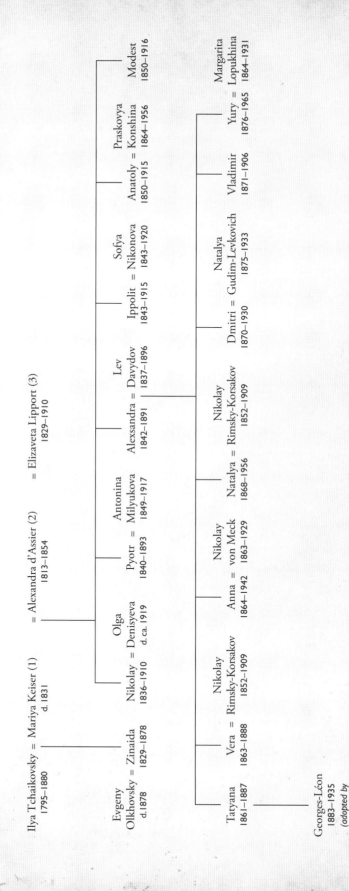

AUTHOR'S NOTE

Tchaikovsky's sexual proclivities can make for uncomfortable reading in today's world. Here I am not referring to his homosexuality, which was officially proscribed in his day and is a taboo subject in Russia even now. There is, however, no denying his predilection for youth. We know from his letters his sexual preference was for teenage boys before and after puberty. He describes the scene at a friend's country estate as a 'pederastic bordello'.

Tchaikovsky believed that his behaviour was morally wrong and struggled with guilt throughout his life. Our knowledge of his actions is incomplete, hampered by censorship, both unofficial by his brother and then official during the Soviet era. He would, we can be sure, be mortified by the accounts of his sexual conduct that have appeared – and will certainly continue to appear – in biographies and biopics.

The question is whether any of this needs to be discussed when examining Tchaikovsky's accomplishments as a composer. I would answer emphatically that it does. My aim, in my series of composer biographies, is to reach the human being behind the music, to present 'the man revealed'. I would go further: it is impossible to separate the man from his music. In Tchaikovsky's case, a single example – the love theme in the Fantasy Overture: *Romeo and Juliet* – will suffice. One might as well try to separate Beethoven's deafness from his late quartets.

While a full account of what we know about Tchaikovsky's life will inevitably include details that might be disturbing, I believe it is important to include them where they help to create as clear a picture as possible of one of our greatest composers.

PROLOGUE

In the early hours of 10 October 1893,[*] Pyotr Ilyich Tchaikovsky arrived in St Petersburg on the train from Moscow. He was met at the station by his brother Modest and nephew Vladimir Davydov, known as 'Bob'.

Tchaikovsky was fifty-three years of age, but he looked seventy. His face was lined and there were bags under his eyes. His white hair was thinning and his teeth were yellow.[1] His character remained youthful, however. Friends frequently remarked on how full of high spirits he was, easily moved to laughter, his eyes sparkling with humour.

The reason for the trip to St Petersburg was for the premiere of his new work, the Sixth Symphony, the *Pathétique*, which, as was now customary with premieres of his orchestral works, the composer was to conduct himself. He remained cheerful, despite a lack of enthusiasm at rehearsals from the orchestra – a disappointment for which there was no obvious reason.

As usual when visiting St Petersburg, Tchaikovsky stayed at Modest's top-floor apartment, on the corner of Malaya Morskaya and Gorokhovaya Street. There he would rise early, before his brother, sit at the dining table and make adjustments to the score of the symphony. At the same time he was revising an opera he had written twenty years earlier, *Oprichnik*, in readiness for a new production.

Evenings were given over to entertainment. There were visits to the theatre, followed by convivial meals at either the Grand Hotel or the Hôtel de France, at which copious amounts of alcohol were consumed. Tchaikovsky, it appears, was the life and soul of the party, always ready with a seemingly endless supply of jokes and stories.

Left

Pyotr Ilyich Tchaikovsky.

---

[*] Dates are given in the Julian calendar, which lagged twelve days behind the Western Gregorian calendar, and was used in Russia until 1918.

Life in St Petersburg, the elegant Russian capital and seat of the Romanov tsar, continued as it always had for the well-off and the nobility, and for many artists, writers and musicians. They were untroubled by the cholera epidemic decimating the lower classes.

For the privileged minority there were two simple rules for steering clear of the epidemic: avoid intimate physical contact with anyone infected with cholera, and drink only boiled water. Cholera was a fact of life in this unhygienic city surrounded by mosquito-ridden marshland at the mouth of the River Neva.

It was said that the city was built on the bones of tens of thousands of peasants forced into construction work. Foetid marshes, dank alleys and extremes of weather provided fertile ground for disease. St Petersburg's climate was described as eight months of severe winter followed by four months of unbearable heat.

Modest would later claim credit for suggesting the subtitle for his brother's new symphony – *Pathétique* – which he said Pyotr Ilyich had adopted with enthusiasm. The premiere took place on 16 October, a Saturday. It is difficult to gauge exactly how the symphony was received. There was, by all accounts, huge interest ahead of the event, and a packed hall to hear the new work by Russia's most acclaimed and most popular composer.

Tchaikovsky's entrance was greeted rapturously, with a prolonged standing ovation. That was not to be repeated, however, at the end of the performance. Unusually for Tchaikovsky, in fact uniquely in his symphonic output, the final bars of the symphony are decidedly downbeat. 'Melancholy' and 'mournful' are words that have been used to describe it.

Composers of the past, none more so than Beethoven, knew how to inspire applause at the end of a symphony. Tchaikovsky, in his Fourth and Fifth Symphonies in particular, showed he too knew what was needed. Yet he did not follow convention for the Sixth. The final movement, with low notes in the minor key on cellos and bassoons, fades away to nothing.

No doubt expecting the usual final flourish, the audience reacted with bewilderment. This was not the Tchaikovsky they knew. The music critics were similarly lukewarm. There was polite respect, certainly, but no ecstatic praise.

Initially disappointed, Tchaikovsky did not remain depressed for long. He knew he needed to make one or two small adjustments to the score, and he had high hopes for the second performance, which he was due to conduct in Moscow three weeks later.

He also had a tour of Europe planned for the following spring, and was considering invitations from a number of other European cities.

Four days after the premiere, on Wednesday, 20 October, Tchaikovsky met with a lawyer to sign the new contract for the revival of *Oprichnik*.

Negotiations had gone better than he could have hoped, with all his demands regarding royalties and rights being accepted.

He was therefore in a particularly good frame of mind that evening when he attended a performance of *The Ardent Heart*, a play by Alexander Ostrovsky at the Alexandrinsky Theatre. One of his companions, a twenty-year-old actor by the name of Yuri Yuriev, described him as being 'in good health and cheerful mood'. In the interval he went backstage to chat 'lightheartedly'[2] with the leading actor, Konstantin Varlamov, in his dressing room.

They discussed spiritualism, which was currently in vogue in Russia. Both dismissed it with mocking laughter. Tchaikovsky described it as a 'snub-nosed horror' that would not come to snatch them off just yet. 'I feel I shall live a long time,' he said.[3]

After the theatre, he strolled along the city's main avenue, the Nevsky Prospekt, with a group of young male friends and relatives. Modest said he would catch up with them a little later. On the spur of the moment Tchaikovsky suggested dinner at one of his favourite restaurants, Leiner's.

There, according to Tchaikovsky's youngest nephew, Yuri Davydov, just seventeen at the time, his uncle summoned a waiter and asked him to bring a glass of water. The waiter returned after a couple of minutes to say that there was no boiled water.

According to Yuri, Tchaikovsky reacted impatiently and told the waiter to bring him 'some unboiled water. Cold.'[4] Yuri and the others remonstrated with him, reminding him of the dangers of cholera. Tchaikovsky waved off their protests as so much superstition.

The waiter left to fetch the water, at which point Modest arrived with the actor Yuri Yuriev, Modest congratulating himself on having presumed this was where he would find them. 'Where else would we be?' asked his brother, laughing.[5]

The waiter returned with a glass of water on a tray. When Modest found out that it was unboiled, he immediately became angry and shouted: 'I strictly forbid you to drink unboiled water!'

Tchaikovsky leapt to his feet. Modest tried to stop him but Tchaikovsky pushed his brother out of the way and drank the water in a single draught.[6]

This was Yuri's version of what happened. Modest later gave his own account, which does not refer to unboiled water – at least not to it being drunk in the restaurant. His account initially accords with his nephew's, with him joining the party in Leiner's an hour later.

He says he was told Tchaikovsky had eaten macaroni, washed down, as usual, with white wine and soda water. No mention of an incident involving unboiled water. They all left the restaurant at around two in the morning. 'Peter Ilich was perfectly well and serene,' according to his brother.[7]

Modest then takes up the story as only he could know it, since his brother was staying in his apartment. The following morning, Thursday, 21 October, when he saw that Tchaikovsky was not at his usual place at the dining table, Modest went to check on him. He found him still in bed, complaining of not feeling well.

Tchaikovsky told him he had had a bad night with an upset stomach. Despite this, according to Modest, he got himself dressed, and at around 11:00 a.m. went out to go and see Eduard Nápravník, chief conductor of the Mariinsky Theatre. But half an hour later he returned, still feeling unwell.

Modest suggested calling for a doctor, but Tchaikovsky expressly forbade it. Modest says he was not overly concerned, since his brother frequently complained about poor digestion and it had never turned out to be serious. Tchaikovsky resorted to his habitual remedy of castor oil.

At lunch the pair were joined by a young relative, Sanya Litke. Tchaikovsky did not eat, says Modest, but while talking he poured out a glass of water and drank it down in a single gulp.

Modest was alarmed by his brother's imprudence, since the water had not been boiled. Tchaikovsky waved away his concern, saying he was not in the least bit worried about contracting cholera.

As the day progressed Tchaikovsky's condition worsened, and Modest called a doctor. The doctor diagnosed cholera. The following day Tchaikovsky seemed to rally, but the improvement did not last.

Kidney failure set in, and there was nothing the doctors – by now there were three in attendance – could do. On the morning of Monday, 25 October, less than five days after the dinner at Leiner's and four after supposedly drinking the water at his brother's, Tchaikovsky died.

In his biography of his brother, Modest wrote: 'At the last moment an indescribable look of clear recognition lit up his face – a gleam which only died away with his last breath.'[8]

1

PYOTR, THE FLEDGLING SEAGULL

In late December 1892, Pyotr Ilyich Tchaikovsky – the most famous living composer in the world, now fifty-two years of age but with the nervousness and apprehension of a small boy – stood outside a humble cottage on rue Clémenceau in the small town of Montbéliard in eastern France, close to the border with Switzerland.

Finally he plucked up the courage to knock. The door was opened by a woman of seventy. Tchaikovsky braced himself for tears, hugs and emotion. It did not happen.

> [She] made no scenes on my arrival, she did not weep, or marvel at the change in me – it was simply as though we had parted only a year ago.[1]

In fact it had been forty-four years ago. Tchaikovsky had not seen Fanny Dürbach, the family's French governess who had looked after Pyotr and his siblings as children, for almost half a century.

The emotional restraint did not last long. Fanny produced letters from many years before, written to her not only by Tchaikovsky and his brother Modest, but also 'wonderfully sweet letters from Mama'. Perhaps most poignant of all for Tchaikovsky, Fanny showed him exercise books he had himself written as a small child. The memories came flooding back for both of them:

I cannot describe the delectable, magical feeling I experienced as I listened to these tales and read all these letters and exercise books. The past in all its detail arose so clearly in my memory that it seemed I was breathing the air of our [childhood] home. I was listening to the voice of Mama . . . At times I was so carried back into that distant past that it became somehow awesome but at the same time sweet – and all the while both of us were holding back the tears.[2]

Tchaikovsky had visited Fanny Dürbach reluctantly, only after she had pleaded with him in several letters to pay her a visit. In a letter to Modest, he confessed he had no desire to see her, expecting her to have aged beyond recognition, even become enfeebled, a shadow of the woman who meant so much to him. He even feared – in an irrationally morbid thought – that on seeing her he would wish her dead. Perhaps he expressed that thought in the joy of having found her rational, full of memories, as kind-hearted as he remembered her, and as willing to indulge in nostalgia as he was himself.

A visit he intended to last no more than a matter of hours extended across two days. On the first day he stayed from three in the afternoon until eight in the evening, and he spent the whole of the following day with her. Without a doubt, the least enjoyable part of the visit for Tchaikovsky was when Fanny insisted on taking him to meet two close friends and a relative, no doubt to show him off to them.

In a touching moment, Tchaikovsky wrote to his brother that at the end of the second day Fanny insisted on sending him back to his hotel for dinner, saying it would embarrass her and her sister, with whom she lived, to try to feed him.

And perhaps only someone who had known the great composer as a child would have the nerve to tell him that although she was proud of his musical achievements, she rather wished he had become a poet instead, for he surely would have become another Pushkin.

At the end of the second day, all nervousness gone, the two parted with kisses. Fanny implored Tchaikovsky to continue writing letters to her, and made him promise he would visit her again in Montbéliard.

The return visit was not to be. Ten months later he was dead.

Almost half a century earlier, as autumn turned to winter in 1844, a carriage drew up outside a large house set among trees in the remote settlement of Votkinsk, which lay around six hundred miles east of Moscow in the western foothills of the Ural mountains.[*]

Three people emerged, with an abundance of suitcases and bags. In charge and directing the others was Alexandra Tchaikovskaya, thirty-one years of age. She was busy checking that her eldest son, Nikolay, then aged eight, had not forgotten anything. The third person was a twenty-two-year-old Frenchwoman she had employed as governess to Nikolay, Fanny Dürbach.

---

[*] The settlement of Votkinsk was not officially granted town status until as recently as 1935 (see p. 246). In the 1970s, during the Cold War, it was the site of the production of the Soviet Union's long-range ballistic missile, the SS-20, and was a 'closed' city.

The journey from St Petersburg, where Alexandra had been visiting relatives and had met and employed Fanny, had taken three weeks – plenty of time, Fanny recalled much later, for her to get to know her employer and the boy who was to be entrusted to her care.

She liked what she saw. Mrs Tchaikovskaya was kind and courteous to her, and Fanny was immediately struck not just by Nikolay's good manners, but by how extraordinarily handsome he was. It boded well, though she confessed to a degree of apprehension. She had yet to meet the head of the family, Ilya Tchaikovsky, and there were two younger children as well. She was also worried about having to adapt to an entirely new way of life hundreds of miles away from home.

The closer she came to Votkinsk, the more her uneasiness grew. But in her own words, 'when we at length arrived at the house, one moment sufficed to show that all my fears were groundless'.[3]

The welcome almost literally knocked Fanny off her feet. So many people rushed out to greet them, she was not sure who were members of the family and who were servants. And if she thought that as a stranger she would be welcomed any less than the mistress of the house and her son, she need not have worried.

There was embracing all round, and one embrace – from the most unexpected quarter – so surprised Fanny that she recalled it in detail more than half a century later: 'The head of the family kissed me without ceremony, as though I had been his daughter.'[4] She felt as if she too had returned home.

Fanny, all her misgivings put to rest, began work the next morning. She was employed to teach not just Nikolay, known as Kolya, but also his young cousin Lidiya. She soon found, though, that she had a third willing pupil on her hands.

Kolya's four-year-old brother Pyotr took a liking to Fanny Dürbach from the moment he set eyes on her. When he discovered that she was to teach Kolya and Lidiya, he pleaded with his mother to be allowed to join the classes. At first Alexandra tried to keep him away, but such was his enthusiasm that Fanny said she was perfectly happy to let him join his elder brother and cousin.

With the natural caveat that Fanny's recollections were written down so many decades later (in fact in the year following Pyotr Tchaikovsky's death, by which time he was the most famous composer in Europe), her memories are still invaluable, the sole source of our knowledge of the composer's earliest years.

Fanny describes how keen Pyotr was to learn – so keen and so naturally talented that he quickly overtook both Kolya and Lidiya. At the age of six, according to Fanny, he could already read French and German fluently.

Above

Tchaikovsky's birthplace
in Votkinsk.

Clearly with a certain amount of hindsight she found 'something original and uncommon' in him, and noted that he possessed 'an indefinable charm [which he exercised] on everyone who came in contact with him'.[5]

Fanny was not entirely uncritical though, which lends credence to her otherwise suspiciously positive memories. A clever young boy Pyotr might have been, but in some ways he suffered by comparison with his elder brother, whose good looks and outgoing personality had clearly earned Fanny's approval:

> *In looks [Pyotr] did not compare favourably with [Nikolay], and was never so clean and tidy. His clothes were always in disorder. Either he had stained them in his absent-mindedness, or buttons were missing, or his hair was only half-brushed, so that by the side of his spruce and impeccable brother he did not show to advantage at first sight.*[6]

But any criticism is tempered by rose-tinted memory:

> *. . . when the charm of his mind, and still more of his heart, had time to work, it was impossible not to prefer him to the other children. This sympathetic charm, this gift of winning all hearts, Tchaikovsky retained to the last days of his life.*[7]

Since Fanny had just that one single meeting with Pyotr after a gap of nearly fifty years, her description of the laudable qualities he retained 'to the last days of his life' is clearly an exaggeration, but surely she can be allowed that.

Fanny's recollections are particularly useful when it comes to anecdotal accounts of young Pyotr's behaviour. He was, she recalled, sensitive in the extreme, far more so than the other children. The slightest criticism, or reproof, would hurt him deeply. He was 'brittle as porcelain', 'a child of glass'.[8] On one occasion, after the mildest of criticisms, he went up to his room and refused to re-emerge for several hours.

He was also very quick-witted. An anecdote that stayed with Fanny all her life, and that one can imagine her retelling with delight, concerned the extreme love the young Pyotr developed for Mother Russia, to the detriment of the rest of Europe.

She recounted how, on one occasion, during a break between lessons, he was poring over an atlas, turning the pages. He came to a map of Europe. He immediately bent down and covered the vast expanse of Russia with kisses. He then spat on all the other countries.

Fanny was shocked:

When I told him he ought to be ashamed of such behaviour, that it was wicked to hate his fellow-men who said the same 'Our Father' as himself, only because they were not Russians, and . . . he was spitting upon his own Fanny, who was a Frenchwoman, he replied at once: 'There is no need to scold me; didn't you see me cover France with my hand first?'[9] *

We know from this little story that the future composer's love for his home country began early, and it was a passion that he would retain for the whole of his life. In middle age he wrote:

I have never come across anyone more in love with Mother Russia than I . . . I love passionately Russian people, the Russian language, the Russian way of thinking, the beauty of Russian faces, Russian customs . . . 'the sacred legends of the dim and distant past' . . . I love even these.[10]

There was, it seems, music in the house in Votkinsk. Fanny recalls Mrs Tchaikovskaya tinkling on the piano for her children to dance to; she

---

* A telling anecdote, when one considers that the most lastingly popular piece of music Tchaikovsky would ever write concerns those two particular countries – to the detriment of one and the glory of the other.

would also sing along. Nothing serious though, according to Fanny, and no one else in the household was any more capable musically.

Things improved when Mr Tchaikovsky returned from a trip to St Petersburg with an orchestrion, a barrel-organ-like instrument that could simulate the sounds of an orchestra. This, Fanny said, transformed Pyotr's life.

The orchestrion was, it seems, highly sophisticated. Its music rolls included arias from the great Italian operas. In this way the young boy first became acquainted with the music of Bellini and Donizetti, and with the composer he would revere above all others for his entire life, Wolfgang Amadeus Mozart.

All the major arias from Mozart's opera *Don Giovanni* were there. This music, and above all Zerlina's aria 'Vedrai, carino', awoke in Pyotr 'a beatific rapture'.[11] Soon, to the surprise and delight of his parents, and of Fanny herself, he was able to recreate on the piano what he had heard on the orchestrion.

Surprise and delight at least initially, but when this musical activity began to get in the way of more 'serious' pursuits, Pyotr's father put his foot down. Often, his brother Modest wrote, Pyotr had to be forcibly dragged away from the piano. He would then, instead, go to the window and drum the rhythm on the pane with his fingers. On one occasion he was so carried away that he broke the glass and cut his hand badly.[12]

But Pyotr's father was not blind – or deaf. Although he allegedly had little musical talent himself, he was astute enough to realise that his youngest son possessed certain unusual qualities. Maybe they should be fostered. And so he engaged a piano teacher, one Mariya Palchikova, to give Pyotr piano lessons.

It was a start, no more than that, but given what was to follow, Palchikova earned her place – albeit a small one – in musical history.* Modest describes her in his memoirs as having only a limited amount of musical knowledge. Within a short time Pyotr could read at sight as easily as she could. Rather witheringly Modest wrote that, later in life, his brother could not remember a single piece she had taught him. Tchaikovsky remained fond of her, though. When she wrote to him thirty-five years later, revealing her financial difficulties, he arranged for money to be sent to this woman, to whom 'I am very, very indebted'.[13]

One story Fanny recounted to Modest seems to be at odds with her general tone when describing the child she knew. She noticed that invariably he became overwrought and distressed after spending any time at the piano. This was the case even when it was not Pyotr himself who was playing the instrument.

One evening the Tchaikovsky family, including the children, were giving a musical soirée. At first Pyotr was enraptured with the music, but he quickly became very tired and went off to bed. After a little while Fanny went upstairs to check that he was all right. He was sitting bolt upright in bed with 'bright, feverish eyes, and crying to himself'. When she tried to find out what was wrong, he sobbed and pointed to his head, saying, 'Oh, this music, this music! Save me from it! It is here, here, and will not give me any peace.'[14]

---

* In a similar but much more important way, Christian Gottlob Neefe has earned his place as the first competent teacher of young Ludwig van Beethoven.

It seems an unlikely reaction from a boy who was already besotted with music. Possibly it is coloured by the fact that Fanny herself had no interest in music and, by her own account, frequently tried to limit the amount of time he spent at the piano. She also made it clear to Pyotr – as she did to Modest all those years later, in correspondence with him following his brother's visit – that her ambition for Pyotr was that he should become a poet. Her nickname for him was 'Little Pushkin'.

Despite Fanny's initial reluctance, Pyotr's competence at the piano eventually left her in no doubt as to where his natural talents lay. A Polish officer who was a friend of the Tchaikovsky family would come to the house and play a selection of Chopin's mazurkas on the piano. Pyotr began to look forward to these visits with a passion, to the extent that he learned two Chopin mazurkas himself and played them for the Polish officer, who was so impressed that he kissed the boy. 'I never saw Pierre [Pyotr] so radiantly happy as that day,' Fanny recalled.[15]

By and large Pyotr was a happy child. He adored his governess, enjoyed being taught by her, and was beginning to indulge his love of music. Life in the Tchaikovsky household was comfortable. Ilya had a responsible position as manager of the local ironworks, and was able to provide for his growing family. His income was sufficient for him to employ staff in the house, in addition to a governess.

In fact Ilya's job was more than responsible; it was prestigious. It brought with it the largest house in the settlement, giving him authority and respect. When a young Alexander Romanov toured the vast country in 1837, including a visit to the Urals and Votkinsk, it was in the Tchaikovsky household that he stayed. Pyotr, born three years after this event, must have heard his father boasting on many an occasion how the future tsar had been his house guest.[*]

As well as his elder brother Nikolay, two years older than him, Pyotr had a sister, Alexandra, almost two years younger, named for her mother and known as Sasha, and another brother, Ippolit, known as Polya, three years younger than him. Twins Anatoly and Modest would follow, ten years his junior. There was also a much older girl, Zinaida, daughter of Ilya's first wife, who was approaching the end of her teenage years.

Zinaida's mother had died when she was an infant. Within two years Ilya had married again. His bride this time was a Russian woman of French descent. Her father's ancestors had fled to Russia a century and

---

[*] Alexander II, known as Alexander the Liberator for his emancipation of the serfs, was assassinated in 1881.

a half earlier, after the repeal of the Edict of Nantes, which revoked Huguenot rights and made Protestantism illegal. Alexandra Tchaikovskaya's maiden name was d'Assier.

Alexandra's father had been born in Russia but was a member of the French nobility and retained the title of marquis. His daughter inherited his elegance and cultured taste. Music had played a central part in her life as a child,[*] and she was talented enough to play the piano and sing as an adult, even if she herself referred to it as little better than tinkling.[16] In remote Votkinsk this was something of a rarity, and the Tchaikovsky house was one of the few in the town – quite possibly the only one – to have musical soirées of the kind that had sent young Pyotr to bed early with his head hurting.

In descriptions of Alexandra, which are always complimentary, the one word that seems conspicuous by its absence is 'beautiful'. 'Those who knew [our] mother describe her as tall and distinguished-looking,' writes Modest, 'not precisely handsome, but with wonderfully expressive eyes. All agreed that there was something particularly attractive in her appearance.'[17]

Modest goes out of his way to mention in his memoirs that Pyotr was entranced by their mother's hands, 'beautiful hands, although by no means small'. He quotes his brother as saying later in life, 'Such hands do not exist nowadays, and never will again.'[18] It is a slightly odd feature to notice, unless you happen to be a pianist yourself.

If we are to believe Modest, Alexandra Tchaikovskaya was a rather unemotional woman, absorbed in her own affairs. He describes her as sparing in shows of affection: 'She was very kind, but her kindness, in comparison with her husband's constant affability toward all and sundry, was austere, and was displayed more in actions than in words.'[19]

If that is true, it did not prevent her second son from openly displaying his affection for her. Pyotr was utterly devoted to his mother, a lifelong devotion that only increased after her early death. We have Modest's word for this, as well as Pyotr's.

Modest recounts how, after their mother returned from a lengthy trip to St Petersburg, Pyotr experienced 'heavenly bliss . . . as he pressed himself against his mother's breast after the three or four months of separation'. After her death, again according to Modest, 'for a very, very long time, even as an adult, [Pyotr] could not speak about his mother without tears, to the point where those around him would avoid bringing her up in conversation.'[20]

---

[*] Her sister went on to become an opera singer of some renown.

10 TCHAIKOVSKY: THE MAN REVEALED

In adult life, every year on 13 June, Pyotr Tchaikovsky noted the anniversary of his mother's death in his diary, often with an added encomium. On the twenty-third anniversary, he wrote:

> *Despite the triumphal strength of my convictions [that there is no eternal life], I can never reconcile myself to the thought that my mother, whom I loved so much, and who was such a wonderful person, may have disappeared for ever, and that I shall never again have the chance to tell her that, even after twenty-three years, I still love her.*[21]

Two years after that he wrote:

> *On this day exactly twenty-five years ago my mother died. I remember every moment of that terrible day as though it was yesterday.*[22]

Even after thirty-two years, in went the entry into his diary:

Anniversary of mother's death.[23]

Ilya Tchaikovsky's family was of Ukrainian origin. The family name was rare, though not unheard of. From his time to ours, it has been assumed by Russians and foreigners alike that the name derives from the Russian *chai*, meaning 'tea'.

In fact the origin is rather more colourful. An ancestor of Ilya had the knack of imitating birdcalls, especially that of the seagull. The Russian word for 'seagull' is *chaika*. The best-loved composer Russia ever produced, the most naturally gifted melodist in all music, is named for the squawking seagull!*

Although Ilya Tchaikovsky was by all accounts a deeply emotional man, given to romantic outbursts and passionate emotions – witness his extravagant greeting of Fanny Dürbach – it seems (at least according to Modest) that Pyotr was never able to form a close relationship with him.

This might have been due to the fact that although he was keen on theatre, Ilya had little more than a passing interest in music – which makes his purchase of the orchestrion all the more commendable. He was not entirely devoid of musical appreciation, though. On occasion he would invite musical friends to play at the house, sometimes joining them on the flute, which he had learned as a youngster although he had not attained a particularly high standard.

Another contributory factor might have been the fact that Ilya was eighteen years older than his wife. He had been forty-five when his second son was born, well into middle age. Perhaps this led to a certain remoteness with Pyotr, a distance he was never able to bridge.

For the moment this was not of concern to the young Pyotr. As he reached his eighth year, he was living a comfortable existence in Votkinsk. He enjoyed lessons with Fanny and, as the family grew and his younger siblings required more attention, he was able to give more and more time to his increasing interest in music.

The idyll, however, was about to come to an abrupt end. Pyotr Tchaikovsky's childhood would soon be over.

---

* These days there are cafés in Moscow and St Petersburg named 'Chai-Koffee-sky', or variations on it, in a mistaken attempt at a double pun.

2

UPHEAVALS
AND LOSS

At the tender age of eight, Pyotr Tchaikovsky became a pupil at the local school alongside his elder brother Nikolay. He was a quick learner and displayed a naturally developing aptitude for music. An emotional child, he was about to experience the first major upheaval in his previously happy childhood. It is not an exaggeration to say he never really got over it.

His father, Ilya Tchaikovsky, had his sights set on higher things than managing a local ironworks, even if that appointment earned him prestige and a comfortable living for himself and his family. Ilya was tiring of the provincial life. He was therefore quick to accept what promised to be a very attractive offer of private employment back in Moscow.

He was in no doubt that the future for him and his family lay in that city. He resigned his post in Votkinsk, renouncing the prestigious rank of major-general that came with it, and prepared the family for the move to Moscow.

This involved taking Nikolay and Pyotr out of the school where they were comfortably settled. Far more of a wrench was their governess, with whom they had formed such a close bond, deciding not to accompany the Tchaikovskys. Instead she would remain in Votkinsk and seek work with another family.

The move took some months to organise. Conscious of Pyotr's emotional fragility and wishing to spare him distress, his parents made the decision – devastating in its effect on the boy – to sneak Fanny out of the house on the day of the move, without any farewells. It was a dreadful miscalculation, resulting in a loss Pyotr was to feel for the rest of his life.

The Tchaikovsky family left Votkinsk in September 1848 and made the six-hundred-mile journey west to Moscow, and a new life. It went wrong from the start. In the intervening months between resigning his post and leaving Votkinsk, Ilya had confided his plans to a friend, only to find that the friend had arrived in Moscow before him and secured the job for himself.

The family was devastated. For Pyotr events had become traumatic. On 30 October he wrote to Fanny back in Votkinsk:

> *We have been in Moscow more than three weeks now, and every day all the members of our family think of you; we are so sad . . . I mustn't recall that life in Votkinsk. I want very much to cry when I think of it.*[1]

The stay in Moscow could not have been more unhappy. Ilya was unable to find work, and there was a cholera epidemic in the city. He told his wife to remain in Moscow with the children while he left for St Petersburg, where he was sure he would secure employment.

Alexandra was ill-equipped to cope on her own with four young children, ranging in age from twelve to five. Zinaida, her stepdaughter, moved in to help, but at the age of nineteen and with no experience of looking after children, she was not able to alleviate much of the burden. Life for the Tchaikovsky family was difficult and uncertain.

Modest would later write in his memoirs that at exactly the moment his brother Pyotr required loving and careful attention, with his father absent and his mother too preoccupied and anxious about the future of the family to spare him much time, he was instead completely neglected.

He even suggests that while Zinaida was kind and loving to the other children, she was much less so to Pyotr, singling him out for harsh treatment. Since Modest cannot have known this at first hand, it presumably must have come from Pyotr himself, many years later, suggesting that the hurt had stayed with him. Whether the harsh treatment was genuine or imagined, we have no way of knowing.

The family stayed in Moscow for less than a month, and it can have come only with huge relief when Ilya told them to leave immediately and come up to St Petersburg, even if it meant more disruption. St Petersburg was at least familiar. It was Alexandra's home city; Ilya knew it intimately, and the family had relatives and friends there. Ilya assured his wife and children they could now settle, since the prospects for employment were good.

As if to underline the family's new circumstances, Nikolay and Pyotr were enrolled in a private school with a fine reputation, the fashionable Schmelling School. From the parents' point of view, this brought some stability and a more regular pattern of life. From their sons' point of view, it was a disaster.

Nikolay and Pyotr had left behind a small school in Votkinsk where they had fitted in easily and had made many friends. They had exchanged that for a class-structured school in the big city, where they stood out because of their provincialism, from their unease at metropolitan ways to the language they used and the way they spoke.

'Instead of their former companions,' writes brother Modest, '. . . they encountered a crowd of urchins who met them, as newcomers, with the usual bullying and drubbing.'[2] Newcomers, outsiders, in a strange school in an unfamiliar place – a situation that causes pain that can last a lifetime.*

---

*As my brothers and I can testify from our own school experiences a century later.

Academically the boys also found themselves at a disadvantage. The move from Votkinsk meant that they had not covered as much of the curriculum as their classmates – something that alienated them from the other boys even further. They had to put in long hours in order to fill in the gaps. They went off to school early, and then, after returning home at about five, spent every evening concentrating on their schoolwork. Sometimes they did not get to bed until midnight, writes Modest. Even if that is an exaggeration, it suggests that Pyotr remembered these schooldays with a shudder.

It should be stressed that everything we know about Pyotr Tchaikovsky's early life – *everything* – is courtesy of his younger brother Modest (including Fanny's later memories, which Modest incorporated into his memoirs). Modest produced three volumes of biography of his elder brother, written fifty years after the events that took place either before he himself had been born or during his infancy. By the time Modest put pen to paper, Pyotr had been dead for several years, and was already revered as Russia's best-known and best-loved composer.

Everything Modest wrote concerning Pyotr's early years, therefore, was presumably as told to him by Pyotr and perhaps by his other siblings. Not only does this mean that his accounts are second-hand, but, since he was conscious of writing for posterity, there remains a suspicion that in some areas he might have stretched the truth slightly to show the family in a better light.

To take one example, all biographies of Tchaikovsky relate the story of Ilya losing the job in Moscow to a friend who betrayed his trust and took advantage of the opening for himself. This is taken entirely from Modest's memoirs. Is it, though, really likely to be true? Would Ilya have resigned his secure and comfortably paid job, employed by the state in Votkinsk, uprooted his large family, taken the children out of school, and moved to Moscow for a job in the private sector that turned out to be no longer on offer because his friend had taken it? It is possible, of course. But I believe it is more likely that Modest is, to an extent, protecting his father's image. Maybe the offer was made but Ilya's credentials were found to be wanting. Perhaps he was less qualified for the post than he thought.

This seems all the more likely since, once in St Petersburg, the family's misfortunes increased. Gainful employment continued to elude Ilya. This, it is easy to imagine, must have caused enormous tension in the Tchaikovsky household, and of all the children it was the emotional and highly sensitive Pyotr who would have felt it most. He was frequently seen in tears, and his behaviour started to become erratic. With increasing frequency he was too unwell to attend school. 'There was also a moral reaction, and [Pyotr] became capricious, irritable, and unlike his former self.'[3]

In December 1848 both Nikolay and Pyotr developed measles. Whereas in Nikolay the illness ran its course, barely interrupting his school life, in Pyotr it had a seriously debilitating effect. It increased his nervousness and unpredictable behaviour. Doctors were called in and Pyotr was diagnosed with a disease of the spinal cord. A word that was becoming fashionable in mid-nineteenth-century Europe was 'neurasthenia', describing a general lassitude coupled with anxiety and depression. Today we would be more inclined to say Pyotr was exhibiting a psychosomatic reaction caused by the tension and upheaval in his life.

All the children, it seems, were suffering, and Pyotr more so than any of the others. Alexandra, their mother, wrote to Fanny, 'He has become impatient, and at every word spoken to him that is not to his liking – there are tears in his eyes and a ready retort.'[4]

So concerned were the doctors about Pyotr's health that they advised he should not attend school. While this no doubt provided the young boy, now eight-and-a-half years of age, with welcome relief, it alienated him still further, not just from other schoolboys but from Nikolay too, the elder brother to whom he had always looked up. The two boys began to grow apart, and there would soon be a parting that ensured they would never regain their early closeness. Pyotr maintained a certain distance from Kolya for the rest of his life.

By contrast he was developing an ever closer relationship with his younger sister Alexandra. Sasha was just two years younger than Pyotr, and it is possible that even at this early age she saw the emotional fragility in her brother and took it on herself to comfort him and care for him as best she could. Certainly their closeness increased with time, and for the rest of his life Sasha was the sibling Pyotr turned to in order to experience the norms of domesticity, as far as he was able.

Amid the turmoil and tension in the Tchaikovsky household in St Petersburg, there was one bright spot for Pyotr. His father arranged for him to have piano lessons with a professional teacher. The lessons were few and interrupted by illness, but they made a lasting impact. In addition to this, despite family hardships, it seems mother and father frequently took their two eldest sons to the theatre and, of more significance to our story, the opera. Modest later wrote that it was during this stay in St Petersburg that Pyotr truly became familiar with music.

As with the brief sojourn in Moscow, the stay in the Russian capital was to be short-lived. Ilya Tchaikovsky still could not find work. This might seem surprising, given his qualifications and experience, not to mention the contacts he must have been able to call on through family and friends. But that was how it was.

Finally, an offer of employment was made. The post was one for which Ilya was well qualified, as the manager of an ironworks. There was only one small problem. The plant was in the remote town of Alapayevsk, three hundred miles east of Votkinsk, on the far side of the Urals. Yet again it meant huge upheaval for the Tchaikovsky family.

The ironworks was privately owned, and the job less prestigious than Ilya's previous position in Votkinsk. To compound matters, it came as no surprise to the family to find that Alapayevsk was small and provincial, populated largely by working-class people and almost entirely devoid of cultural activity. It made them pine for Votkinsk, and what they had left behind.

Once again, it was Pyotr who was most affected, for there was something else – or, more accurately some*one* else – missing from his life. His elder brother Kolya remained in St Petersburg. He was approaching the end of his time at school and, following in his father's footsteps, had been accepted into the St Petersburg Mining College.

The two brothers had begun to grow apart back in St Petersburg. This might have been partly attributable to Kolya's popularity with everyone he met. We have Fanny's account of how he charmed her, and in her memoirs Pyotr comes off the poorer in comparison with his elder brother.

Modest is in no doubt about who the star performer among the children was back in those early days: '[Kolya was] the most brilliant in appearance . . . Adroit, handsome, refined, a passionate lover of physical exercise.'[5] He was also, it seems, making more progress in music than any of his classmates.

Music was not something Kolya was to pursue, but his talent might well have spurred his younger brother on in his own musical activities. It might also have encouraged a certain hero worship of his elder brother to develop into a kind of jealousy, which Kolya's absence from Alapayevsk now reinforced. Unquestionably Pyotr missed Kolya's companionship but we can be confident he was relieved no longer to be compared unfavourably with him, even if letters came regularly from St Petersburg saying how well he was doing.

In one area, though, Pyotr now experienced extreme disappointment. His parents no longer seemed so enthusiastic about his passion for music. In the first place, they recalled how musical activities in the past had led to him becoming nervously excited, exacerbating his highly strung nature, frequently leading to tears and exhaustion. They did not want a repetition of that.

In addition, on a more practical level, any thought of a career in music was out of the question. It simply would not be an appropriate profession

Above

The Tchaikovsky
Commemorative
Museum, established
in the family home
at Alapayevsk.

for a young man from a middle-class family to pursue. Musicians had no social status and the music schools needed to train them had yet to be established. Music was essentially a domestic activity for the gentry, predominantly pursued by women and girls. Professional concerts, ballets or opera were the province of visiting European companies and musicians.[6]

This time no music teacher was to be engaged, nor, it seems, was Pyotr enrolled in school. Zinaida, his much older half-sister, undertook to educate him. It was a poor decision by his parents. Zinaida had never really liked her younger half-brother, who suffered once again in comparison with Kolya. To compound matters, Zinaida had no experience or qualification as a teacher. She was unsympathetic, frequently reporting to her parents that the boy was lazy and uninterested in learning.

Pyotr was now nine years of age. Votkinsk, and the joy of his early childhood in the company of Fanny Dürbach must have seemed a distant memory, whereas it was, in reality, not that long ago. In that time the family had uprooted first to Moscow, then to St Petersburg, and now to Alapayevsk.

Also in that time he had lost Fanny; he had lost his elder brother, and he had suffered nervous illness. Now there was about to be even more upheaval.

On 1 May 1850 Alexandra gave birth to twin boys, Anatoly and Modest. The family was now made up of one elder half-daughter and six children – five boys and a girl. If neither parent had found much time for Pyotr before, there was even less now, perhaps something for which Pyotr might have felt grateful. If he was denied the music he so craved, he could at least lose himself in books, a lifelong passion.

Soon, though, the parents were to turn their attention back to their son, and his future. They made a decision that would affect the rest of Pyotr's life. He looked back on it with horror until the day he died, and it marked the point at which his childhood truly came to an end.

Ilya and Alexandra decided that their son should become a civil servant.

3

AN UNBEARABLE FAREWELL

Pyotr Tchaikovsky, just past his tenth birthday, was enrolled in the prestigious Imperial School of Jurisprudence in St Petersburg. This involved two years of study in the school's preparatory class, to prepare him for the entrance exams.

More change for the young Pyotr, this time of an even more dramatic nature. For the first time he was to be separated from his family. In all the moves so far – Votkinsk to Moscow, then to St Petersburg and on to Alapayevsk – he had remained with close family members.

Now he was following in his elder brother's footsteps. He too was about to begin life in St Petersburg, as a boarder at a school 800 miles from his family home. The knowledge that Kolya was already in the city must have been some consolation to Pyotr, even if they would be at different schools and their relationship was not as warm as it had once been. Maybe he even felt a certain amount of pride, a sure sign that he was no longer a child, old enough now to fly the nest? Such a reaction would be understandable in a child such as Kolya certainly, but would be less so in a highly emotional boy easily moved to tears.

Pyotr's parents were aware of this, and made the decision that Alexandra would accompany her son to St Petersburg. This would mean leaving the three-month-old twins behind, a decision that might seem rather strange to us today but was less so in a country and in an era in which household staff, nannies and wet nurses were common even in middle-class families. Zinaida and Pyotr's younger sister Sasha would also accompany them.

Anyone who has left home for the first time at a tender age will remember the pit in the stomach that Pyotr must surely have felt. It was no doubt compounded by memories of their last sojourn in the capital city, and his experience at the Schmelling School.

With the twins back in Alapayevsk, Alexandra's absence might have been expected to be as short as she could make it, but it appears there never was any intention of a swift return. Alexandra was back in the city of her birth, and there were people to see and places to go.

Her priority, of course, was her son, and the desire to see him well settled at his new school. She did not stint as far as her maternal duties were concerned. According to Modest, she visited her son at every opportunity. 'At first, all his Sundays and half-holidays were spent with his mother . . . so that in the beginning he did not feel the transition from home to school life so severely.'[1]

One event in particular stayed in Pyotr's mind. On 22 August he went with his mother to see Glinka's opera, *A Life for the Tsar*, which, with its theme of nationalism, much impressed him. He wrote to his mother a year later to remind her of their outing. Decades later he would say that it continued to hold a special place in his heart.

But this is to view the past through rose-tinted glasses. Again, any young school boarder who has known that Sunday-afternoon feeling when a parent says goodbye will identify wholly with the sadness that engulfed the sensitive Pyotr at each parting. Worse was to come, however, with a day that was so traumatic for Pyotr that for the rest of his days he looked back on it with horror.

Alexandra's departure from St Petersburg could not be put off any longer, and both parents were aware of how difficult it would be for Pyotr to say goodbye. Ilya wrote to his wife from Alapayevsk:

> *Darling [Pyotr] is accustomed to the caresses of his father and mother, but now will be a long time without this happiness – and as he is sensitive and finds it difficult to part with people, you must naturally instil in him* courage.[2]

This is accurate although slightly curious wording on Ilya's part. He had never had a particularly close relationship with their second son, showing more interest in his eldest son Nikolay. Pyotr's younger siblings, born swiftly after him, added to the claims on Ilya's attention. He was also trying desperately to secure employment, uprooting his family time and time again – something for which it is quite possible Pyotr nursed a deep, if subconscious, resentment.

Left
Programme for Glinka's
opera *A Life for the Tsar.*

Until now Pyotr's relationship with his mother had not been so different, despite his affection for her. Alexandra had a growing family to look after, several moves to plan and put into action. Beyond perhaps keeping an eye out for her second son, encouraging his musical activities as had his father, at least in the early days, she did not seem particularly devoted to him.

'Caresses' therefore might be slightly overstating it, given the tenderness the word conjures up, even if Ilya's description of Pyotr's sensitive nature is spot on.

That all changed in St Petersburg. Maybe it was the frequent visits by his mother, the exeats from school when she had nothing to distract her from her son, when she was able to devote her entire attention to him, that strengthened the bond between them.

The day for Alexandra's departure was set for the end of September, after a sojourn in St Petersburg of almost two months. Pyotr travelled with his mother and two sisters as far as the turn-off for Moscow, where it was traditional for departing friends to be waved off. Also accompanying them was a relative, Ilya Keiser, and a family friend, Modest Vakar, both of whom lived in St Petersburg. The two men would accompany Pyotr back to the city.

If the adults thought Pyotr might take the parting rather badly, they can hardly have been prepared for what happened. We have, once again, only Modest Tchaikovsky's account, as relayed to him by his brother many years later. The fact that Pyotr recalled it in such detail, and with such horror, tells its own story, even if the passage of time might have lent it extra drama.

In the early stages of the drive, Pyotr sat in the carriage quietly crying and staring through the window into the distance. At the turnpike junction the family dismounted from the carriage. Alexandra and the two girls began their goodbyes. At this point Pyotr totally lost control.

Suddenly Pyotr flung his arms round his mother, clinging to her tightly. The others tried to prise him away but he clung on, crying inconsolably. Nothing they could say or do would convince him. 'He saw nothing, heard nothing, but hung upon her as though he was part and parcel of the beloved presence.'[3]

There was no alternative but to use force. The task fell to Ilya Keiser. He grabbed Pyotr by the arms, and physically tore him away from his mother. Pyotr reached out with his hands, trying to hold on to any part of her, but Keiser dragged him away.

Pyotr sobbed uncontrollably as he watched his mother and sisters get into the carriage for Moscow. The driver whipped the horses, and the carriage began to move. With a sudden twist of his shoulders, Pyotr broke free from Keiser. He ran after the carriage, screaming aloud, and hurled himself at it in desperation. But the horses gathered speed and Pyotr watched the carriage draw further and further away through a veil of tears and uncontrollable sobbing.

'To his life's end Pyotr could never recall this hour without a shiver of horror,' wrote Modest.[4] Many times in the ensuing years he would pass the spot on the turnpike where the drama occurred, and even thirty years later he still remembered 'that mad despair that possessed me when the carriage carrying everything most dear to me disappeared from sight.'[5]

Young Pyotr had experienced yet another devastating farewell. But these farewells were not over yet. He could not know it, but the most traumatic loss of his entire life was less than four short years away.

Over the course of the two years that he was a pupil in the preparatory class of the School of Jurisprudence, Pyotr poured his heart out to his parents in letters overflowing with emotion. It might not be too wide of the mark to imagine that at this young age he was writing words in a similar fashion to how he would one day write musical notes.

There were thirty-nine letters, in which we read sentiments such as: 'Dear wonderful and beautiful Mama and Papa'; 'I kiss your little hands, your little feet, and all of you warmly, my darlings'; 'I kiss your hands a million times and ask for your blessing'; '[I long to] cover you both together with kisses'; '[I have tried] to be good all the year so that I might kiss both my angels together'.

When there is a suggestion of a visit by his parents, he writes in similarly effusive and emotional language, but there is a telling twist at the end:

> [I] shall cover you with kisses so that you will not go back any more to nasty [Alapayevsk], but stay here to live forever. However, maybe Papa has again changed his mind and again will not wish to come and see his chicks.[6]

The strong emotions and sensitivity that Fanny Dürbach noted in Pyotr the child are taking firm root as he moves towards his teenage years. So noticeable is this in the letters he wrote home that Modest draws a distinction with elder brother Kolya, whose letters, says Modest, are less sensitive and display a formality and coldness. Pyotr, by contrast, writes 'not only by his mind, but also by his heart'.[7] You could say exactly the same about the music he would go on to compose.

We know little about the two years Pyotr spent in the preparatory class of the School for Jurisprudence, except that academic study was all-consuming. There are no accounts of any visit to concerts, opera or ballet.

Not that music was entirely absent from Pyotr's life. On one occasion, as he recounted in a letter home, he was playing a humorous polka on the piano while other pupils danced, making such a noise that one of the teachers came into the room to remind them angrily that dancing was forbidden.

The boys fled, leaving a solitary Pyotr at the piano. When the teacher demanded to know the names of the boys who had broken the no-dancing rule, Pyotr haltingly replied that there had been so many, he could not remember their names.

Interestingly, in recounting this tale to his parents, Pyotr stresses the guilt he felt at having lied to the teacher, who was one of his favourites.

Considerably more guilt attached to him when a scarlet fever epidemic broke out at the school, and the Vakar family took Pyotr into their home to protect him. He did not contract the disease, but it seems he carried it into the Vakar household. The eldest son Kolya, five years of age and 'the pride of the home', contracted it, and four weeks later he died.

In a letter home Pyotr pours out his grief. He stresses that the Vakars did not blame him in the least, 'not a word of reproach', but guilt suffuses every word. Modest writes:

> *[Pyotr] could not rid himself of the sense that the parents must regard him with secret bitterness. It is not surprising that just at this time life seemed to him cold and cheerless, and that he longed more than ever for his own people.*[8]

That longing was about to be fulfilled. Ilya had paid a quick visit to St Petersburg a year after Pyotr had begun in preparatory class, to check out employment prospects, and eight months later moved the entire family – once more – back to the capital city.

Ilya's circumstances are not entirely clear. It appears he was again tiring of provincial life. He now had a large family and Sasha and Ippolit were approaching school age. Ilya apparently resigned his post at the ironworks, and in May 1852 the Tchaikovsky family left Alapayevsk to take up residence in St Petersburg.

Whether Ilya found employment we do not know. Modest writes in his memoirs that his father's meagre savings and his government pension (presumably from running the state-run ironworks in Votkinsk) enabled him to retire, which seems unlikely given how many children he had to support.

The knowledge that his family would shortly be joining him and his elder brother Kolya in St Petersburg was exactly the fillip Pyotr needed as exams approached for entry into the senior part of the School of Jurisprudence. In May 1852, at around the time of his twelfth birthday, Pyotr sat the all-important entrance exam and passed easily, coming third in his class.

The weeks that followed were truly happy. Pyotr was reunited with his family; his father rented a house in the countryside north of the city, and the family spent a joyous summer there, joined by Ilya's two young nieces, Lidiya and Anna, who would remain close to Pyotr for the rest of his life.

Anna gives us an illuminating description of Pyotr. He struck her as 'a thin, nervous, extremely sensitive boy . . . notable for his affectionate sensibility, in particular toward his mother'.[9] The word 'nervous' is interesting; it seems Pyotr was unable to relax totally, even in the familiar company of his family. Yet his love for his mother is so noticeable that Anna remarks on it. The boy who had thrown himself at the departing carriage was determined not to lose her again.

Pyotr Tchaikovsky began at the senior School of Jurisprudence in the autumn of 1852, a few months past his twelfth birthday. The school was unashamedly elitist. Pupils wore a green three-quarter-length quasi-military jacket with a gold-braided collar – the junior school's collar was silver-braided – brass buttons and an elaborately adorned cocked hat. The school motto was *Respice finem* ('Remember your objective'), and that objective was 'love and devotion to God, throne and motherland'.[10]

Graduation after a seven-year course of study in a curriculum that included physics, natural history, mathematics, geography, languages and literature, with legal studies in the final three years, was a guarantee of a privileged position in the civil service.

Pyotr, already used to boarding, now had the added pleasure of knowing that his family was living in the same city as him, no longer hundreds of miles away beyond the Urals. From the corner window in his dormitory he could see across the street to the house where his aunt, his mother's sister, lived. When he knew his mother was about to visit, he would wait to blow kisses and wave at her. There must have been times when he longed to escape back into the bosom of his family, since life at the School of Jurisprudence was undeniably harsh.

The day began at 6 a.m. and lasted until 10 p.m. six days a week. The daily schedule included seven hours of classwork and three hours of prep in the evening. Parental visits were restricted to one short visit a week.

Discipline was strict and ruthlessly enforced. Canings were almost commonplace, and inflicted with cruelty coupled with humiliation. A boy who was caught smoking – strictly forbidden to pupils in the younger classes – had his trousers pulled down to his ankles, was made to bend over a bench and was given sixty strokes in front of the whole form. One of the boys who was watching burst into sobs and was threatened with a similar thrashing unless he stopped.

On another occasion, recounted in memoirs of the school forty years later by a pupil, the perpetrator of some minor offence refused to confess to it and the director of the school worked himself into a frenzied hysteria and ordered every boy in the class to be stripped naked and publicly flogged.

It seems that Pyotr Tchaikovsky, during his entire time at the school, was never beaten. By all accounts he was the model of good behaviour, liked by his teachers and by the other pupils, even if his dishevelled appearance, general disorganisation and forgetfulness were evident enough to be remarked on. His only 'vice' – his own word – was smoking, which was allowed once a pupil moved up to the senior classes, and which would remain a lifelong habit.

Many years later, once Tchaikovsky had achieved fame, some of his schoolmates wrote their reminiscences of him. One described him as

"Always pensive, preoccupied with something or other, with a slight but charming smile and girlishly pretty."

Description of Tchaikovsky by an old schoolfriend.

'always pensive, preoccupied with something or other, with a slight but charming smile and girlishly pretty'.* [11]

It was a source of obvious joy to Pyotr that there was a piano in the school. The same pupil writes that Pyotr 'would appear among us in his little jacket with the sleeves rolled up and spend hours on end at the piano in the music room'. [12] He entertained them by asking for tunes, then playing them with the keyboard covered with a cloth – as he knew his hero Mozart had done. The writer admits, though, that none of them had any inkling of what a great musician their friend would become.

Although music was not a regular part of the curriculum, it played an informal role in school life. Dancing lessons were held once a week, with boys dancing in pairs, one assuming the male role, the other the female.

We learn from pupils' reminiscences that the boys lived closely and intimately. Baths were taken communally. As adolescence took hold, banter between the boys became more sexual, with the emphasis on the purity of relationships between men. By contrast that between a man and woman was so 'dirty, cynical, revolting and ugly that I would have considered merely touching a woman the greatest of sins,' wrote one former pupil, Vladimir Taneyev.† [13]

Unsurprisingly liaisons were formed at the school, between teachers and pupils, and between the pupils themselves. While homosexuality was technically illegal, it was widely tolerated not just at the School of Jurisprudence but in other institutions such as the military and prisons.

Only when scandal threatened was action taken. One pupil at the school was reported by his own family for an 'unspecified sickness' – almost certainly masturbation – and the school was forced to take action; it expelled him. On another occasion an older pupil waylaid a younger boy in a park outside the school grounds and raped him. Other pupils formed a protective 'wall' around both boys so the incident would not reach the school authorities. Instead they took action of their own, voting to ostracise the perpetrator.

It is as Pyotr Tchaikovsky reached adolescence at the School of Jurisprudence that we have the first real signs of the homosexuality that would become such a vital feature of his life.

---

* Poznansky reports that this description was later redacted from the files at Klin. It was more recently reinstated.

† Vladimir Taneyev was elder brother of Sergey Taneyev, who would become Tchaikovsky's star pupil at the Moscow Conservatory, as well as a future composer and lifelong friend.

4
GUILT AND THE CRUELLEST LOSS

hile there has been little doubt about Tchaikovsky's sexual orientation from his own day to this, extraordinary measures were taken to hide and even deny it. In a country where homosexuality was not only illegal but condemned throughout society and where its discovery could destroy reputations and careers, this secrecy is to a degree understandable. But that it has prevented us from fully understanding the true nature of a musical genius is surely unforgivable.

If blame is to be apportioned, then it attaches to Tchaikovsky's own family as much as the authorities. Right at the start, the man whose ambition it was to make Tchaikovsky's life known to posterity, his own brother Modest, went to inordinate lengths to conceal his brother's sexuality – and his own. This was continued in the twentieth century by the Soviet authorities who, well aware of the truth, were determined to prevent what they viewed as a sullying of the reputation of a Russian hero.

Only in recent years, with the release of hitherto suppressed documents, have we been able to gauge the depth of the relationships and liaisons that Tchaikovsky forged at the School of Jurisprudence, and how important they were to him. Some, we now know, lasted a lifetime.

Modest's magisterial three-volume biography of Tchaikovsky, the most comprehensive account we have, was published between 1900 and 1902. His purpose in writing about his famous brother was simply to portray him

Above

The Imperial School of Jurisprudence in St Petersburg.

in the best possible light, even if that meant glossing over and omitting certain aspects of his life.

Not once in any of the volumes is there even a nod to Tchaikovsky's sexuality. In order to hide it Modest expurgates and censors correspondence, in some cases distorting its meaning. He mentions the names of several fellow pupils at the School of Jurisprudence with whom his brother formed friendships. There is not a single word or suggestion that these might in any way have been sexual liaisons.

Towards the end of his life, aware that he might have done a disservice to posterity for which sooner or later he would be reproached, Modest began writing an autobiography, as if to reveal the full truth about his brother in an account of his own life might somehow lessen the impact. At the very start of his autobiography he writes:

> *If some day people glance at this manuscript, as I am counting on, though I almost have no hope that they will – may they be rewarded for the interest they take in my obscure existence by what I have to say about my brother Pyotr.*[1]

He was certainly correct in his final wish, though he could not of course know the lengths to which the authorities would go to suppress what he had written. Modest never completed his autobiography, but what he did write reveals more about his famous brother than any other words written by family or friends. While the formal biography of his brother reveals not a hint of Tchaikovsky's sexual encounters at the School of Jurisprudence, in his own autobiography he goes to the other extreme.

In the portion of the autobiography that has so far been made public,[*] we are left in no doubt that the most intense attachment Tchaikovsky formed was with a fellow pupil by the name of Sergey Kireyev. In the biography Kireyev merits a single brief mention, which is a bizarre mixture of the unintended and the deliberately misleading.

Modest recounts how his brother told him that on one occasion he was walking through the dormitory of the junior course with one of his friends – 'unfortunately I do not recall his name'.[2] His use of the word 'dormitory' is highly significant, and I believe it is likely to be a slip of the pen that he would have corrected at a later stage.

Kireyev, four and a half years younger than Tchaikovsky, was in the junior school. There was very little interaction between pupils in the junior and senior schools. Seniors were rarely seen in junior classrooms, and although it was considered something of a badge of honour for a junior to be seen strolling in the corridors with a senior, we can be sure that visiting a dormitory together was strictly against the rules.

As for being deliberately misleading, Modest certainly did recall his name. He knew exactly who his brother was talking about. This is made more than clear in his explicit description of the relationship in his autobiography.

Modest does not stint in the language he uses. His brother's relationship with young Kireyev 'was the strongest, most durable, and purest amorous infatuation of his life'.[3] He repeats this for good measure: 'There was no stronger, more enduring and agonising love in all his life.'

Well might he have used the word 'agonising'. Modest knows he is treading on dangerous ground here, and confronts it head on:

> I would ask those who dare to call such a love 'dirty' whether among their kind they will find many who, without daring to hope for a kiss, receiving only now and then the reward of a slight brush of the hand of their adored beloved, have managed to cherish such a feeling for more than ten years.

---

[*] Many more pages remain held at the Tchaikovsky Archive in Klin, still not released for publication.

There is a suggestion here that the relationship was not physical, at least while both were students – just the occasional 'brush of the hand' – and this is reinforced later when Modest writes:

> *The fact that the object of his love was beyond all reach eliminated the possibility of disillusionments and served to idealise the [love], turning a tender affection into an ardent and enthusiastic adoration, so sublimely pure that it did not even cross his mind to hide it.*

It is possible that even in his autobiography, since it was clearly intended for publication, Modest is being cautious. He states himself that his brother was sixteen and Kireyev just twelve when they first met. Kireyev was a child.

It is uncertain whether the relationship was ever fully physical, but Modest claims there was an abusive element to it – in an unlikely direction. He describes how his brother's feelings towards Kireyev were 'maidenly pure and sublime', and that this either failed to satisfy the young boy, or led to him being teased by his classmates. This caused Kireyev to begin to resent Tchaikovsky's attention, which led to him treating his admirer 'with contempt and hostility'.

According to Modest this manifested itself in outright cruelty on the part of Kireyev towards Tchaikovsky. One moment he would treat his admirer with unexpected tenderness, 'as if he were afraid [Tchaikovsky] might be unfaithful to him', then in the next he would 'plunge his victim into despair by equally unexpected coarse mockery'.

On one occasion Kireyev is described as having boasted to his classmates that Tchaikovsky would put up with anything from him – even a slap in the face. He waited for Tchaikovsky to walk over to him 'trustfully', as he knew he would, then Kireyev swung his arm and slapped Tchaikovsky's face in front of everybody.

The boy was right, says Modest. 'Misunderstood and insulted, the poor admirer suffered all the more because he had always been so pampered by the sympathy of everyone around him.' He adds, significantly, 'But instead of quenching his love, these sufferings just stirred it up further.'

Given that Modest can have heard this only from his brother many years later, and his avowed intention of portraying Pyotr in the best possible light, some exaggeration is to be expected. However, it is surely fair to assume more than a degree of truth in the incidents described.

In a relationship that lasted for ten years, an inordinately lengthy period of time (as Modest is at pains to point out), it is hard to believe there was no physical element. Even if that was the case, Tchaikovsky by no means abstained from forming other relationships, as Modest describes in a particularly flowery passage in his autobiography:

I should like to say that just as knights of the Middle Ages, whilst still worshipping the fair lady of their hearts, would often betray her in carnal love and take wives, so Pyotr at the same time as his adoration of SK had many amorous infatuations of a different sort, to which he would abandon himself irrepressibly, with all the ardour of his passionate and sensual nature.

In the unlikely event that the reader has still not grasped the nature of Tchaikovsky's sexual orientation, Modest writes, 'Women were never the object of these infatuations; they repelled him physically.'

Sergey Kireyev.

In later life Tchaikovsky was to see Kireyev a couple of times more. Now the boot was very much on the other foot. Tchaikovsky was a famous composer, with many admirers competing for his attention. Meanwhile Kireyev, it appears, had lost his looks: 'The other day I met Kireyev at the opera,' Tchaikovsky tells his brother. 'How sweet he is, though not so handsome as before.' And a little later, Modest describes Kireyev as 'a very prosaic man, incapable of instilling anything other than the most sober friendliness in his former admirer'. Tchaikovsky's ardour had cooled, and Kireyev finally passed out of his life for good.

It is worth stressing again that Modest did not personally witness any of the interactions he describes between his brother and Kireyev at the School of Jurisprudence. All the information has come from Tchaikovsky himself, recalled much later in life.

If Tchaikovsky's relationship with Kireyev remained 'pure' and non-physical, the same was almost certainly not true of another schoolboy liaison he formed, with the future poet Alexei Apukhtin.

Apukhtin was an entirely different character from the young and impressionable Kireyev. Just six months younger than Tchaikovsky, Apukhtin was a somewhat overbearing character, universally disliked for his arrogance. He had cause enough for self-confidence. Precociously gifted, he possessed an exceptional memory, allowing him to quote vast tracts of Pushkin by heart.

Tchaikovsky was soon in thrall to the intellectually superior Apukhtin, admiring his impressive knowledge of literature. A strong friendship quickly formed, all the more unlikely if, as Modest claims, the two teenage boys possessed radically different temperaments.

It was their shared love of poetry that brought them together, and Apukhtin would delight in demonstrating his considerable skills as a poet with verses written for his friend, one beginning:

You remember how, hiding in the music room,
Forgetting school and the world,
We would dream of an ideal glory –
Art was our idol.

And ending:

. . . I guessed the spark of divinity
In you, then scarcely glimmering,
Now burning with so powerful a light.[4]

Even in his poetry a measure of arrogance comes through, Apukhtin here claiming credit for recognising Tchaikovsky's artistic talent. The poem had the desired effect. Tchaikovsky wrote to his brother that the poem caused him to shed many tears.

Although the relationship with Kireyev remains the only one explicitly detailed by Modest in the portion of his autobiography that has been released, it is more than likely that it was Apukhtin who introduced Tchaikovsky to a physical relationship.

Their radically different temperaments – one outgoing and brimming with self-confidence, the other almost painfully shy – were also evident in the two individuals' attitude to their sexuality.

Apukhtin was in no doubt that he was homosexual from the time of puberty; he was openly gay for his whole life. At the School of Jurisprudence, Tchaikovsky was far from being the only object of his affection. He had relationships with at least four other pupils, and continued to be overtly promiscuous on leaving the School. Contemporaries described him as polite and courteous in the company of women, but coming alive as the wittiest of storytellers in the company of men.

Opprobrium did not deter him. Fellow pupil Taneyev, also homosexual, wrote scathingly of the man Apukhtin became:

On leaving school . . . he spent his time in the most evil and despicable
society, made up of everything that was the very worst of societies – the
Russian aristocracy and the guards.[5]

We can be fairly confident that at some stage when both boys were around fourteen or fifteen years of age, Apukhtin seduced Tchaikovsky. Tchaikovsky's most comprehensive modern biographer, Alexander Poznansky, goes further, suggesting that it was with Apukhtin that the teenage Tchaikovsky not only first recognised and acknowledged his own desires, but that Apukhtin helped an initially reluctant Tchaikovsky to recognise and justify them.[6]

Apukhtin led a dissolute life, according to Taneyev, and this affected his creative powers. He failed almost entirely to fulfil his early literary promise and became obese in middle age, which caused him chronic shortness of breath. He achieved little literary success despite publishing a number of prose works and collected poems.

As for Tchaikovsky's relationship with his former fellow pupil, this would endure for the lifetime of the two men, albeit not entirely amicably nor without interruption. Apukhtin will reappear at one of the most critical

junctures in Tchaikovsky's life. In the end the two men would die within two months of each other.

We will never know for sure how many friendships developed into intimacy in the seven years Tchaikovsky was a pupil at the School of Jurisprudence. We can know only what Modest has relayed to us and a handful contemporaries have written – all of them aware that such sexual activity was illegal and guaranteed to destroy reputations. It is more than likely that more will come to light if and when further writings by Modest are allowed into the public domain.

One other name, however, does feature in what is already publicly available, and it affords us a fascinating insight into the character of the young Tchaikovsky. It involved an aristocratic pupil by the name of Prince Vladimir Meshchersky, who even at the School of Jurisprudence had acquired a reputation for flamboyance and promiscuity.

Meshchersky was sixteen months older than Tchaikovsky, and two classes ahead of him. The older boy swiftly saw the delicately featured, sensitive younger pupil as an amorous target.

Although Modest, in his three-volume biography, affords Meshchersky only a single brief footnote, there is little doubt from other pupils' memoirs and writings that Meshchersky pursued Tchaikovsky and that the two went on to remain friends for life.

We have copious evidence of how Meshchersky, in a similar way to Apukhtin, was disliked from his schooldays onwards. Given his aristocratic origins, he moved in the highest circles: his younger sister was lady-in-waiting to Tsar Alexander III's mother. Members of the royal circle in St Petersburg were well known in high society as being flamboyantly open about their sexual orientation, enjoying colourful lifestyles.[7] Even so, Meshchersky's behaviour was so shocking that he was involved in several scandals, alienating everyone close to him. One described him as 'Prince of Sodom and citizen of Gomorrah'.[8]

Later in life he was an adviser to the last two tsars, Alexander III and Nicholas II, both of whom had to protect him from public disgrace. This did nothing to enhance his popularity, and by the end of his life he was widely despised.

Not though, it seems, by Tchaikovsky, and here is where we gain an insight into his trusting, forgiving nature. Even after leaving the School of Jurisprudence, he continued to count Meshchersky as a friend. He must have been one of the few who did so.

That Tchaikovsky formed an enduring relationship with Meshchersky, which began at school, is not in doubt, and – like Apukhtin – he would resurface at one of the most critical junctures in Tchaikovsky's life.

A hallmark of these relationships for all involved, including Tchaikovsky, was their lack of exclusivity, both at school and in adult life. It was seemingly of no concern to any of the participants that their relationships were not monogamous. There is evidence of petty jealousies and the occasional squabble, but sharing lovers was the norm.

Tchaikovsky's homosexual liaisons at the School of Jurisprudence reveal him to be the pursued rather than the pursuer (with the exception of the relationship with Kireyev), a rather vulnerable youth who was already developing the tortured attitude towards his sexuality that would stay with him for his whole life. There is one obvious contributory factor for this vulnerability. If Pyotr was by nature an emotional and sensitive boy, easily moved to guilt, those traits were soon to be compounded by the saddest of circumstances.

The year 1854 began with much rejoicing in the Tchaikovsky household. The eldest daughter, Zinaida, married a certain Colonel Yevgeny Olkhovsky. It was one less dependant for Ilya Tchaikovsky to provide for.

Kolya was firmly established at the Mining College. Pyotr himself was two years into the seven-year course at the School of Jurisprudence. Sasha and Ippolit were at school, and Ilya would soon be thinking of schooling for the twins, Anatoly and Modest, now aged four.

Then, with no warning, barely a month after Pyotr's fourteenth birthday, Alexandra Tchaikovskaya contracted cholera. At first it did not seem serious. She quickly rallied, but then suffered a relapse. The last-resort treatment for cholera was to be lowered into a scalding hot bath to reactivate the kidneys. Alexandra experienced this – exactly as her son Pyotr would almost forty years later – but to no avail.

Alexandra died so suddenly that none of her children were able to be at her bedside to bid her farewell.

Pyotr's world was turned upside down. His mother was the person he loved more than anyone else in the world, from whom he could not bear to be separated, from whose side he had had to be torn, whose departing carriage he had chased after. This time it was a parting from which there could be no return. She was gone from his life forever.

The dreadful day of her death – 13 June 1854, at the age of just forty-one – was to stay with Tchaikovsky for the rest of his life. He could never let the date pass unmarked. It is not an exaggeration to say that from this moment on, added to his natural reserve and sensitivity was a large measure of the torment from which he would never be free. And he associated this torment with his sexual orientation. Towards the end of his life he wrote, 'My whole life has been a chain of misfortunes because of my sexuality.'[9]

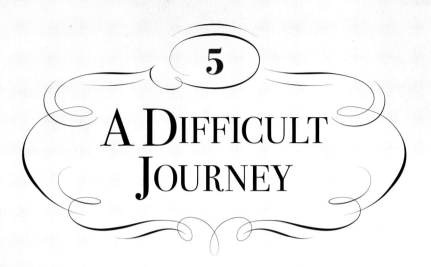

5

A DIFFICULT JOURNEY

Pyotr **Ilyich Tchaikovsky** graduated from the School of Jurisprudence on 13 May 1859, just two and a half weeks after his nineteenth birthday. The twentieth class to graduate in the school's brief history posed for a group photograph.

Seated to the right of centre in the front row, directly in front of the principal and another teacher, sit two graduates, one with his hand resting on the other's arm in an overt display of affection. On the right is Tchaikovsky; it is not known who the other is, pressed up against him. None of the other thirty-two graduates are in such close physical contact, nor is anyone else in the photograph paying any attention to the intimacy between Tchaikovsky and his friend.

Tchaikovsky graduated thirteenth in his class, none of the subjects having caused him particular problems, except mathematics at which he struggled somewhat. He had earned the rank of titular counsellor, the very lowest rung on the civil service ladder. Three weeks later, in early June, he began work as junior assistant to the head of the administrative department at the Ministry of Justice in St Petersburg.

He wrote later that he was a bad civil servant, but official records describe him in favourable terms, and two months after beginning work he became a senior assistant. His main job was to prepare documents of

Above

Tchaikovsky in his 1859 graduation photograph, sixth from the right in the front row.

various sorts, and he would remain at this level, with the same duties, for the following three years.

The work was routine and undemanding, leaving Tchaikovsky plenty of free time to indulge his passion. Surprisingly, at the time this appears not to have been music – or at least there is little evidence of musical activity in trips to the opera or theatre involving Tchaikovsky himself.

The passion he now pursued was physical, and he pursued it relentlessly. In his published biography, Modest paints a vivid picture, while managing to reveal nothing too intimate:

> *With the change from youth to manhood came also the desire to taste the pleasures and excitements of life. The future appeared to him an endless carnival and, with nothing in his young life as yet to disabuse him, he surrendered himself to this seductive illusion. With his impulsive temperament, he took life easy: a good-natured, carefree young man, unencumbered by serious interests or aspirations.*[1]

We learn more from this about the character of Pyotr than we do about his activities, but Modest clearly allows the reader to read between the lines. Tchaikovsky was now, in Alexander Poznansky's words, a 'man about town'.[2] Relishing his freedom, he was at liberty to indulge his desires in any way he wished. As a close friend of Apukhtin still, he had the entrée into any homosexual set he desired.

It is paradoxical, but true, that although homosexuality was against the law in Russia and exposure guaranteed to ruin a career, it was more openly practised than in many a Western European country where there was seemingly more tolerance. It was one response to the despotic rule of the tsars. As long as it never entered the public domain, the authorities were content to turn a blind eye. As long as the only person whose reputation could suffer from exposure was the homosexual himself, there was no inherent threat to the political system.

And so Tchaikovsky set out to enjoy himself. Again, Modest confirms this, again using neutral language, though contemporary readers are left in no doubt as to the hidden message:

> In the elegant salons, at the theatre, in restaurants, and on strolls along the Nevsky Prospekt and in the Summer Garden at fashionable times of the day, in everything, everywhere [Pyotr] sought and found the flowers of life's joys. The field of these flowers appeared boundless to him and there seemed to be enough of them for him to pick for his entire life, and nothing else did he know or wish to know.[3]

Just as at the School of Jurisprudence, he was enormously popular, exuding a great deal of charisma. One friend described how hard it was to resist that natural attraction:

> It was impossible not to love him . . . Everything, starting with his youthful appearance and his marvellous, intense gaze, made him irresistibly attractive . . . Everyone felt, in talking with him, a special warmth and caress in the sound of his voice, in his words, and in his glance.[4]

Modest confirms his brother's popularity. In fact, Tchaikovsky did all he could to attract other men, his party piece – as it had been at the School of Jurisprudence – being to pretend to be a female dancer. This he did openly, giving 'full-scale performances that everyone applauded and no one saw as unsuitable for a boy'.[5]

The 'man about town' life was about to come to a rather abrupt end. One evening Tchaikovsky, Apukhtin and a number of homosexual friends were having dinner at the Chautemps restaurant in St Petersburg. The exact circumstances of what happened are not clear, since police files for the period were destroyed during the turmoil of the Revolution in 1917.

It appears, from Modest's papers in the Tchaikovsky Archive in Klin, that the group was denounced in public and that their names were published throughout the city. Those involved 'acquired for ever the reputation of buggers'.[6] As homosexuality was broadly, if not officially, tolerated, this came as a shock to the young men.

Tchaikovsky, as might be expected, was more deeply affected than his companions:

> *It was the first time that he had faced cruel injustice on the part of people who despised and were indignant about a situation that might have caused, if the matter had been clearly understood, at worst regret with regard to an irreversible natural defect.*[*7]

Modest goes on to write that the incident did not change Pyotr's inclinations in any way.

This was the first time Tchaikovsky had felt such vilification. He became more cautious in his amorous adventures, even avoiding company that might lead to more criticism and damage his reputation. For instance, we know that Tchaikovsky was attracted to a sixteen-year-old boy at the Department of Justice, 'in the expression of whose eyes something special was to be felt'. He was also drawn to another youth, 'an attractive dark-haired young man with a flat Tartar face and small eyes'.[8]

We know no more than that. Whatever might have happened between Tchaikovsky and these youths, or indeed anyone else, remains a secret. From now on, according to Modest, the 'young rake and socialite' had modified his behaviour. At the same time, since this is what was important to his brother's reputation, 'a bad public officer was transforming into a good musician'.[9]

Modest is compressing events slightly. As yet, music had not become the dominant activity in Tchaikovsky's life, though it was soon to do so. Before that the young man was to have his first real taste of the outside world, of life outside Mother Russia.

It is at this stage in his life, twenty-one years old and working as a civil servant at the Department of Justice, that we have the first evidence of Tchaikovsky's desire to make music his profession, with the revelation that he is studying musical theory at the same time as carrying out his civil service duties.

---

* Modest's use of the words 'natural defect' gives an insight to how he and his brother viewed homosexuality.

It comes in a letter to his sister. Sasha had recently married Lev Davydov, whose full-time job was to manage his family's extensive estate at Kamenka near Kiev, and a smaller one at Verbovka, in Ukraine. In years to come Tchaikovsky would spend a lot of time composing at Kamenka – a welcome escape from the city – and become very close to his sister's children.

Sasha was pregnant with her first child when her brother wrote to her in March 1861. Although Tchaikovsky never developed a particularly close relationship with his father, it seems Ilya by this point was not wholly averse to his son pursuing a musical career, even at the expense of his civil service one. It is typical of Tchaikovsky, here writing to Sasha, that he plays down his own musical ability:

> *At supper my musical talent was discussed. Papa assures me that it isn't too late for me to become a professional musician. It would be splendid if that were so – but the point is this: if there is talent in me, it is still most likely that it's impossible to develop it by now. They've made a civil servant out of me – and a bad one at that. I try to improve as best I can, to do my job more seriously – and suddenly, at the same time, I am studying thorough-bass.*[10]

It must be rare in the annals of classical music that a father has had a change of heart and encouraged his son to pursue a full-time career in music, over the son's doubts, rather than the other way round – as witness the examples of Vivaldi, whose father trained him for the priesthood; Handel, whose father wanted him to become a lawyer, and Berlioz, whose father wanted him to follow in his footsteps and become a doctor.

Yet that is the rather comfortable position Tchaikovsky found himself in – despite his own modest misgivings – so it must therefore have been with little hesitation that he applied for leave of absence from his job at the ministry, when the chance of an extensive foreign trip came up. It is perhaps a measure of the mundanity of his work that leave was granted without question.

The opportunity had arisen because a friend of his father, an engineer by the name of Vasily Pisarev, was about to make an extensive tour of European cities and required an interpreter and secretary. Tchaikovsky had a good command of French and was passable in German – his early lessons with Fanny Dürbach paying dividends. He was the obvious choice.

The itinerary was extensive and exciting – Berlin, Hamburg, Antwerp, Brussels, London and Paris. Tchaikovsky regularly wrote letters to his father and sister detailing his progress* and it is possible to piece together much of what happened in the three months he was away – on a trip that by turns he found exciting, boring and ultimately traumatic, but that also afforded him a mental break with the past and led to a new direction in life.

The thrill of adventure is there in every word he wrote to Sasha just before leaving:

> *As you probably have heard already, I am to go abroad. You can imagine my delight . . . This journey seems to me at times an alluring, unrealisable dream. I shall not believe in it until I am actually [on my way].*[11]

---

* Reminiscent of Mozart's letters home to his father while touring Europe.

The pair left St Petersburg in the middle of July 1861. It is easy to imagine the excitement, mixed with trepidation, as they crossed the border, leaving their homeland behind. Even the border guards seemed to pity them for leaving Mother Russia:

> Everyone crossed themselves, and the last Russian sentry shouted to us, 'God be with you', solemnly waving his hand.[12]

On 18 July Tchaikovsky and Pisarev arrived in Berlin – a city, if Modest is to be believed, universally loathed by Russians, thanks to the growing power of Prussia and its threat to Russia. Pyotr contributed his due, his brother claims, finding the city old-fashioned and overbearing.

This applied to its musical offerings as well. Tchaikovsky went to a performance of Offenbach's *Orphée aux enfers* (*Orpheus in the Underworld*) and was unimpressed, dismissing it out of hand. German women, he wrote to his father, did not appeal to him; nor did the food, though the helpings were copious. The two men stayed in Berlin for just four days, and it was enough: 'Now we know our Berlin thoroughly, and have had enough of it!'[13]

They moved on to Hamburg, which afforded a thoroughly different experience. A considerable improvement, Tchaikovsky wrote to his father. Given his reference to prostitutes, and his previous comment about the women of Berlin, it has to be wondered whether he was making such statements to conform to his father's image of him as a young man finding out about life, and the delights it was able to offer:

> Hamburg is incomparably better than Berlin . . . In general the week there flew by; there were a great number of amusements. We spent each evening very pleasantly, sometimes taking a walk, sometimes going to a dance with women of doubtful morals (this town abounds in them), sometimes visiting places where the inferior part of the population enjoys itself. It's all extremely jolly and varied.[14]

Should we really believe that Tchaikovsky, even in the company of an older man, went dancing with prostitutes? Quite possibly this is how Pisarev amused himself, but it is difficult to imagine Tchaikovsky following suit – particularly given what was to come very soon.

That he enjoyed Hamburg more than Berlin, though, rings true. A port city no doubt thronging with seafarers of many nationalities, a fish market renowned throughout northern Germany, bristling with dockside restaurants, it was much more characterful than Berlin, the landlocked capital city of Prussia.

Moving on through Cologne to Antwerp, once again Tchaikovsky was unimpressed, as he was with Brussels, in both cities being left to his own devices while Pisarev took care of business matters. From Antwerp to Ostend, which was – literally – a breath of fresh air for Tchaikovsky. His first sight of the open sea thrilled him, and he took full advantage of what it had to offer:

> *I love the sea terribly, especially when it roars, and these last days it has been furious . . . I have bathed very industriously. Men and women bathe together in the open sea.*[15]

From there the two men travelled to London, arriving on 8 August. They did the tourist trail during the week of their visit, and Tchaikovsky was impressed and disappointed in equal measure.

They visited Westminster Abbey, the Houses of Parliament, and twice visited the Crystal Palace, built ten years earlier to house the Great Exhibition. Tchaikovsky found the building magnificent from the outside, but declared that the interior failed to match the exterior splendour.

On the second visit he heard Handel's 'Hallelujah' Chorus performed by a choir of 'several thousand voices', and confessed himself 'overwhelmed by the effect'.[16] He also attended a recital given by a young Adelina Patti, just beginning to make a name for herself on the opera stage. He was not convinced by her performance, though later in life he was to become an ardent follower.

Overall London was not a huge success. It was interesting, he conceded, but made a 'gloomy impression' on his soul. He was not the first visitor to comment on the weather, before or since, though he was more positive about the cuisine, which appealed to him:

> *The sun is never seen; it rains all the time. The* food *is very much to my taste. It's simple, even unsubtle, but liberal in quantity, and tasty.*[17]

There was one more stop on the itinerary, and it was to be the jewel in the crown. Tchaikovsky found his excitement increasing as the time approached. It was as if he knew he would love the city, and that Paris would remain in his heart for the rest of his life.

They arrived on 14 August, and Tchaikovsky was soon extolling the virtues of the French capital to his father:

> *In general life in Paris is extremely pleasant. There you may do everything you like: the only thing that's impossible is to be bored. Get up and out onto the boulevards – and already you are gay.*[18]

If his letter is to be believed, he and Pisarev went to the theatre every day. Even if that is an exaggeration to impress his father, we know they – or Tchaikovsky alone – saw two performances of opera, Verdi's *Il trovatore* and Meyerbeer's *Les Huguenots*.

Regrettably he does not give a detailed account of the performances, though he does write (presumably to please his father) that the productions were good, albeit much inferior to those back home in St Petersburg.

What now begins to become apparent is a certain tension arising between the two men, Pisarev and Tchaikovsky, separated not just by age but also by interests and, more than likely, by sexual inclination.

Another factor began to come between them, this time financial. Pisarev had agreed with Tchaikovsky's father in advance that he would meet Tchaikovsky's expenses. Ilya had also given his son some pocket money, but it appears that by the time they reached Paris, or at least soon after, Tchaikovsky was beginning to run up a debt. He owed at least three hundred roubles to Pisarev.

How this happened, what he spent money on, beyond living expenses that Pisarev covered, we do not know. He does not enlighten us. Nor can we be certain about what exactly happened next between the two men, other than that there was a catastrophic break between them.

Our knowledge of the incident comes entirely from a letter that Tchaikovsky wrote to his sister Sasha once he had returned home to St Petersburg. The letter is lengthy and heartfelt. Although he says nothing explicit, he uses very strong language, leaving us in no doubt that Pisarev did something that utterly appalled his young companion.

> *What is there to tell you about my journey abroad? It's better not to talk about it. If ever I committed any colossal folly in my entire life then this journey is it. You remember Pisarev? Imagine that beneath that mask of* bonhomie, *from which I took him to be an unpolished but worthy gentleman, there are hidden* the most vile qualities of mind *[my italics]. Up till then I had not suspected that* such incredibly base persons *[my italics] existed on the earth.*

In the following sentence he resorts to irony and exaggeration:

> *Now you will have no difficulty in appreciating what it was like for me to spend three months tied inseparably to such a pleasant associate.*[19]

Irony because he clearly found Pisarev anything but pleasant; an exaggeration because the two men went their separate ways before the three-month trip was over.

What led to such an outburst of invective on the part of the mild-mannered and unfailingly courteous Tchaikovsky? Unless and until more papers from the archive at Klin are put into the public domain, we cannot know for certain; even then no more light may be shed on the incident.

Biographers have almost always been drawn to the same, seemingly inescapable, conclusion, namely that Pisarev made an unwanted sexual

"It was as if he knew he would love the city, and that Paris would remain in his heart for the rest of his life."

advance towards the younger man. David Brown goes further: given the strength of Tchaikovsky's language, he suggests it might even have amounted to an assault.[20]

Anthony Holden takes an opposing view: given Pisarev's blatant taste for the low life, as evinced in Tchaikovsky's account of dancing with prostitutes, could Pisarev have shocked the younger man by suggesting some unpalatable *heterosexual* adventure?[21]

Although we do not know the exact date they parted, we have to assume they had been travelling together, in close and even intimate circumstances, for at least two months, quite possibly sharing hotel rooms, and certainly sharing a railway sleeping compartment.

Whether or not Pisarev was gay would undoubtedly have been known to Tchaikovsky, and Pisarev must have been aware of Tchaikovsky's sexual orientation. Even if the latter had been endeavouring to hide it, his descriptions of women of various kinds indicate the two men were at least together in the company of females. It is a fair assumption that their sexuality was known to each other.

Although, at least for the time being, no details can be confirmed, Tchaikovsky's language surely indicates a sexual outrage of some kind. Given what is known of Tchaikovsky's attitude to his own sexuality – his feelings of guilt, even shame – a sexual assault on the part of Pisarev, perhaps particularly violent in nature, certainly seems possible.

All that is truly certain is that the two men parted acrimoniously in Paris, even though Tchaikovsky remained in debt to his companion. Tchaikovsky's letter to Sasha makes it clear he felt embarrassed by this, and he suggests – albeit in guarded language – that the debts might have been incurred because of his propensity to spend on sexual pleasures, even when he knew he could not afford them:

> *You know my weakness? When I have money in my pocket I sacrifice it all to pleasure. I know it's shameful, it's foolish. Strictly speaking I cannot have any money for pleasure; there are exorbitant debts that demand repayment, there is need of the most basic essentials — but I (again through weakness) take account of none of these, and enjoy myself. Such is my character. How shall I end up? What does the future promise for me? It's terrible to think of it. I know that sooner or later (but, more likely, sooner) I shan't have the strength to cope with the hard side of life, and I shall be broken into smithereens. But until that happens I am enjoying life as best I can, and sacrificing all to pleasure.*[22]

'Sacrificing all to pleasure' – telling words. Tchaikovsky is revealing his intimate thoughts to his sister – and there was more. His money troubles were compounded by problems in his love life, though he makes only the briefest reference to this:

> *. . . the last two weeks have been unpleasant in every way. At work it's gone extremely badly, my roubles have long since evaporated – unhappiness in love. But all this is nonsense: the time will come when things will be cheerful again.*[23]

The reference to his work going badly was not an exaggeration. There was a vacancy at the ministry at a more senior level than he currently held, and he had high hopes of securing it – promotion would mean more responsibility and higher pay.

In the event he was passed over, which hurt him greatly. The Justice Ministry's loss would be music's gain.

At the end of that scorching letter to Sasha, Tchaikovsky writes:

I have begun studying thorough-bass, and it's going extremely well. Who knows, perhaps in three years you'll be hearing my operas and singing my arias.[24]

Another letter to Sasha, written six weeks later, was redolent with the modesty regarding his talent that was second nature to him:

You'll agree that, with my tolerable talent (I hope you won't take this as boasting), I should be ill-advised not to try my luck in this field. The only thing I fear is lack of will power: perhaps laziness will claim her own, and I shan't hold out. However, if the opposite happens, then I promise I'll become something.[25]

Tchaikovsky had finally made his mind up. For some months past he had been attending classes at the newly formed Russian Musical Society in St Petersburg. This was where he had been studying thorough-bass, as well as music theory, harmony and counterpoint, while developing his piano-playing technique.

Events were now playing into Tchaikovsky's hands. The Russian Musical Society had been established only two years earlier. If that was fortuitous, the timing of the next development could not have been better for him.

On 8 September 1862 the St Petersburg Conservatory opened its doors. Tchaikovsky was one of the first students to enrol. His mind was made up. His days as a civil servant were behind him. From now on, he would devote his life to music.

6
PYOTR CHOOSES MUSIC

Pyotr Tchaikovsky the music student was an altogether different individual from the Pyotr Tchaikovsky of earlier months, even years. He applied himself in a way he had never done before. He had found his calling.

His self-doubt might not have left him – it never really did throughout the course of his life – but he was clear now about his ambitions. Writing to his sister Sasha, he has no doubts about the future, although he still cannot help putting himself down slightly:

> *Now you will want to know what will become of me when I have finished my course. One thing I know for certain. I shall be a good musician and I shall be able to earn my daily bread. The professors are satisfied with me, and say that with the necessary zeal I shall do well. I do not say all this in a boastful spirit (it is not my nature), only in order to speak openly to you without any false modesty.*[1]

In the same letter, he assures Sasha that he has no intention of getting into debt, having given up all luxuries and amusements. His natural desire to avoid a repeat of the debt he had run up to Pisarev was compounded by the fact that his father, Ilya, had retired from his position as director of the Technological Institute. With the twins Anatoly and Modest in their early teens and still at school, it was a surprising decision, possibly made

due to ill health. Tchaikovsky was aware that from now on he had to pay his own way.

In spite of his assurances to Sasha that he had renounced amusements, he did not entirely give up his homosexual dalliances, but from now on he was both more selective and more discreet. We know from fellow students' accounts that several young and attractive men crossed his path, and it is beyond doubt that he formed a close and enduring relationship with a sixteen-year-old by the name of Joseph Ledger, who was half German and half English.

At the other end of the scale he mixed openly with the homosexual Prince Alexei Vasilyevich Golitsyn and his circle, even to the extent of spending the entire summer of 1864 at the prince's family estate near Kharkhov in Ukraine. In this case, any potential scandal was averted by the prince's standing in the aristocracy, a milieu where homosexuality was not uncommon and generally tolerated, and homosexuals protected. He also continued to see Apukhtin on a regular basis, though he was by now more in control of the relationship than he had been when they were both younger.

Of most importance, however, is that from now on, with music at the centre of his life, all extra-curricular activities were subordinated to it. There was no question of neglecting his studies in pursuit of pleasure. It was remarked on, both by professors and fellow students at the Conservatory, that he applied himself zealously throughout the three years that he studied there. 'Zeal' is the word that crops up again and again, and one that he himself used in his letter to Sasha. He was an exemplary student in all disciplines. Pyotr Tchaikovsky had made up his mind; he clearly *wanted* to become a professional musician.

A new character now enters Tchaikovsky's life, and in one way or another – not always to Tchaikovsky's advantage – will never leave it. Anton Rubinstein, almost eleven years older than Tchaikovsky, was the best-known musician in St Petersburg. If that was probably true before September 1862, it was most definitely true thereafter.

Rubinstein, composer, pianist and conductor, not only founded the St Petersburg Conservatory in that month but was also its first director, and the recruiter of a formidable array of musical talent to its ranks, both as teachers and students. He was already a legend in musical circles, having performed in the capitals of continental Europe, as well as before Russian royalty in St Petersburg. He was lauded as one of the most celebrated pianists in Europe.

At the age of just eleven, he gave a recital in Paris. In the audience were Chopin and Liszt. Both men were hugely impressed. Chopin invited the boy to his studio and played for him. Liszt encouraged him in his efforts to study composition.

As a youth Rubinstein met musicians who had known Beethoven. All were stunned at the physical resemblance. Rubinstein, from an early age, had a mop of uncontrollable hair, and leonine features set off with piercing eyes. In photographs of him in early adulthood and middle age he could be mistaken for Beethoven. Like Beethoven's, his fingers were short with square ends, and he played with them stretched flat over the keys. His little fingers were said to be as thick as his thumbs.

His natural style of playing was to pound the keys heavily, though he was capable of lightness of touch. 'Strength with lightness' was how he described his playing, but there was more strength than lightness, because he knew that was what his audience had come to hear.

His style of playing was so dramatic and intense that it was frequently said that he was Beethoven come back to life. Like Beethoven, his forte was improvisation. But his compositions, both for piano and orchestra, were not in the same league. Liszt, who as a boy had known Beethoven, nicknamed him 'Van II', both for his physical resemblance to the master and his style of musicianship. The future great pianist and composer Sergey Rachmaninov met Rubinstein as a young man, and reported that Rubinstein advised him to play 'until the blood oozes from your fingertips'.[2]

In terms of character, Rubinstein also shared qualities with Beethoven. He was biting in his criticism of other musicians, even offending the 'grand old man' of Russian music, Mikhail Glinka. For some his style was overbearing; others were held spellbound by his virtuosity. An American pianist who came to hear him said she could take him for a few pieces, but a whole evening would be too much.

True to his character, Rubinstein ran the St Petersburg Conservatory with a rod of iron. He was scathing of any student's attempts at composition that fell short. Similarly with performance, his criticism was biting and often hurtful.

One student, recognised as hugely talented, played the first movement of Beethoven's 'Appassionata' Sonata as if he was playing for 'Auntie and Mamma', in Rubinstein's words. He told the student to begin again, and then after a few minutes said, 'Have you started yet?'

'Yes, master, I certainly have.'

'Oh, I hadn't noticed,' replied Rubinstein with studied ennui in his voice.[3]

At the end of the movement Rubinstein offered advice that the young man remembered for the rest of his life: 'My boy, don't you ever forget what I am going to tell you. Beethoven's music must not be studied. It must be reincarnated.'[4] The recipient of both sides of Rubinstein's tongue was the future internationally acclaimed pianist Alfred Cortot.

Beyond his unbounded admiration for the man who changed the course of music, Rubinstein was surprisingly unadventurous in his teaching. Apart from Beethoven, he stressed the importance of Chopin, Schumann and Mendelssohn, but few other composers. It was a complaint among students, though never stated to Rubinstein's face, that their musical education was too narrow.

Too narrow in scope, maybe, but in other ways it was valuable and stimulating. Rubinstein had a habit of beginning a class by reciting a poem, then instructing his students to sketch out a vocal setting there and then, and produce an orchestrated composition the next day.

These he would critique brilliantly, striding in front of the class, compositions in hand, pointing out errors, demonstrating at the piano. Repeatedly he would instruct his students to take their courage in both hands and write what came from their heart as well as from their head.

It is hardly surprising that the naturally timid and modest Pyotr Tchaikovsky would have contradictory feelings towards Rubinstein. His admiration for Rubinstein's musical skill bordered on hero worship. He later wrote:

> [Rubinstein was] not only . . . a great pianist and a great composer, but also . . . a man of rare nobility, sincere, honest, magnanimous, alien to any baseness or vulgarity, with a clear, straightforward mind and infinite kindness – in short a man superior to all other mortals. As a teacher, he was incomparable. He got down to business without bombast or lengthy perorations, but always with a very serious attitude toward the business at hand.[5]

Tchaikovsky is clearly allowing his admiration – adoration, almost – to run away with him. 'Infinite kindness' is not a description many would ascribe to Rubinstein. Yet Tchaikovsky was also genuinely frightened of Rubinstein. He dreaded being made to play the piano in front of him, wilting under the criticism that this so often unleashed. He withered in the face of Rubinstein's overbearing and extroverted personality.

Rubinstein's bark could be worse than his bite. He recognised Tchaikovsky's skills at the keyboard and arranged for him to give piano lessons, which brought in a modest income. Rubinstein was less kind when it came to the matter of composition, something on which he placed the highest emphasis, arguing that it was composition, not performance, that would ensure lasting approbation.

During the summer of 1864, which Tchaikovsky spent at Prince Golitsyn's family residence, he took with him a task he had been set: the composition of an overture to a play by Alexander Ostrovsky, *The Storm*.

Modest recounts that Tchaikovsky, despite pledges to renounce sybaritic pleasures, spent a hedonistic summer among Golitsyn's homosexual set. For a start he was unused to the lavish opulence on display – 'something out of a fairy tale', in Modest's words.[6]

Despite the many temptations, it was here that he developed a love for walking alone through the countryside of Ukraine, content to keep his own company until dinner. In the evening he would entertain on the piano. It was a thoroughly welcome break away from the city and the rigours of Conservatory study.

For Tchaikovsky's name day, 29 June, Golitsyn had prepared a day to remember. Tchaikovsky was honoured at an al fresco breakfast, and later that day was driven through the forest, down a torchlit path leading to a clearing in the woods, where the prince had laid on 'a sumptuous supper' in a splendid marquee for his visitors and serfs alike, with Tchaikovsky as guest of honour.[7]

Given such distractions, Tchaikovsky might have been excused if he did not devote his mind entirely to composition. He completed the overture but it is possible that he knew he wasn't realising his full potential.

Partly for this reason, and partly out of his fear of his teacher's reaction, Tchaikovsky did not submit the piece directly to Rubinstein, but asked a good friend of his and fellow student, Herman Laroche, to hand it in for him.

If Tchaikovsky was dreading Rubinstein's verdict on the Overture: *The Storm*, his anxiety proved justified. The terrifying Conservatory director castigated it, in particular for breaking away from the traditional conventions of composition to which he adhered so strictly.

His reaction might have had something to do with Tchaikovsky's decision to delay returning to St Petersburg, pleading toothache, which was unlikely to have fooled Rubinstein. There is also a suggestion in Modest's memoirs that Rubinstein, who would shortly marry and produce three children, had a streak of homophobia.

History, on the other hand, has been rather more kind to Tchaikovsky's first substantial orchestral work, recognising in it several qualities that he would later use to greater effect, to the extent of salvaging one of the themes for incorporation into his First Symphony. But so stung was Tchaikovsky by Rubinstein's criticism that he refused to give the piece an opus number.

Left
Ludwig van Beethoven.

If Tchaikovsky found that criticism hard to accept, it was nothing compared to what followed a year later. He was approaching the end of his time at the Conservatory. For his graduation exercise, Rubinstein set Tchaikovsky a fiendishly difficult task: to compose a cantata on Schiller's poem 'An die Freude' ('Ode to Joy'). Given that Beethoven had set the same poem in the final movement of his Ninth Symphony, the 'Choral', Tchaikovsky knew from the start Rubinstein had handed him an impossible task that he was destined to fail.

From childhood Tchaikovsky's musical hero had been Mozart. Beethoven had never truly appealed to him, and Rubinstein's possession of so many of Beethoven's characteristics – musical and physical – must have made him only the more nervous. The overt praise he used to describe him was of the sort he might have accorded Beethoven himself just as easily as Rubinstein. It shows deference, even reverence, rather than a personal attachment or intimacy.

Tchaikovsky was given the assignment in late October, with a date for the public performance set a mere eleven weeks later, on 29 December 1865. It was a daunting challenge, even without such a short timescale.

Mindful of the mauling his overture to *The Storm* had received, this time Tchaikovsky stuck strictly to convention. No rules bent or broken, no stepping outside the norms of tradition so assiduously espoused by the Conservatory director.

Now more than half a year past his twenty-fifth birthday and still not in possession of his true musical voice, Tchaikovsky produced a cantata that he again felt was not of a sufficiently high quality – so much so that in an echo of the toothache ploy, he decided to stay away from the performance of his *Ode to Joy* at the graduation concert.

Rubinstein was so furious he seriously considered denying Tchaikovsky his diploma. But he relented in the end; in fact he did more than that. Finally putting aside his own prejudices, Rubinstein awarded Tchaikovsky the silver medal, the first the Conservatory had bestowed, allowing his name to be carved in marble on the Conservatory's grand staircase.[*] Since there was as yet no gold medal, it was the highest award the Conservatory could offer.

The cantata is a substantial work, no fewer than 115 pages, but that did not endear it any the more to one particular critic. César Cui was a trained soldier who had turned to musical criticism and become one of the most respected – and feared – critics in St Petersburg. He was scathing, subjecting Tchaikovsky to insults and barbs the composer never forgot:

> *The Conservatoire composer, Mr Tchaikovsky, is utterly feeble. His composition was written under the most difficult circumstances it is true: to order, to a deadline, to a pre-ordained theme, and with strict adherence to familiar forms. If he had any talent at all, nonetheless, it would surely at some point in the piece have broken free of the chains imposed by the Conservatoire.*[8]

It caused friction between the two men that would last a lifetime, without ever being fully resolved.

---

[*]Where it remains to this day.

By contrast, Tchaikovsky's friend and unfailing supporter, his fellow student Herman Laroche, leapt to his defence. Proving himself a better critic than musician – as indeed he would go on to be – he praised Tchaikovsky's cantata to the skies, which, given the circumstances, can surely be excused. His prediction, though, is spot on:

> *This cantata is the greatest musical event in Russia since [Serov's] Judith. I will tell you frankly that I consider yours the greatest talent to which Russia can look for its musical future at present. More powerful and original than Balakirev, more lofty and inventive than Serov, far more refined than Rimsky-Korsakov. In you I see the greatest – perhaps the only – hope for our musical future.*

What he goes on to say is truly prophetic and does him great justice:

> *Your own really distinctive voice will probably not emerge for another five years or more. But these ripe and classic works will surpass everything we have heard since Glinka. To sum up, I honour you not so much for what you* have *achieved, as for what you soon* will. *The proofs you have offered us so far are but solemn pledges to outshine all your contemporaries.*[9]

Cui's blistering criticism aside, further proof of Rubinstein's recognition of Tchaikovsky's musicianship came with his recommendation that he should now leave St Petersburg and go to Moscow, where he would be able to secure him a post as teacher of musical theory at the Moscow branch of the Russian Musical Society which, fortuitously, was run by Rubinstein's younger brother, Nikolay. It was common knowledge that in Moscow, as in St Petersburg, the Musical Society would soon become the Moscow Conservatory.

In another sign that Tchaikovsky's talent was beginning to be noticed, even before the graduation concert he had received word that an earlier composition of his, the *Characteristic Dances*, had found its way into the hands of a Viennese musician making a fine name for himself with concerts in Pavlovsk Park, close to St Petersburg and frequented by the aristocracy seeking entertainment.

The performance by Johann Strauss II and his orchestra was the first public performance of any of Tchaikovsky's works.

In his personal life, things were settling down for Tchaikovsky. If he was still not comfortable with his sexuality, he was at least perhaps aware that it was a part of him that he was powerless to alter. It is evident, however, that a sense of deep guilt was still present. From a letter Tchaikovsky wrote to Modest, it is clear that he regarded masturbation as a homosexual curse, and that he deplored it.

Modest, and his twin Anatoly – Tolya – were now in their mid-teens, and both had clearly passed through puberty. Tolya was heterosexual, but Modest had confided in his elder brother that he was not. This must have shocked Tchaikovsky, even upset him, given that he clearly regarded homosexuality as a deviance. As for the activity he so closely associated with it, it disgusted him.

He wrote to Modest in February 1866:

As for Tolya's nagging you to stop indulging in masturbation, it is I who encourage him in this. Only by constant surveillance and even actual pestering can you be cured of this shamefulness . . . In general, masturbation should be seen as an abominable habit that can become very deep-rooted, and therefore, it is better to offend at times your self-esteem and to cause some slight annoyance than to allow your ruin. *10

Tchaikovsky perhaps reveals more about his own behaviour in this letter than his brother's. There is no question, though, that their shared sexual orientation brought the two brothers closer, and it is not unreasonable to wonder whether Modest's unstinting admiration for his elder brother had some influence on his own sexual development.

Further evidence comes later that Tchaikovsky was constantly trying to 'cure' his younger brother. In a letter to him dated 13 January 1870, in response to one in which Modest clearly states his preference for men, he wrote:

If there is the slightest possibility, try to be [word deleted, probably 'normal']. This is very sad. At your age one can still force oneself to love [words deleted, probably 'a woman']. Try at least once, maybe it will work out. †11

Once again, Tchaikovsky tells us more about himself than about Modest. In a few short years he would follow his own advice, with disastrous results.

Until now Tchaikovsky had been living with his father in St Petersburg which might have led to tension, though we have no evidence of any problems. This arrangement would now need to change. His father, Ilya, had remarried.

---

* Poznansky makes the point that this passage was missed by Soviet censors in early editions of Tchaikovsky's letter, but redacted in later ones.

† Poznansky agrees with speculation that it might have been Modest himself who later struck the words out of the original letter.

Elizaveta Lipport became Ilya's third wife. For her, a widow, it was a second marriage. We have evidence from a later letter written by Tchaikovsky that initially he and his siblings were against his father remarrying, even though it was twelve years since their mother had died. But in the same letter he goes on to say that they all came to love their stepmother very much. Pyotr certainly, and probably his siblings, had a (probably private) nickname for her: 'Dumpling', because of her rotund shape.

Given that the house might have become a little overcrowded, it was fortuitous that the offer of a job in Moscow materialised for Pyotr soon after his father's marriage. In some respects the move heralded a new Tchaikovsky.

He was now a distinguished graduate of the St Petersburg Conservatory, with an established reputation as a pianist, a lesser one as flautist and timpanist (he had studied both instruments, as well as piano), and a growing, although not uncriticised, reputation as a composer.

Tchaikovsky was assuming the demeanour of an artist. He had always been fond of clothes and careful about his appearance but now he adopted a studied inelegance. He allowed his hair to grow long, and wore clothes that had seen better days. He had also developed an eccentric habit in the course of the few occasions he had taken to the podium to conduct.

According to a fellow student, Tchaikovsky disliked conducting so much that he feared his head would fall off under the strain of appearing in front of an audience. To prevent this happening, he would clutch his chin with his left hand to hold his head in place, while conducting with his right.

It is difficult to know whether he really believed this. Could it simply have been a casual remark when someone asked why he held his chin? It is an endearing and intriguing image: the young musician clutching his chin and explaining, possibly with a grin, that it is to stop his head falling off while conducting the orchestra.

It is certainly the case that Tchaikovsky had abhorred conducting during his years at the Conservatory – one reason for his decision to stay away from the graduation concert – and had never considered himself to have a talent for it. His grades in the final exams in every subject were 'good' or 'very good'; it was only conducting that was given a 'satisfactory'.

In January 1866, the twenty-five-year-old Tchaikovsky was about to leave the city he knew better than any other for one he had only spent a few months in as a boy of eight. He would be away from his family and the musical friends he had made in St Petersburg.

Given his sensitive nature, the trepidation with which Tchaikovsky set out on the journey south to the old Russian capital can be imagined. But he was a teacher now, no longer a student. He had served his time as a musical apprentice; now came the chance to practise his chosen profession.

"Tchaikovsky was now a distinguished graduate of the Conservatory, with a growing reputation as a composer."

Central to this was the younger of the two Rubinstein brothers, Nikolay, who would have a much more profound impact on Tchaikovsky's life than the older Anton – both personally and professionally.

The coming years would be the making of Tchaikovsky. His status as the leading composer of his generation would be assured, even as his personal life descended into chaos, turmoil and recrimination.

7

TCHAIKOVSKY, MUSIC TEACHER

*S*eparated by a mere **450 miles** in a country that stretches nearly 6,000 miles from west to east, Moscow might have been situated in an entirely different universe from St Petersburg.

The ancient capital of the Grand Duchy of Moscow, the city was rambling and provincial, a warren of narrow streets surrounding the Kremlin. This ancient seat of power boasted a profusion of onion domes, evidence of the influence of Byzantine architecture from Constantinople, centre of Orthodox Christianity, from which the Russian Orthodox Church evolved.

Entirely lacking the sophistication of St Petersburg, which had displaced it as capital, it was also resistant to the western trends and ideas that had encroached upon the new, upstart city on the edge of the Baltic. If St Petersburg, Peter the Great's 'window on the western world', was intended to be a European city, Moscow represented ancient Russia.

St Petersburg consisted of streets laid out at right-angles in a regular grid pattern, a city suited to the modern world. Moscow, by contrast, began as a small trading post and fortress, growing outwards from the Kremlin, the fortress, at its centre.

Frequently the object of conquest and invasion from the east, by the Golden Horde from the Mongol empire, the city of Moscow and its people were a cosmopolitan blend of west and east, absorbing cultures and traditions from far-off places. By contrast, to use modern terminology, to the people of Moscow the residents of St Petersburg were, like the French, mostly 'faux' aristocrats and 'nouveau riche'.

Culturally the two cities were totally different as well. Moscow had the Bolshoy Ballet, but the Mariinsky Ballet in St Petersburg was proud of being half a century older. St Petersburg had a profusion of orchestras; Moscow lacked even a single ensemble of a professional standard.[1] St Petersburg was ahead of Moscow with its Russian Musical Society, and then its Conservatory.

It is small wonder that in the dozen or so years Tchaikovsky was largely resident in Moscow he never came to like the city. He was a man of St Petersburg through and through:

> Yes, [Tchaikovsky] revered Moscow's ancient monuments, and he enjoyed the picturesque views of the Kremlin and other historic parts of the city. But he couldn't stand the dirty, swampy pavements, and the lack of facilities for citizens of very limited means . . . In all his truest sympathies he remained a son of St Petersburg, which had long since surpassed Moscow in these elementary amenities.[2]

Tchaikovsky's inbuilt sensitivity, his tendency to self-pity and introspection, were in full flow as he prepared to leave the city he loved for one he did not know, but already disliked. He wrote to his sister Sasha in Kamenka that he was suffering from 'a disease of the spirit', 'incredible depression' and 'hatred of the human race'.[3]

To add to this, he must have been nervous about the prospect of trying to please another ferocious Rubinstein, Anton's younger brother Nikolay, who on Anton's recommendation was offering him a teaching post, with the expectation of a professorship. In the event Tchaikovsky was to find Nikolay far easier to get along with, though their relationship would have to survive some tense moments. It is fair to say that Nikolay would in fact become the single most important and enduring musical influence on the mature Tchaikovsky.

Modest was in no doubt:

> No one, artist or friend, did so much for the advancement of [Tchaikovsky's] fame, gave him greater support and appreciation, or helped him more to conquer his first nervousness and timidity, than the Director of the Moscow Conservatory . . . It is not too much to assert that, during the first years of Tchaikovsky's life there, all Moscow was personified in Nikolay Rubinstein.[4]

Nikolay was five years younger than his brother and only five years older than Tchaikovsky, though the relationship of director to employee made the gap seem larger. Modest attributes this to Nikolay's forceful personality, in contrast to Tchaikovsky's, which he describes as 'yielding and submissive'.

Forceful Nikolay might have been, but he was mildness itself compared with his elder brother. He was, for a start, diminutive in height and stoutly built. He had 'curly hair . . . a dreamy expression, languor of speech, and an air of aristocratic weariness', in Modest's words.[5]

There was no resemblance to Beethoven, either in appearance or pianistic skills. He was unquestionably a virtuoso, but his style was less showy than Anton's. He could pound the keys when it was required, but he was capable of great delicacy as well.

Tchaikovsky, in a letter to his twin brothers, was effusive about his new employer:

Above

Entrance to the grand hall of the Moscow Conservatory.

[Nikolay Rubinstein] is a very kind and sympathetic man. He has none of his brother's unapproachable manner, but in other respects he is not to be compared to Anton – as an artist.[6]

In one other quality Nikolay differed markedly from his elder brother. He seems to have been universally respected, even loved, by his students, even when he chastised them. Tchaikovsky had reason to feel the same way from the moment he arrived in Moscow.

Rubinstein insisted Tchaikovsky move into his house. This Tchaikovsky gladly accepted, though he wrote to his brothers that the wall dividing their rooms was very thin, and he was worried that even the sound his pen made when writing would bother his host.

Tchaikovsky was not the only student to have a room in his employer's house. Rubinstein had a habit of giving lodging to poorer students who could not afford accommodation, and it was remarked on how deeply he cared for his students, acting like a 'nanny' towards them. He even 'forced' a dozen new shirts on Tchaikovsky, and insisted on taking him to his tailor to order a frockcoat.

There is no suggestion of any ulterior motive on Rubinstein's part. He would go on to marry but the marriage failed after two years, because of the opposition of his wife's family to the match. Even after marriage, there is no indication that Rubinstein was attracted to men – he was considered by female students to be quite the 'ladies' man'.

Rubinstein was extremely well known in Moscow, in both artistic circles and beyond. His gregarious nature meant that his home was always full of artists of one kind or another. Dinners, musical recitals and card games were a frequent occurrence in the evening. Occasionally there was dancing, from which Tchaikovsky usually took pains to absent himself.

Through Rubinstein, Tchaikovsky became familiar with the leading artistic figures of the city. It was a wonderful introduction to artistic life in Moscow, even if Tchaikovsky complained to his brothers that he found the evening engagements, the constant socialising and entertainment, unappetising and exhausting.

His duties at the newly opened Conservatory were far from demanding. At least initially he was required to lecture on only two mornings a week, Tuesdays and Fridays, before a late lunch in the mid-afternoon. A few more hours' work on his own projects followed, before an evening meal out with friends and a visit to the theatre.

He had already acquired a habit, which would stay with him, of reading in bed into the small hours; the works of Charles Dickens were a firm favourite. This was both the cause and the effect of chronic insomnia, which plagued him. He described 'sleeping abominably' in letters to Modest, accompanied by 'little apoplectic fits', which seemed to be getting worse and came on unpredictably. 'Two days ago I did not sleep almost the entire night,' he wrote. 'My nerves are again utterly shot.'[7]

Around this time, four lifelong 'vices' now established themselves – coffee, liquor, cigarettes and card games – although in a letter from this period, probably with a certain amount of bluff, he tells Modest he has given up vodka, wine and strong tea.

Interestingly Tchaikovsky was by this point in a milieu that thronged with young women. He might have been able to avoid them at dances either at Rubinstein's home or formal occasions the director took his teaching staff to, but he could not do so in classes at the Conservatory.

He wrote to Sasha, who was not yet aware of his homosexuality, that 'many pretty girls presented themselves'[8] in his classes. He also wrote to his new stepmother, clearly not wishing to enlighten her either:

Yesterday I had to give an examination to everyone who had entered the course. I confess I was terrified at the sight of such an enormous number of crinolines, chignons, etc. But I still hope that I shall manage to captivate these fays [fairies], since in general the local ladies are awfully passionate.[9]

His father is absolutely delighted that Pyotr is surrounded by young women, and teases him mercilessly:

I imagine you sitting at the rostrum. You are surrounded by rosy, white, blue, round, thin, chubby, white-faced, round-cheeked maidens desperately in love with music, and you lecture to them like Apollo sitting on the hill with his harp or lyre while around him the Graces, just like your listeners, only nude or draped in gauze, listen to his songs. I should be very curious to see you sitting there, blushing in confusion.[10]

As far as we know, Tchaikovsky had not yet enlightened his father about his sexuality, though it is always possible of course that he had his suspicions. Indeed, Ilya would go on to encourage his son to find a wife.

Certainly, given his character, Tchaikovsky is likely to have dealt with the female attention he was now getting in a gentler way than the director of the Conservatory. In the same letter to his stepmother he says that Rubinstein has no idea how to rid himself of 'the whole army of ladies who offer him their . . . charms'.[11]

However, that description appears to be somewhat misleading. Certainly Rubinstein had a disdain for his female students. He believed they merely wished to be taught the rudiments of music and had no intention of seeking a career in music. In his reminiscences, published many years later, he describes them misogynistically as behaving 'as though they were quite mad', and in class they would 'shout, grimace, be obstinate, mince, swoon, even run out of the classroom, and altogether exasperate the professors'.

But he believed he had the measure of them and in response to any such conduct, he would have the woman removed. If that was ineffective, he would order a glass of water to be poured over her head.[12]

Despite the unnerving presence of female students, Tchaikovsky was settling into a routine as a music teacher and seeming to enjoy it, even if the city was not to his liking. In early February 1866 he wrote to Modest:

I am gradually becoming accustomed to Moscow, although sometimes I feel very lonely. My classes are very successful, to my great astonishment; my nervousness is vanishing completely, and I am gradually assuming the airs of a professor. My homesickness is also wearing off, but still Moscow

is a strange place, and it will be long before I can contemplate without
horror the thought of remaining here for years – perhaps for ever.[13]

Given that the classes he was scheduled to take did not require much
of Tchaikovsky's time, he had plenty of opportunity to work on his
own compositions. Back in St Petersburg he had composed two further
overtures, as well as the ill-fated overture to *The Storm*. Both had been
performed by a student orchestra but neither, predictably, had impressed
Anton Rubinstein.

Now Nikolay told Tchaikovsky he would conduct the better of the
two, a free-standing Overture in F, providing Tchaikovsky made substantial changes to it. He set about the task with relish, helped by Rubinstein's
unfailing encouragement, an attitude in marked contrast to his brother's.

Tchaikovsky completed the revision, and at a concert on 4 March
1866 Rubinstein conducted the Overture in F. The trepidation with which
Tchaikovsky approached this performance, given the mauling he had received at earlier performances of his music in St Petersburg, can only be
imagined, though it can be assumed that it was tempered with relief that he
was not conducting himself.

This time things were very different. Tchaikovsky's compositional skills
had clearly improved; Rubinstein was a competent conductor, and the

orchestra would have played to a higher standard under his more collaborative guidance.

Whatever the reason, or combination of reasons, the performance was an outstanding success. Two days later Tchaikovsky wrote to the twins, Tolya and Modest:

> *My overture was performed on Friday, and had a good success. I was unanimously recalled, and – to be grandiloquent – received with applause that made the welkin [heavens] ring. More flattering still was the ovation I met with at the supper which Rubinstein gave after the concert.*[14]

Pride, softened with modesty, comes bursting through every word of his description of that after-concert dinner.

> *When I walked into the room, the last to arrive, it was to the sound of prolonged applause, during which I could only blush and bow clumsily in all directions. At the end of the meal, a toast was drunk to Rubinstein, after which he himself proposed another to me, and applause again broke out. I tell you all this in such detail because the evening amounted to my first real public success, and was therefore a very special one for me. (Another detail: the orchestra too applauded me, at rehearsal.) I will not pretend that this has done anything but raise my regard for Moscow and all its charms.*[15]

The words ring so true. It is easy to picture him blushing as he bows awkwardly, then blushing again at the applause after the toast. Probably of equal significance to him, though he puts it in parentheses, is the approval of the orchestra, who applauded him at rehearsal. Approbation from musicians: he could not have asked for more. As he wrote, this marked the first time his music had met with public success. It was a heady feeling that he must have wondered if he would ever experience. Now he knew what it felt like.

It was the success of this performance, coupled with Rubinstein's encouragement, that led Tchaikovsky to consider whether the time was now right to attempt a major work.

He was settled in Moscow; he was lauded in musical circles; he could put the brickbats he had received in St Petersburg behind him. As much to test himself as for any other reason, he made the decision to embark on a full-scale composition.

He had two choices. Which should it be, an opera or a symphony? Rubinstein favoured an opera and furnished Tchaikovsky with several librettos. None of them pleased him. That, coupled with the fact that for some months past he had been making sketches for a possible symphony, decided him.

He would compose his First Symphony. Newly emboldened, he set to work. But, from the very start, it was to be a struggle.

8

THE LADIES' MAN

Tchaikovsky was pushing himself hard. He was by this point embarking on his first major work, and it was proving to be more difficult than it ought to have been if he was to have a professional career as a composer and musician.

Unable to sleep, he frequently worked through the night, suffering from severe headaches and depression. By the end of the summer of 1866, the doctors pronounced that he was heading for a nervous breakdown. He was experiencing hallucinations, and complaining of numbness in his hands and feet.

Work on the symphony proceeded slowly and painfully, and even more so once the doctors had ordered him to stop working at night. But could the strain and effort of composing a symphony, for a musician for whom the act of composition was later to become almost second nature, really be the sole cause of what threatened to be a physical and mental breakdown?

Almost certainly not. There was an added ingredient in the mix, and it was something that would affect him – even come to haunt him – through-out his life. He was having 'woman trouble'.

Pyotr Tchaikovsky, whether he liked it or not, and it was something of which he was certainly aware, was enormously attractive to women. He had soft, sensitive features, and a character to match. He was by nature kind, with a ready smile, and popular in company.

If that smile was unable to conceal entirely a certain amount of anxiety, even pain, perhaps it served only to make him more attractive to the opposite sex. And when he finally sat at the piano, after genuine protestations of modesty, the unintended seduction would be complete.

Despite his tortured attitude towards his own sexuality, he was well aware that any potential liaison with a woman was ultimately doomed, though that would not prevent him making attempts to establish such a relationship in the future, with predictable results. But now, at the age of twenty-six, he was determined to avoid any such thing.

That is not to say that this is how he wanted to be seen by those closest to him. Quite the contrary. He regarded it as essential that his true desires should remain secret, even from close family, and he went to great lengths to keep them hidden.

Take the case of a certain Elizaveta Dmitrieva, known as Mufka to her family. Nikolay Rubinstein, now a close friend of Tchaikovsky as well as his employer, had had a fleeting relationship with Mufka, the niece of a family with whom he was acquainted, and it seems he attempted to pass her on to Tchaikovsky. We cannot know for sure whether Rubinstein was aware of Tchaikovsky's homosexuality. Given the closeness of their relationship, it seems likely; if so, it is possible he was trying to 'tempt' Tchaikovsky by introducing him to Mufka.

Whatever the case, it seems Mufka had no inhibitions. She fell quickly for Tchaikovsky, and made it clear she was ready for a relationship. Tchaikovsky panicked – at least inwardly. Outwardly he took the opposite approach, which made his life all the more difficult.

He wrote to Modest that he found Mufka 'more charming than anything I've seen'. Even more than that: 'To tell the truth, I am quite preoccupied by her, which allows Rubinstein occasion to pester me in the most awful manner.'[1] There has to be, surely, an element of 'tongue in cheek' about this, the homosexual Pyotr writing to his homosexual brother as if he had eyes only for women.

He goes even further in a letter to his father, who is genuinely excited at the prospect that his son might be in love, and that it might lead to something more permanent. Tchaikovsky's letter is lost, but his father replied effusively:

> I shall tell you frankly: in your letter I liked best of all the niece. She must be most pretty, most lovely, and certainly quite clever. I have so fallen in love with her that I wish to see her without fail. Please afford me this opportunity when I come to Moscow.[2]

Inevitably his father was to be disappointed. Over his next few letters to his brothers Tchaikovsky denied having any romantic feelings for Mufka;

in fact his attitude to the young lady seems to have hardened as he wrote: 'I have utterly cooled towards Mufka . . . In general, I am very much disappointed in her.'[3] Was the entire affair simply an attempt to disguise his true feelings, with Tchaikovsky using the young lady as cover? Or might it be more accurate to say the converse had happened, that on discovering his predilection for male relationships, it was Mufka who had cooled towards Tchaikovsky?

With Mufka no longer in the picture, Tchaikovsky finally completed his First Symphony. He called it 'Winter Daydreams', giving the second movement the heading 'Land of gloom, land of mists', which certainly matched his mood during its composition. That movement is rich in melody, and the third contains a waltz, a sign of things to come.

Given the performance history of the First Symphony, it seems certain that Tchaikovsky himself was not entirely satisfied with it. Which makes his decision to send the score to Anton Rubinstein in St Petersburg – even before he had entirely completed it – particularly surprising.

Rubinstein, never one to mince his words, told Tchaikovsky it was dreadful. A composition professor at the St Petersburg Conservatory, under whom Tchaikovsky had studied, also looked at it and concurred with Rubinstein's verdict.

Tchaikovsky, predictably, was hurt to the core; not the first time Anton had had that effect on him. But a sign that Tchaikovsky might not have been entirely surprised was that following the symphony's first performance in February 1868 he revised it substantially before publication in 1875, and it did not receive its second public performance until 1883. He would come to dismiss it as an immature work, and in fact it has not found a regular place in the repertoire to this day.

Having thus far chosen to write a symphony rather than an opera, Tchaikovsky now decided to turn his attention to that other large musical form. With an unsuccessful symphony the only major work the twenty-six-year-old had under his belt, taking on a work as demanding as an opera might be considered very ambitious.

The opportunity came to him, rather than the other way round. A sign of how much better appreciated Tchaikovsky was in Moscow than in St Petersburg (even if he had not yet enjoyed unqualified success) was that the leading playwright of the day, Alexander Ostrovsky – author of nearly fifty plays, described as the most remarkable body of dramatic work in Russian – offered to write a libretto based on his play *The Voyevoda* ('The Provincial Governor') for Tchaikovsky to set.

Right
Alexander Ostrovsky.

Tchaikovsky was flattered, even overjoyed. True to his word, Ostrovsky delivered a libretto of the first act and Tchaikovsky set to work. Once again, his demons haunted him. Still in a state of nervous exhaustion, the effect of intensive, and ultimately unsuccessful, work on the First Symphony, coupled perhaps with the strain of handling unwanted female attention while pretending to others to be interested, hampered him both creatively and practically.

To his huge embarrassment, he managed to lose the libretto, and try as he might he could not find it. He had no alternative but to contact Ostrovsky and own up to his carelessness. Penitently he asked the famous playwright if he would mind writing it again from memory.

All we know of Ostrovsky's reaction is that he agreed to do so, but the second version was a long time coming, and when it finally arrived it was incomplete. Ostrovsky had clearly lost interest and moved on to other things. Tchaikovsky had done himself no favours, and knew he had no choice but to try to complete the libretto himself.

At that point the chance to get away from Moscow presented itself, exactly what he needed to apply himself to the task in hand. But his attempt to focus on his work was to be seriously hampered.

Tchaikovsky's sister Sasha was holidaying with her family – husband Lev Davydov and three young daughters – at Hapsal* on the Estonian coast. Also in attendance was Lev's younger sister, Vera, who was head over heels in love with Tchaikovsky.

It was not a new infatuation. Tchaikovsky had met her at earlier family gatherings, and such had been her attraction to him that it had been common parlance in the family for the past several years that she was in love with him.

Sasha had even written to her brother commenting on the situation after one summer at Kamenka (their home in Ukraine), causing Tchaikovsky to reply in indignant, oblique, and at the same time disingenuous, language:

> As regards what you wrote to me concerning memories left in Kamenka, I refuse to believe it, this never entered my head, and if it were true, that is, serious, then it would affect me in the most unpleasant way.[4]

If he knew Vera was going to be in Hapsal in the summer of 1867, it might legitimately be asked why he chose to go there – as Sasha clearly did later by letter. Tchaikovsky's reply illuminates his character as if with a spotlight, even if he does not intend it that way. Carefully avoiding using Vera's name, he portrays himself as confused by her attention, refusing to believe there is anything serious in it, and falls back on his habitual penchant for running himself down:

> You ask why I decided to go to Hapsal, knowing that a person was living there for whom my presence was not without its dangers. In the first place, because there was nowhere else to go; secondly, I wanted to spend the summer with them all; and thirdly, because it seemed to me that, if what you suggest is really the case, then my absence would be more harmful to her than my presence.

Really? Hard though it may be to take him seriously, he actually claims that he is such an appalling human being that only by seeing him close-up will a woman who loves him realise the folly of her ways. Only because she sees him rarely could she believe herself in love with him:

---

* Now Haapsalu.

When I'm not there my person can, very likely, be imagined as worth loving. But when a woman who loves me has daily contact with my far from poetic qualities, such as slovenliness, irritability, cowardice, triviality, self-esteem, secretiveness, and so on – then, believe me, the halo that surrounds me when I'm afar will evaporate very quickly.[5]

Even by Tchaikovsky's standards, this is an extraordinarily graphic piece of self-critique. He concludes by admitting it might make him seem 'blind and foolish', but really all he has perceived in Vera's behaviour is 'simple friendliness'. In which case, Sasha might be forgiven for telling him he was indeed being blind and foolish.

In a further illumination of Tchaikovsky's character and his apparent inability to behave decisively towards women, during his stay in Hapsal he composed a set of three piano pieces, *Souvenir de Hapsal*, and dedicated them to Vera. The third of these, *Chant sans paroles* ('Song Without Words'), was to become one of his most famous and best-loved pieces.

If she regarded the dedication as an indication that, regardless of his protestations, he was in fact in love with her, who could blame her? This she did, and took it further. It is clear from a letter that the horrified Tchaikovsky wrote the following spring that Vera was assuming they were to be married.

She had good cause to believe it. Astonishingly, in that same letter Tchaikovsky reveals he and Vera have often discussed the farm on which they would end their days together, and he says he was quite serious about it. It is yet further evidence of the ambivalence Tchaikovsky held towards his own sexuality. Again, in direct contradiction to this, he cannot resist a little self-deprecation:

I am too lazy to form new ties, too lazy to start a family, too lazy to take on the responsibility of a wife and children. In short, marriage is to me inconceivable.[6]

There, at last, in those five final words, is the truth – at least for now. We do not know exactly how Tchaikovsky was finally able to convince Vera that a relationship was out of the question. He must have done it with a certain amount of diplomacy and sensitivity, because the two retained a lasting friendship, and Vera went on to marry a naval officer, a future vice admiral.

As with his First Symphony, conditions could certainly have been better in the period Tchaikovsky was writing his opera, *The Voyevoda*. The emotional turmoil of yet another strained relationship was far from conducive to the creative process.

It was not until 30 January 1869, two years after that summer stay in Hapsal, that the opera was first staged – evidence in itself of the difficulties Tchaikovsky had encountered in bringing it to fruition.

The opening night at the Bolshoy Theatre was judged to be a success. An enthusiastic audience gave Tchaikovsky fifteen curtain calls, and presented him with a laurel wreath. The all-important critics, though, were disappointed and said so. They accused Tchaikovsky of falling too much under the influence of German and Italian composers.

Tchaikovsky was able to derive some small comfort from the fact that, on the whole, the critics reflected the audience's enthusiasm to the extent that they suggested Tchaikovsky possessed as yet unrealised talent. It has become clear how easily Tchaikovsky was hurt by criticism, and in this case it shattered him.

Particularly hurtful was the fact that his old friend and fellow student at the St Petersburg Conservatory, Herman Laroche, who had so encouraged him to compose and who had himself now forsaken composition to become a music critic, was unsparing in his assessment.

He accused Tchaikovsky of showing an ignorance of Russian folklore, coupled with repeated mistakes in musical technique. It was a withering review, and it led Tchaikovsky to declare that he would have nothing more to do with Laroche. He stuck to his word for a considerable period of time.

Relations between the two men were later restored somewhat, but they were never quite the same again.

Tchaikovsky took the criticism to heart, despite attempts to dismiss it. Maybe he was aware he had still not composed to the best of his ability. After only four more performances – five in all – Tchaikovsky not only withdrew *The Voyevoda*, but destroyed the score.[*]

The gestation period for *The Voyevoda* was long and difficult. It was not solely due to his entanglement with Vera, but given the difficulties he had encountered there, it might have been expected that Tchaikovsky would avoid any further demands on his attention while concentrating on the mammoth task of bringing his opera to fruition.

Far from it. In the space of just a few months over the summer and autumn of 1868, as he was busy composing, Tchaikovsky would begin two intensive affairs – one homosexual, the other heterosexual. And in the case of the latter, he was so infatuated that this time it was he who would propose marriage.

---

[*] Not until 1933 was it restored from surviving orchestral parts. It still failed to make an impact.

9

A Most Unlikely Affair

Tchaikovsky may have become more careful in his choice of partners as his musical reputation spread, but he by no means eschewed liaisons with other men altogether. In Moscow's musical circles he was becoming the subject of gossip: at times he did little to prevent this and his behaviour positively encouraged it.

As professor at the Moscow Conservatory, he formed a close friendship with a fellow professor of piano and music theory, Nikolay Kashkin. The relationship was not physical. Kashkin was married, and we owe one of the most colourful of all anecdotes about Tchaikovsky to his daughter Sofiya.

It was no secret that Tchaikovsky loved a practical joke – as a youth he was constantly playing tricks on his siblings, a favourite being to perch a bucket of water on top of a door he knew one of his brothers was about to open. His predilection stayed with him in adult life.

On one occasion Tchaikovsky and his friend Kashkin were both invited to attend a masked ball. Tchaikovsky hated such occasions, and probably to assuage his natural reluctance to attend, he persuaded Kashkin that both would dress in disguise. They made a bet that each would not recognise the other.

Kashkin's disguise was simply to shave off his beard. While waiting for Tchaikovsky to arrive, all eyes were drawn to the entrance of a tall, elegant lady wearing a luxurious loose-flowing cloak, which covered her head and incorporated a mask that hid the upper part of her face. She was wearing diamonds and carrying an ostrich-feather fan. She was led into the room on the arm of a male guest.

It was well known in aristocratic circles in Moscow that the cloak was the only one of its kind, made specially to order for a wealthy Moscow lady. It so happened that this lady had told her husband she was feeling unwell on this particular evening, and would not be attending the masked ball.

Her husband, enjoying his freedom, was openly flirting with an actress. Realising his wife had entered the ballroom unexpectedly, he scuttled away, hoping he had escaped her notice. The actress in question was not short of attention, and soon found herself being paid court by another man.

The lady in the cloak was led round the room by her male partner, to the universal admiration of the guests. Walking past Kashkin, she suddenly turned and exclaimed loudly, 'Idiot I am! Of course he would have shaved!'

The lady – no doubt to the errant husband's relief – was instantly recognised as Tchaikovsky.

Neither Tchaikovsky nor Kashkin, it seems, recognised the other, at least to begin with. Sofiya does not tell us who was judged to have won the bet, but does say the unmasking of both men caused amusement all round.[*]

Such pranks served only to increase rumours about Tchaikovsky's sexuality. More serious was the close relationship he formed with a teenage boy at around the same time, one that would endure – though not without tension and occasional estrangement – for the rest of his life.

The composer had first met Vladimir Shilovsky when he was twenty-six and Vladimir was a boy of fourteen. He was introduced to the Shilovsky household – mother, stepfather and two sons – by a mutual friend so that he could meet the younger of the two boys, Vladimir, who was showing a prodigious talent for music.

Tchaikovsky was instantly impressed – and not solely by the boy's musicality. A photograph taken a decade or so later shows a broad sensitive face, deep dark eyes, full lips, and a luxuriant head of wavy hair, parted in the middle. A year later, Vladimir gained a place at the Moscow Conservatory. Tchaikovsky became his professor of music theory and composition, and a close relationship developed between the two.

---

[*] A similar anecdote from another occasion, which has Tchaikovsky dressed in a rich black frock with long train, flicking a fan of black feathers encrusted with gold, 'so inimitably grand and so unrecognisable that we greeted him with a burst of unanimous applause', is related in Poznansky, *Tchaikovsky Through Others' Eyes*, pp. 99–101.

Modest described Shilovsky as being 'unusually attractive, his manners most spontaneously charming, and his mind, despite his poor education, sharp and observant'. He also had, by all accounts, a less attractive side to his personality but, according to his brother, Tchaikovsky 'was bound to his pupil . . . by that love verging on adoration which he instilled in the boy'.[2]

Shilovsky came from a wealthy family, and in May 1868, at the age of sixteen, he embarked on an extended European trip with his stepfather and a family friend. Shilovsky invited Tchaikovsky to accompany them, offering to cover all Tchaikovsky's travel expenses.

Tchaikovsky accepted, though with a certain reluctance. He knew from his previous travels that he was prone to homesickness whenever he left

Above

Berlin's Zoological
Gardens.

Russia, and this trip would be no exception. There was also the fact, which would be known to those involved, that he was being subsidised by a teenage boy.

The group left for Europe, but their trip was marred by a series of unwelcome events. In Berlin, they visited the Zoological Gardens. Keepers in the reptile house offered to demonstrate to them how the giant boa constrictor was fed. A live rabbit was placed in the boa's cage. It immediately stood up on its hind paws and stared at the snake, frozen to the spot. The boa locked its jaws instantly round it, and devoured the hapless animal.

Three of the four Russians cried with delight. Tchaikovsky, though, let out a scream and broke down in tears, sobbing hysterically. He had to be taken straight back to the hotel. All efforts to calm him failed and he shook uncontrollably for the whole evening, refusing to eat.

After a week in Berlin the party moved on to Paris, and there Shilovsky fell ill. He became so unwell that the rest of the trip had to be abandoned and they remained in Paris for five weeks, to Tchaikovsky's frustration, before returning to St Petersburg in early August. A small consolation was that he met the elderly French composer Daniel Auber, composer of more than thirty comic operas, whom he found utterly charming.

It is not known for certain whether Tchaikovsky and Shilovsky began a physical relationship during this trip, but Tchaikovsky's later correspondence with Modest makes it clear that at some point a relationship began. It was to last, on and off, for the rest of both their lives. Like Tchaikovsky's other relationships, it conformed to a pattern: Shilovsky, belonging to a higher social class, was able to be more open about his homosexuality than Tchaikovsky.

The ill health that Shilovsky suffered on the trip to Europe continued to plague him throughout his life, and he never managed to fulfil his musical potential. He died at the age of forty-one, five months before Tchaikovsky.

Shortly after his return to St Petersburg, Tchaikovsky became involved in another relationship. This time it shocked those who knew him to the core, causing them to question what they knew of him. Likewise it forces us today to re-evaluate our own judgements.

Tchaikovsky fell head over heels in love and, for the first and last time in his life, it is clear that his emotions were aroused by a woman.

It is hard to know what was going on in his mind at this point. Perhaps it suggests that, at the age of twenty-eight, Tchaikovsky was still not utterly convinced his sexual orientation was fixed. Homosexual leanings, he clearly still believed, might be something that could be 'cured' by the right behaviour. This would remain the case, in even more dramatic circumstances, nine years later, when he would take the most drastic 'remedial' action possible.

The woman in question was a Belgian operatic soprano, born Marguerite Joséphine Montagney, who was famous throughout Europe under the stage name of Désirée Artôt. In his memoirs, Modest described her – a little ungallantly – as:

> . . . not good-looking. At the same time, without recourse to artificial aids, her charm was so great that she won all hearts and turned all heads, as though she had been the loveliest of women. The delicate texture and pallor of her skin, the plastic grace of her movements, the beauty of her neck and arms, were not her only weapons.[3]

Others were less polite. Tchaikovsky's friend Laroche saw her as 'a thirty-year-old spinster with a plain and passionate face who was just beginning to grow stout'. Another noted that 'her nose was broad and her lips somewhat too thick'.[4]

Her voice, however, was universally hailed as her greatest asset. According to Modest, it had the timbre more of the oboe than the flute, giving it a penetrating clarity, and was particularly good in the lower register, allowing her to sing mezzo-soprano roles as well as soprano.

Among those who were instantly captivated was Pyotr Tchaikovsky. It has become standard practice for his biographers, in describing this unexpected relationship, to state that Tchaikovsky fell in love with the artist more than he did with the woman.

Certainly that is the impression Tchaikovsky himself gave when describing her to Modest, focusing on her accomplishments:

> *Ah! . . . If you knew what a singer and actress is Artôt! Never yet have I been under so strong a spell of an artist as this time. And it is such a pity that you cannot hear or see her. How you would admire her gestures and the grace of her movements and poses!*[5]

However, if there was any doubt that Tchaikovsky had fallen in love with the woman as well as the artist, it was soon dispelled. It was evident to all who knew him. They described the longing looks the two exchanged, with 'beaming delight' in their eyes. Rumours of marriage soon circulated, even reaching his family back in St Petersburg.

Tchaikovsky was not put off, though. He described himself in one letter as loving Artôt very, very much. Exactly how and when he proposed marriage to her we do not know, but we know that he did. We know too that she accepted.

But the couple faced a number of challenges. In the first place Artôt was five years older than Tchaikovsky, at the height of a career that she could not be expected to curtail after marriage.

Tchaikovsky's friend and mentor Nikolay Rubinstein was dead set against the union. He warned Tchaikovsky that he would have to follow her across Europe while she worked, give up his own musical ambitions and be financially supported by her, and that once the first flush of passion had inevitably faded, he would be left with only 'broken pride, despair, and ruin'.[6]

Rubinstein, it seems, was not the only sceptic. Both Tchaikovsky's twin brothers pointed out to him in letters from St Petersburg the folly of a course of action that was so alien to his natural instincts, with an underlying suggestion that they believed the whole enterprise was another of Tchaikovsky's practical jokes.

His sister Sasha, too, wrote from Kamenka that she was feeling feverish and having trouble sleeping, because her joy was mixed with anxiety. In a slightly strange choice of words, she said she was experiencing the same trepidation as a mother would feel giving away her sixteen-year-old daughter in marriage.

Only one person, predictably, was thoroughly delighted. If Ilya was still harbouring doubts about his son's sexuality, particularly after the relationship with Vera had come to nothing, then marriage to Désirée would put

his mind to rest once and for all. 'With such a person as your "Desired" you will rather perfect than lose your talent,' he wrote to Pyotr in Moscow. 'Why assume that you will be deprived of the opportunity to proceed along your own path?'[7]

Our knowledge of what happened next is based largely on an account by a friend who, at the time, was very close to Tchaikovsky – in fact the same friend who first introduced him to Vladimir Shilovsky, and was one of the party on the fraught European trip – the actor and singer Konstantin de Lazari. Despite some rather bizarre elements to his account, we have no reason to doubt it. What follows is based on his memoirs.

Tchaikovsky, it seems, had a rival for Artôt's affections, an Armenian gentleman who had also fallen victim to her charms. In a calculated move, the Armenian set out to befriend the singer's mother, while also taking every opportunity to undermine Tchaikovsky, even convincing her that Tchaikovsky was the son of a Polish writer and mercenary – definitely several rungs down the social ladder from a Russian.

The malicious campaign was yielding results. Aware of the influence Artôt's mother had over her, Tchaikovsky realised he was rapidly falling out of favour. Having pressed her on the matter, she admitted that her mother did not look kindly on his suit. She reassured him, though, with loving words. 'Whatever they may tell me, however they may try to separate us, please know that I shall always be true to you and shall never belong to anyone but you.'[8]

Désirée did not keep her promise. In early 1869, after her opera company moved to Warsaw, she abruptly, and to everyone's surprise, married one of its other performers, a Spanish baritone named Don Mariano Padilla y Ramos.

Both Tchaikovsky and the Armenian had lost their suit. Tchaikovsky tried to brush it off with sarcastic humour, belittling Artôt for marrying a man whom she had apparently previously scorned. He wrote to Modest in February 1869:

> *The business with Artôt has resolved itself in the most amusing manner. In Warsaw she fell in love with the baritone Padilla, who here had been the object of her ridicule – and she marries him! What sort of lady is that! . . . This denouement is ludicrous.*[9]

An indication, perhaps, that Tchaikovsky was indulging in a little bit of wishful thinking, trying to convince himself that it was all to the good, even if he knew deep down he had been humiliated, came shortly before this, when things were going rapidly downhill. He dedicated his melancholic Romance in F minor, Op. 5, to her.

In fact he must have been anticipating an end to their relationship, as he had only recently reported to Anatoly:

Concerning the love affair that you know happened to me in the early winter, let me tell you that it is very doubtful whether my entry into the bounds of Hymen will take place; this affair is beginning to fall apart somewhat.*[10]

Still, he clearly continued to appreciate Artôt's talent as a performer. When she sang in St Petersburg, Tchaikovsky wrote to Modest advising him to go and see her.

The affair was over; there was to be no marriage. But Tchaikovsky was not yet done with the duplicitous singer. It appears he really did harbour a lasting love for her, or at least had not entirely got over her. She too was deeply affected by their relationship.

They met again, six years later. It was a chance encounter, and both were thoroughly shaken by it. Kashkin recounts that when he and Tchaikovsky went to see Nikolay Rubinstein at the Moscow Conservatory, they were standing patiently outside his office, waiting for him to finish a meeting with a 'foreign lady'. When the door opened and Artôt walked out, Tchaikovsky 'jumped out of his seat and turned quite pale'.

Artôt gasped and was so disorientated that she walked straight into a wall rather than through the door. Then, once she had managed to locate the door, disappeared through it as quickly as she could.

Tchaikovsky shrugged off the encounter with a laugh, exclaiming, 'And I thought I was in love with her!' he said.[11]

The embarrassment of the moment must have rekindled some painful memories, however, as he was withering and unkind in his assessment of a performance he attended not long after: 'Yesterday Artôt premiered here. She has grown fat to the point of ugliness and has nearly lost her voice, but her talent could still be felt.'[12]

The two would meet again, in Berlin in 1888. On this occasion it seemed enough time had now elapsed for bygones to be bygones. Witnesses described the encounter as entirely friendly, all past transgressions and animosity appeared to have been forgotten. Later that same year he even dedicated a second piece to her, his Six French Songs, Op. 65.

That Tchaikovsky was deeply affected by his love for Artôt cannot be doubted. It is impossible to know, of course, to what degree his sexuality was responsible for the ultimate failure of their relationship.

---

*The Greek god of marriage ceremonies.

De Lazari does not say so, but it is more than likely that Nikolay Rubinstein had a quiet word with Désirée's mother, tipping her off that Tchaikovsky was gay. That would certainly account for her sudden coolness towards him. If that is the case, did she in turn enlighten her daughter?

Given what is known of Tchaikovsky's personal life – in particular of events to come – it was probably best for all concerned that the marriage to Artôt did not take place. The whole affair has such obvious echoes of his failed relationships with both Mufka and Vera that it seems likely that Tchaikovsky was trying to suppress his sexuality. Could marriage really be the solution? Once again he had tried, this time coming closer than before, but once again a heterosexual relationship had eluded him. It would not be the last time he would try.

It might be expected that the emotional turmoil of a failed relationship would affect Tchaikovsky's creativity, even to cause a block. In fact the opposite was true, which is all the more surprising given that, only weeks after learning of Artôt's sudden marriage, he was to face the failure of his opera *The Voyevoda*, after its long and difficult gestation period.

But a significant event in his life was about to occur. Within a matter of months he was to meet one of the most prominent names in Russian music – an encounter that led to Tchaikovsky composing his first true masterpiece.

But even then Tchaikovsky was struggling constantly with his sexuality. At the time he was writing an extraordinary piece of music concerning a doomed love affair, he would once again embark on exactly such a liaison, and this time its dénouement was to devastate him.

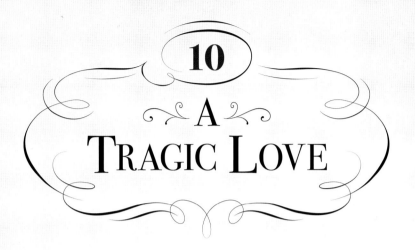

10

A
TRAGIC LOVE

With Glinka dead for more than a decade, the mantle of 'grand old man' of Russian music now fell on Mily Balakirev. Despite being only four and a half years older than Tchaikovsky, he was seen as the senior figure in Russian musical circles. A fierce nationalist who made his name with works based on Russian themes, he headed the group of what would become known as the Five, or the Mighty Handful, which included such composers as Mussorgsky, Borodin and Rimsky-Korsakov.

Tchaikovsky never joined the group – in fact he had strained relationships with some of the members – but he respected and admired Balakirev, who in turn seemed happy to take him under his wing.

It is not known exactly when the two met but it was certainly around the time that Tchaikovsky was recovering from Artôt's rejection, because he asked Balakirev to accept the dedication of a symphonic poem he had written, which he called *Fatum*. The title, meaning 'fate', was no coincidence, given the trauma of his love life.

Balakirev accepted, and conducted the second performance of the piece to a lukewarm reception. Although Balakirev was grateful to Tchaikovsky for the dedication, he castigated the work mercilessly. It is a sign of the respect in which Tchaikovsky held Balakirev that he was not offended. He did not, though, take Balakirev's advice on how to rework it. Instead he destroyed it.*

A similar fate befell a full-length opera Tchaikovsky worked on feverishly at around this time, bringing it to fruition in a mere six months. The title was *Undine*, and the plot was based on a German folk tale in which a lovelorn nymph metamorphoses into a fountain.[1]

The Imperial Theatres, for whom it was written, at first shelved and then rejected the work. Tchaikovsky, again, destroyed the score. He was at a low ebb. Two unsatisfactory compositions, yet another failed love affair – and seemingly also a failed attempt to 'cure' the homosexuality about which he felt so conflicted.

Even Balakirev was beginning to get on his nerves. Tchaikovsky wrote to Modest that he disliked the narrowness of Balakirev's views, an undoubted reference to the fact that Balakirev believed that Russian composers should compose Russian music, uncontaminated by foreign influences.

Nevertheless his admiration for the older composer was not lessened. In the same letter, he wrote, 'Although [Balakirev] has sometimes bored me, I must in justice say that he is a good, honourable man, and immeasurably above the average of an artist.'[2]

This was something of an understatement. Shortly before leaving Moscow, during a long walk they took together, Balakirev suggested that Tchaikovsky should compose a piece of music based on Shakespeare's *Romeo and Juliet*. Tchaikovsky had resisted taking advice from fellow musicians, ever since he had felt the sharpness of Anton Rubinstein's tongue. It is a measure of his respect and admiration for Balakirev that – surprisingly – he pursued the idea.

In late September 1869, Tchaikovsky set to work on composing a stand-alone piece, an overture based on the story of the tragic, star-crossed lovers. It had been two months since he had composed anything, and with Balakirev in St Petersburg, Tchaikovsky isolated himself from outside interference and waited for inspiration. It was slow to come.

A full week went by with not a note written. This fed into Tchaikovsky's depression, causing him to sink close to despair. If we take the words he wrote to Balakirev at face value, he believed this marked the end of his life as a composer. It had all come to nothing. His muse had deserted him; it might never return:

> *I didn't want to write to you until I had sketched out at least some-*
> *thing of the overture. But just imagine, I'm completely played out,*

---

*The score was reconstructed from the original orchestral parts after Tchaikovsky's death.

and not one even mildly tolerable musical idea comes into my head. I'm beginning to fear that my muse has flown off to some distant place . . . and perhaps I'll have to wait a long time for her to return — and that's why I have decided to write forewarning you that I have become a museless . . . musician.[3]

Writing to Balakirev was the best thing he could have done. By nature Balakirev was a better teacher than he was an original composer. It was he after all who had mentored the composers of the Five. He now counselled Tchaikovsky by letter from St Petersburg, and was unstinting in his encouragement.

He told Tchaikovsky how he himself had struggled at first to compose his own overture to *King Lear*, explaining how he set out a 'ground plan', fitting themes to characters and plot. He suggested to Tchaikovsky that he should 'inflame' himself with

Above
Mily Balakirev.

a plan, and followed this with some delightfully practical advice: 'Then arm yourself with galoshes and a stick, set off for a walk along the boulevards . . . and I'm convinced that before [long] you'll have some theme or at least some episode.'

Balakirev even confessed himself inspired on Tchaikovsky's behalf, and sketched out four bars representing 'a fierce allegro with sword clashes' that he thought should open the piece. If Tchaikovsky were to carry that around deep within his brain, then Balakirev was certain there would issue something 'alive and feasible'.[4]

It seems Balakirev unlocked something within Tchaikovsky. Three weeks after receiving Balakirev's letter, he was able to inform him by return that the overture was progressing rapidly. He is effusive in his gratitude to the older man, employing colourful language:

The greater part is already composed in outline, and if nothing happens to hamper me I hope it will be ready in a month and a half. When it's crept out of my womb you'll see that, whatever else it may be, a large portion of what you advised me to do has been carried out as you instructed.[5]

Tchaikovsky included with the letter several of the themes he had composed. One in particular caught Balakirev's fancy, and responding to Tchaikovsky's choice of imagery he uses particularly sensuous language, teasing Tchaikovsky over his failed love affair with Désirée Artôt:

> *The second D flat tune is simply* delightful. *I play it often, and I want very much to kiss you for it. Here is tenderness and the sweetness of love . . . When I play [it], then I imagine you are lying naked in your bath and that the Artôt-Padilla herself is washing your tummy with hot lather from scented soap.*[6]

It is significant that this theme is the soaring love theme at the heart of the work, for which Tchaikovsky had chosen the 'soft' key of D flat.[*]

Despite the colourful language, Balakirev was critical too. In fact he advises nothing less than a complete rewrite. It can be assumed that Tchaikovsky's readiness to rewrite large portions was as much to do with his own awareness that the work was not yet up to scratch as it was about following Balakirev's advice.

He revised the overture after its first performance, which was conducted by Nikolay Rubinstein, and then again two years later. Significantly, Tchaikovsky substantially rewrote the ending of the piece eight years after that.

By then Balakirev had passed out of Tchaikovsky's life. Tchaikovsky had now outgrown his mentor and was refusing to make changes the older composer suggested.

Balakirev had fallen on hard times, and in the spring of 1871 he suffered a nervous breakdown. After he recovered, friends found he had lost his energy and drive and become largely silent. Borodin suggested to Rimsky-Korsakov that Balakirev was now insane.

He underwent a religious conversion. A former atheist, he committed himself to the Russian Orthodox Church so intensely that he could not pass a church without crossing himself. He became a strict vegetarian, eating fish only if they had died naturally and not been killed.

His compassion for animal life became obsessive, to the extent that if he saw an insect in a room, he would carefully catch it and put it out of the window, saying – according to Rimsky-Korsakov – 'Go thee, dearie, in the name of the Lord, go!'[7]

Balakirev – who as far as is known never married or had children – continued to compose, even after his nervous breakdown, but his works were slight compared with his earlier compositions. His style also be-

---

[*] D flat major uses all five black keys on the piano keyboard.

longed to a bygone era. His importance lies in the encouragement he gave to younger composers, and in particular to Tchaikovsky.

Without Balakirev, we might not have the Fantasy Overture: *Romeo and Juliet*. True, the finished work we know today is far removed from Balakirev's early advice, not all of which Tchaikovsky followed. But given the depths of despair to which Tchaikovsky had descended, had Balakirev not encouraged him to the extent that he did, Tchaikovsky might never have undertaken the composition.

By the time he had finished the revisions, Tchaikovsky had produced his first mature masterpiece. He knew it himself, describing it many years later as the best work he had ever done.

In the Fantasy Overture he portrays perfectly in music the psychological drama of Shakespeare's tragedy. He captures the sense of inevitable doom that surrounds the young lovers: theirs is a passion that will end in death. The warring families of the Montagues and Capulets are searingly depicted, while Friar Laurence imparts wise advice and reason. The truly dramatic sequence of chords, in syncopated rhythm, that ends the piece was Tchaikovsky's final addition.

At the heart of the work sits that soaring love theme, which survived all the revisions. It is as if Tchaikovsky had poured his heart into that theme. Could it be that it did indeed come from his heart, that he was himself once again in love?

At exactly the time that Tchaikovsky was composing *Romeo and Juliet*, he was falling deeply in love with a fifteen-year-old boy by the name of Eduard Zak. All his life, Tchaikovsky considered this to be the age at which boys were at their most beautiful.[8]

Eduard might have been one of Tchaikovsky's pupils at the Conservatory, or perhaps he was related to one of Tchaikovsky's pupils. Modest does not mention him once in his writing. It is possible that Soviet censors have excised any mention of him, and that more information might emerge in the future.

Nevertheless, Eduard Zak was, as Alexander Poznansky states, 'one of the great passions of Tchaikovsky's life'.[9] The evidence is there in the composer's own letters.

It seems Tchaikovsky's elder brother Nikolay (Kolya) had given Eduard a job – perhaps Tchaikovsky had even suggested it – working on the railway in a provincial location. While he is pleased Eduard is employed, he misses him deeply and worries about the conditions he is working in.

He is grateful to Nikolay for sparing Eduard exhausting work in the

"Tchaikovsky had produced his first mature masterpiece, describing it many years later as the best work he had ever done."

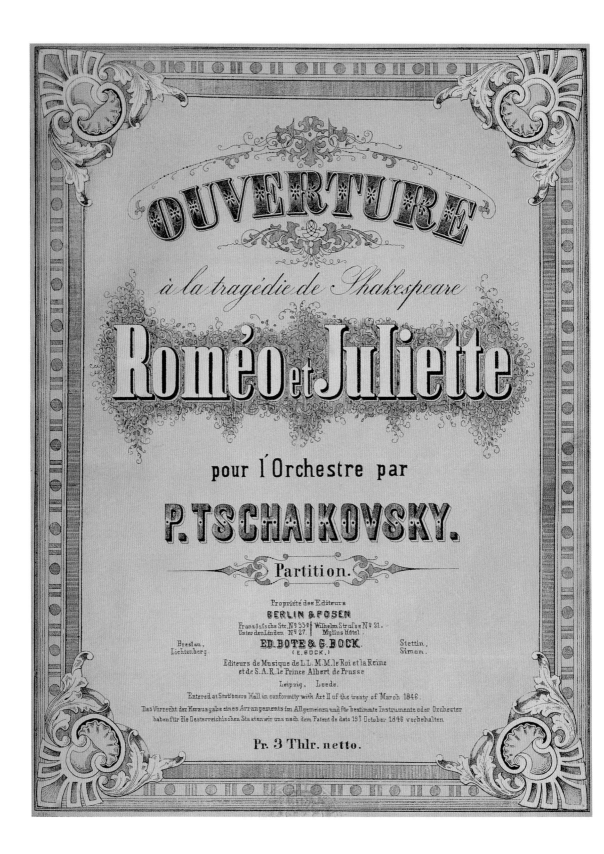

depths of winter – again, probably at Tchaikovsky's request – but implores him to allow the boy to take a short holiday so he can return to Moscow. He writes:

> *In doing this you will also give me great pleasure. I have missed him terribly and fear for his future . . . It is absolutely essential for me to see him. For God's sake, work it out.*[10]

There is no proof of Eduard's sexual orientation, although by 1873 he was associating with Shilovsky and his crowd. That, together with the amorous attention Tchaikovsky clearly accorded him – whether it developed into a physical relationship or not – suggests that he was homosexual.

His altruism towards Eduard is persuasive evidence of his deep affection towards him. Did Eduard inspire the soaring love theme in the Fantasy Overture: *Romeo and Juliet*? We can only speculate, but I would suggest there is a direct connection. We can draw such a conclusion only with hindsight, able – as we are – to look back at Tchaikovsky's life in its entirety.

On 2 November 1873, Eduard Zak committed suicide. None of the circumstances of why or how he took his own life are known. Perhaps the details remain under censorship, in which case more might be revealed at some future time.

We most certainly do know how this tragic turn of events affected Tchaikovsky, however. He was devastated almost beyond words, so much so that a full fourteen years later, he is still haunted by Eduard's death, writing two emotional diary entries. On 4 September 1887 he wrote:

> *Before going to sleep, thought much and long of Eduard. Wept much. Can it be that* he *is truly gone??? Don't believe it.*

The next day, Eduard still dominating his thoughts, the words of grief poured from him:

> *Again thought of and recalled Zak. How amazingly clearly I remember him: the sound of his voice, his movements, but especially the extraordinarily wonderful expression on his face at times. I cannot conceive that he should be no more. His death, that is complete non-existence, is beyond my comprehension. It seems to me that I have never loved anyone so strongly as him. My God! No matter what they told me then and how I try to console myself, my guilt before him is terrible! And at the same time I loved him, that is, not loved, but love him still, and his memory is sacred to me!*[11]

Tchaikovsky uses the word 'guilt'. It is quite possible that he seduced the

Left

Title page of the score for the *Romeo and Juliet* overture.

fifteen-year-old boy, in which case perhaps he felt that he was responsible for 'converting' Zak to homosexuality, perhaps ultimately for his death? That must remain speculation. Whatever the truth, the intensity of his feelings towards Eduard can be in no doubt, given that Tchaikovsky lay in bed thinking of him, and woke up the next morning thinking of him, fourteen years after he died.

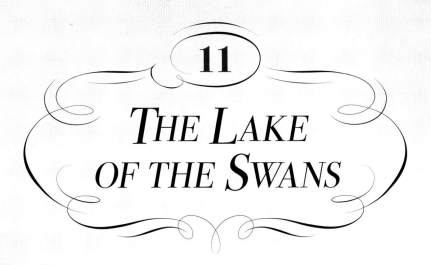

11

THE LAKE OF THE SWANS

efore Eduard Zak's suicide clouded Tchaikovsky's life, the composer was enjoying musical inspiration. As he so often did when he needed peace and quiet to work, he spent the summer of 1871 at his sister Sasha's estate in Kamenka in Ukraine.

Peace and quiet might not in fact have been in plentiful supply, given that she and her husband Lev Davydov had four children under ten years of age, and Sasha was pregnant with a fifth. This fifth, who would be born in December, was Vladimir, known as Bob, to whom Tchaikovsky would become deeply attached. After Bob, the Davydovs would have a sixth child, Yuri, who lived into the mid-1960s and the height of the Cold War.

Mindful of her brother's need for isolation so that he could compose his music, Sasha gave him an attic room with its own separate entrance. Tchaikovsky made full use of this to continue working on a full-scale opera he had begun the year before. It was called *The Oprichnik* ('The Guardsman') and was based on a melodramatic tale set in the time of Ivan the Terrible by a respected but little-known Russian playwright. Tchaikovsky wrote the libretto himself.

Progress initially had been slow. In a pattern that would be repeated many times, Tchaikovsky found that inspiration came in the bucolic surroundings of Kamenka. He rapidly completed the bulk of the work, leaving the finishing touches until his return to Moscow.

Above

Stage design for
The Oprichnik.

In Kamenka he also entered into family life, something he always enjoyed, perhaps mindful he was unlikely to have a family of his own. Modest was also in Kamenka that summer, and one can imagine much happiness, even rowdiness, as two adoring uncles indulged themselves with their four young nieces.

There was much musical activity. Although Tchaikovsky was fully engaged on *The Oprichnik*, he still found time to compose a miniature ballet for the children – and their uncles – to perform. Not only did he compose the music for the ballet, but he choreographed it as well.

One of the nieces has left a beguiling description of how the staging was done entirely by 'Uncle Pyotr'. To demonstrate the dance moves, Uncle Pyotr, 'red in the face, wet with perspiration as he sang the tune', danced the steps himself, arms above his head, pirouetting.

Uncle Modest danced the part of the Prince, and the eldest niece, Tatyana, was Odette. It all presented a 'pretty amusing sight', she recalled, and she and those of her siblings old enough would remember it for the rest of their lives.[1]

Where did Tchaikovsky find the inspiration for this little ballet? Most likely from a stretch of water on the estate, and the birds that made it their home. He called his ballet *The Lake of the Swans*, and it did indeed contain the famous melody, the Swan's Theme, that would form the heart of the immortal ballet he would write five years later.

At the end of the summer idyll Tchaikovsky returned to Moscow in changed circumstances. He was finally able to move out of Rubinstein's home into an apartment of his own.

It was modest in the extreme, consisting of just a kitchen and two rooms, and one of his friends described it as 'very tiny'. But it marked a change in status for the aspiring composer, who was now thirty-one years of age.

It marked a change in lifestyle too; living alone he was able to entertain his guests away from prying eyes and detractors. He took in a succession of lodgers, and they were exclusively male.

One was an architect by the name of Ivan Klimenko. Although Klimenko would go on to marry and father children, he makes it clear in his later memoirs that Tchaikovsky's invitation to move in with him was erotically charged and that they enjoyed a physical relationship.

He quotes letters from Tchaikovsky in which the composer feminised his name to 'Klimenka' or 'Klimenochka', something Tchaikovsky regularly did when writing to homosexual friends.[*] He even did it to his brother Modest, addressing him as 'Modestina' and signing the letters with a feminisation of his own Christian name, 'Petrolina'.[2]

One particularly graphic letter, written in September 1871, redacted by Soviet censors from Tchaikovsky's correspondence, but contained in Klimenko's own memoirs (which the censors missed), is replete with barely disguised sexual double entendres and innuendos.

Tchaikovsky calls Klimenka 'the most beloved of the concubines of my harem', and describes his newly upholstered divan 'drooping out of longing for you', and inviting him 'to soothe your tired limbs on its resilient shoulders newly furnished with fresh springs'. Should Klimenka not heed his call, Tchaikovsky, the 'voluptuous Sultan', would ensure 'penalty of death by impalement'.[3]

Another long-term, on-and-off lodger was a man by the name of Nikolay Lvovich Bochechkarov. Modest describes him as rather stout and sporting a small 'Regency' moustache, with the venerable characteristics of an important but old-fashioned and out-of-touch dignitary living in

---

[*] Anthony Holden states that Soviet censors removed all trace of feminised names from Tchaikovsky's correspondence, but missed the references in Klimenko's own memoirs.

Above
Modest Tchaikovsky.

retirement. He peppered his speech with tiny French phrases, despite not understanding a word of that language. It seems that he was introduced to Tchaikovsky by Shilovsky or one of his set.

Bochechkarov was some years older than Tchaikovsky, and Modest is clear that he too was homosexual. No one knew exactly what he did as a profession; Modest describes him as clownish and a freeloader, always borrowing money that he had no intention of repaying, and wearing 'a mask of satisfaction with life and of well-being'.[4]

There is a suggestion that, in return for lodgings, Bochechkarov acted as a pimp for Tchaikovsky, procuring for him young male lovers.[5] What he certainly did do was to keep Tchaikovsky in touch with the homosexual underground of Moscow. Tchaikovsky writes as much: '[Bochechkarov] appears periodically with a supply of gossip.'[6] Around this time Tchaikovsky now begins to use for the first time in his letters the word *tyotki*, or 'aunties', a slang term for passive homosexuals.[*]

Meanwhile his home quickly became crowded. Soon after moving in, Tchaikovsky employed a live-in manservant by the name of Mikhail Sofronov, a twenty-three-year-old from the country town of Klin,[†] around sixty miles north-west of Moscow, who was recommended to him by a fellow Conservatory professor.

Sofronov, it seems, lived in the kitchen, bedding down there at night. It soon became apparent that he was not the most efficient of housekeepers, with Tchaikovsky limiting his duties to general tidying, and the cooking of 'buckwheat kasha [grains boiled in water] and cabbage soup', which was the sole dish in his culinary repertoire.[7]

Given that Tchaikovsky's small flat was already overcrowded and that he did not need much looking after, it might seem strange that shortly after employing Mikhail Sofronov, Tchaikovsky also employed his younger brother Aleksey.

Aleksey was just twelve years of age when he moved into Tchaikovsky's apartment, too young to have had experience in any kind of housekeeping,

---

[*] In letters kept by others, thereby evading Soviet censorship.

[†] Where Tchaikovsky would later purchase a substantial property and spend the final years of his life.

indeed too young to be expected to perform such tasks. Poznansky suggests the sole reason for Tchaikovsky taking him in was that Mikhail was already past the age that Tchaikovsky would consider attractive, unlike Aleksey.[8]

The brothers Sofronov would, over the years, establish an enduring relationship with the brothers Tchaikovsky. While Tchaikovsky may have reserved his affection for the younger brother, Mikhail found an admirer in Modest. It has also been suggested by Holden that Mikhail, whom Tchaikovsky at one time compares to Leporello, the manservant in Mozart's *Don Giovanni*, might have procured boys for Tchaikovsky, as Leporello procured women for his master.[9]

It is clear that the relationship with Aleksey – Alyosha or Lyonya as Tchaikovsky referred to him in letters – quickly turned physical. In various letters he records such sentiments as: 'The very thought of Alyosha causes a painful longing in me . . .'; 'I . . . am quite heartsick that my dear Lyonya . . . is not with me as he was last year . . .'; 'My dear Lyonya, I have missed you terribly [*redacted*] . . .'.[10]

In December 1877, in the aftermath of his disastrous marriage, Tchaikovsky wrote to brother Anatoly, 'He [Alyosha] has understood exceptionally well what I need from him right now, and he more than satisfies all my demands.'[11] The sexual implication of this is clear and, as Poznansky points out, it is hardly surprising that Soviet censors would redact the passage from later editions of Tchaikovsky's correspondence.

Within a few short years, Tchaikovsky was to dismiss Mikhail, but he would keep Aleksey on for the rest of his life, bequeathing him an enormous and valuable legacy, which would cause jealousy among Tchaikovsky's relatives.*

Despite the obvious pleasures to be derived from pursuing amorous activities in his own apartment, Tchaikovsky was far from being a happy soul. Life at the Moscow Conservatory was becoming increasingly irksome.

He was teaching several different courses – harmony, orchestration and composition – and regularly spending up to thirty hours a week in the classroom.[12] He clearly did not enjoy it, as one male student later recalled, painting a vivid impression of the future great composer as reluctant teacher, not to mention the generally rundown state of the prestigious Conservatory:

---

*Aleksey would outlive Tchaikovsky by more than thirty years, regarding his sole purpose in life as to protect his master's legacy.

Tchaikovsky would enter the classroom in a rush, always somewhat em-
barrassed and irritable, as if annoyed at the tedium to come. He hated
the mundane furnishings of the theory classroom with its school desks
and ordinary old dilapidated yellow piano with jangling yellowing keys,
and the blackboard with its red lines. I remember the squeamish gesture
with which, after tossing away the chalk and grey dust cloth, he would
wipe his fingers on his handkerchief.[13]

This student, Rotislav Genika, goes out of his way to stress how gentle, delicate and patient Tchaikovsky was with his male students, while he was irritated by the slowness of the majority of the female students.

This misogynistic attitude is borne out by a female student, Alexandra Amfiteatrova-Levitskaya, who quoted another female pupil telling her that Tchaikovsky was a terrible fault-finder. He flew into a rage, putting a pencil through a whole page of her work, simply because she had put tails on the wrong side of individual quavers.

Tchaikovsky's musical advice, though, was appreciated by all. As Geni-ka wrote, 'Simplicity, clarity of thought, smoothness of form, transparency, lightness in the scoring, were the ideals towards which Tchaikovsky made his pupils strive.'[14]

Always liberal with his money among his coterie of friends, Tchaik-ovsky frequently found himself short of cash, particularly now with rent and servants to pay. For a while he took a job as music critic, first for the journal *Contemporary Chronicle*, then for the newspaper *Russian Register*. It was a useful way of keeping in touch with musical developments in Mos-cow, as well as bringing in a little extra income, but he found his views being openly disputed, which he did not enjoy, and his life as critic soon came to an end.

As the Moscow winter began to bite hard in December 1871, Tchaik-ovsky might have been expected to welcome an invitation from Vladimir Shilovsky to spend Christmas and New Year with him in Nice on the French Riviera, as before with all expenses paid. In fact the opposite was the case. The prospect exacerbated his depression. He was aware by now that home-sickness would set in as soon as he left; he also knew that to travel abroad with his homosexual friend would inevitably invite rumour and comment.

Initially he turned the invitation down, but Shilovsky would not take no for an answer. Finally he relented. He wrote to his brother Anatoly urg-ing him not to tell anyone where he was going, but instead to say he was spending the festive season with his sister Sasha in Kamenka.

Leaving Moscow did nothing to lift his melancholy. He wrote again to Anatoly:

On the very day I left Moscow I was gripped by an all-consuming depression which stayed with me right through the journey and has not left me even now.[15]

Once he had arrived in Nice, Tchaikovsky derived some comfort from the warm weather and the colours of nature, but he could not fully conceal his loneliness:

How curious it is to arrive from the depths of a Russian winter in a climate where I can step outside without an overcoat, where oranges, roses and lilacs are in bloom, and the trees are covered in leaves. [I am enjoying] many pleasant hours, especially those in the early morning, when I sit alone by the sea in the warm, but not too warm, sunshine. *[16]

Tchaikovsky indulged in a little light composing while on the French Riviera, writing Two Pieces for Piano, Op. 10 – one of them the ever popular *Humoresque* – which he dedicated to Shilovsky.

Predictably the absence from his homeland began to tell on Tchaikovsky. Shilovsky suggested they take a circuitous route home, by way of Genoa, Venice and Vienna. Once back in Moscow, Tchaikovsky wrote to his father to say how the idleness had begun to weigh heavily on him, and he was pleased to get back to his home city.

In the familiar surroundings of his own apartment, tolerating the grind at the Conservatory, Tchaikovsky worked through the spring to put the finishing touches to *The Oprichnik*. He delivered the completed opera not to the Moscow Theatre for which he had written it, but to the Imperial Theatres in St Petersburg. There, in the city he knew so well, where he had made so many lifelong friends, he felt his opera would receive a more sympathetic hearing.

That task out of the way, his restlessness got the better of him once again. As he had the previous summer, he spent several weeks with his sister and her family in Kamenka, followed by stays at the nearby country estate of one of his friends, Nikolay Kondratyev, finally visiting Shilovsky, who was staying at his estate at Usovo near Kiev.

The warmth and relaxation of Ukraine clearly worked wonders on Tchaikovsky's mental as well as physical health. In a matter of weeks, seemingly with no struggle, he all but completed an entire symphony, his second. This would be one of his most carefree works. Redolent with themes and melodies from Russian folklore and popular folk songs, Tchaikovsky was

"Despite the obvious pleasures to be derived from pursuing amorous activities, Tchaikovsky was far from being a happy soul."

---

* Given Tchaikovsky's predilection for pre-pubescent boys, Holden draws parallels with Aschenbach in Thomas Mann's *Death in Venice*.

particularly pleased with the Ukrainian folk song 'The Crane', which had been sung to him by one of the servants at Kamenka, and which he had incorporated into the final movement.

Tchaikovsky knew right away he had written something that would be popular, and not just with the traditionalists of the Five, whose ideal was for Russian music to be consistently more Russian. When it was close to completion, he wrote to Modest that Kondratyev had already called it a work of genius, and he added, with his usual touch of humility, 'I think this is my best work with respect to perfection of form, a quality in which I have not shone before now.'[17]

If there is a distinct lack of angst in this work, it might have something to do with a delightful incident that occurred between the main composition and the orchestration, and that explains a lot about Tchaikovsky's character – his sense of humour, his love of a practical joke, his self-deprecation and relish of the absurd, all of which, in a sense, could be said to have found their way into the 'Little Russian'.

At the end of the summer, Tchaikovsky was returning to Moscow in the company of Modest. At the final staging post in northern Ukraine, before the coach ride to Vorozhba, from where they would take the train to Moscow, the two brothers spent a convivial evening at the local inn, and got drunk.

After dinner Tchaikovsky called for the horses to be harnessed for the final coach leg to Vorozhba. The postmaster told him in no uncertain terms that it was too late, and he and his brother would have to stay overnight and wait for the coach the next morning.

Tchaikovsky, in high spirits, slipped easily into practical-joke mode. He demanded to be given the complaints book. After entering his complaint he signed his name: 'Prince Volkonsky,[*] Gentleman of the Emperor's Bedchamber'.

The postmaster saw the name, apologised to 'Your Royal Highness' most profusely, bowed and scraped, and ordered the horses to be harnessed immediately. Within minutes the brothers Tchaikovsky were on their way, with much mirth and merriment inside the carriage.

That soon changed when Tchaikovsky, suffering from the combined effects of too much alcohol and the over-hasty departure, realised on arrival in Vorozhba that he had left his briefcase containing 500 roubles and all his documents behind at the inn.

---

[*] Is this a pun on Prince Bolkonsky, one of the heads of family in Tolstoy's *War and Peace*, which had been published just a few years earlier? Possibly.

Not in itself a major problem, other than time lost to return to retrieve it. However, either Tchaikovsky would now have to give his real name to show it matched the documents inside and that he was the legitimate owner, or the postmaster would have already examined the contents of the briefcase and discovered his real name. One way or the other, an awkward scene was certain to ensue.

Modest revelled in his brother's embarrassment, as siblings are inclined to do, and continued blithely on his way to Moscow, leaving his elder brother to sort out his own problems. Tchaikovsky, unable to face the prospect of confessing to the postmaster, gave a few roubles to a local chap in Vorozhba and persuaded him to return to the inn and collect his case.

Tchaikovsky spent an uneasy night in a dirty, rat-infested attic – the only space available at such short notice in Vorozhba – and looked forward to the return of the emissary, and his briefcase, in the morning.

Far from the hoped-for resolution, matters got even worse. The postmaster had firmly informed the emissary that he would place the briefcase belonging to such an eminent figure only into the hands of 'His Royal Highness' himself.

Tchaikovsky had no choice but to return to the staging post. Either the postmaster would still be none the wiser as to his real identity, or a grovelling apology would have to be made.

In the end, the story concluded in anticlimax. When Tchaikovsky arrived, he was again subjected to much grovelling on the part of the post-master, who had clearly not had the temerity to open the briefcase and examine the documents. With profuse apologies, delivered in the language and manner of high aristocracy, Tchaikovsky was reunited with his precious briefcase.

Relieved and happy, 'Prince Volkonsky' fell into casual conversation with the postmaster before he left, and asked him his name. 'Tchaikovsky, Your Royal Highness,' the delighted postmaster replied.

For a moment Tchaikovsky must have wondered if his ruse had been discovered and the postmaster was having fun at his expense, which in the circumstances would have been well deserved.

Tchaikovsky beat a hasty retreat, and continued on his journey home. Once back in Moscow, he made enquiries as to the identity of the postmaster at that staging post in northern Ukraine. The official did indeed bear the name 'Tchaikovsky'.

A delighted Tchaikovsky would tell this story – no doubt with added embellishments over time – for the rest of his life.[*] Is it too fanciful to believe that he was smiling at it even as he orchestrated his Second Symphony, and put the finishing touches to it? I do not think so.

The smile would be short-lived, though. Tchaikovsky still, it seemed, had not mastered the art of composing opera.

---

[*] Echoes of the anecdote Giuseppe Verdi would tell into old age of how, as a child, he had cursed a priest who had humiliated him in front of the church congregation, calling on God to strike him dead with lightning, which God duly did. See John Suchet, *Verdi: The Man Revealed*, pp. 10–11.

12

UNEXPECTED INSPIRATION

In **August 1872,** back in the city of Moscow, the first thing Tchaikovsky did was move into a larger apartment. A government grant to secure the future of Moscow Conservatory had allowed Rubinstein to increase Tchaikovsky's salary by more than 50 per cent. Accompanying him were the two Sofronov brothers and a stray dog named Bishka that he had found in Moscow.

It was time to put the summer behind him and work on his music. It took him just a few weeks to bring the Second Symphony to fruition, working intensively on the orchestration and completing it by November.

One might think that this combination of factors – a salary increase, a larger apartment, and musical progress on a major composition – would improve Tchaikovsky's mood dramatically. That appears not to have been the case. Tchaikovsky frequently yielded to bouts of depression. Now the low mood seemed to hang over him almost permanently, as if he was unable to shake it. More than anything, he wrote to his architect friend Klimenko, it was his teaching duties that got him down:

> *Day after day I go to the Conservatory, day after day we meet up to get drunk, Jurgenson* above all, and day by day I grow more depressed*

---

* A friend of Tchaikovsky, music publisher and director of the Russian Musical Society.

. . . On the whole, depression gnaws away at me largely because I am growing older, all too aware that every passing day brings me closer to the grave.[1]

However much we might or might not take Tchaikovsky's words at face value, given that he was working hard on his Second Symphony at the time, the final line of his letter rings with truth:

As for me personally, to tell the truth I have only one interest in life: my success as a composer.[2]

Word must have spread that he was working on a new symphony – probably through the musical communities of the conservatories in each city – because the following month, back in St Petersburg to discuss arrangements for staging his opera *The Oprichnik*, he was guest at a party in the home of Nikolay Rimsky-Korsakov.

To his embarrassment, he was asked to sit at the piano and play something from his new symphony. Given Tchaikovsky's natural humility and reticence, he must have taken some persuading, but finally he went to the piano and played the final movement of the new symphony.

One can imagine the delight with which the host and his guests greeted 'The Crane', when they recognised it woven into the music. Rimsky-Korsakov, a leading light of the Five – that group of famously nationalistic Russian composers – must surely have been particularly impressed.

Tchaikovsky's own judgement, quoted in the previous chapter, that he had written his best work to date, was borne out by the reception in Rimsky-Korsakov's house. In Tchaikovsky's own words to brother Modest: 'The entire company almost tore me to pieces in their enthusiasm.'[3]

Back in Moscow, the first public performance was given on 26 January 1873. It was a *succès fou*. If ever Tchaikovsky needed a musical success in his life, it was now, and that was what he got.

It was more than just a success; it was a triumph. Writing to his father, he described how he was called out to take applause several times, and that he was going to be awarded a gift and 300 silver roubles for another performance at the Russian Musical Society.

Even his old student friend turned critic Herman Laroche, with whom relations had become frosty after his scathing review of *The Voyevoda*, could hardly contain his enthusiasm:

Not in a long time have I come across a work with such a powerful thematic development of ideas and with contrasts that are so well motivated and artistically thought out.[4]

Given the predominance of Ukrainian folk themes in the symphony, Tchaikovsky's friend (and fellow practical joker) Nikolay Kashkin named it the 'Little Russian' – Little Russia being the nineteenth-century name for Ukraine – and it stuck. To this day Tchaikovsky's Symphony No. 2 is known as the 'Little Russian'.*

Tchaikovsky's mood lifted in the light of such adulation. He sent a typically teasing letter to Modest:

> *. . . the time is drawing near when [brothers] Kolya, Tolya, Ippolit, and Modya will no longer be the Tchaikovskys, but merely the brothers of the Tchaikovsky. I shall make no secret of the fact that this is the desired*

---

* Despite the plaudits, Tchaikovsky himself was less than happy with the finished work. Seven years later he completely rewrote the first movement. The revised version is the one normally performed today, though there is a body of musicological opinion that rates the original version superior to the revised one.

end of all my efforts. To grind into the dust everything around one by one's own greatness – is not this supreme pleasure?! So tremble, for soon my fame will crush you.[5]

He could not possibly have known how accurate that flippant prediction in the final sentence would prove to be.

In the wake of the success of the 'Little Russian', Tchaikovsky began to compose at a more prolific rate than at any time in his life up till now, all the while waiting for the premiere of *The Oprichnik*, the work that he hoped would finally establish him as a composer of opera.

He accepted a commission from a friend of his, the dramatist (and stepfather to Shilovsky) Vladimir Begichev, to write incidental music for a Bolshoy production of Ostrovsky's new play, *The Snow Maiden*.

In the event the music Tchaikovsky composed received more praise than the play itself. Tchaikovsky wrote it at lightning speed – in just three weeks. Unusually for him, he never rewrote it; in fact he had plans to turn it into a full-length opera, plans he was sad to discard when Rimsky-Korsakov got there first.

The music was not good enough, however, to satisfy his old adversary, the influential critic César Cui, who had given his early attempt at a cantata on Schiller's 'Ode to Joy' such a mauling. He was no kinder now. 'The ideas are banal, the harmony trite, the finish (or absence of finish), rough and clumsy,' Cui wrote.[6] Tchaikovsky, as always, took the criticism to heart.

Following *The Snow Maiden*, the music critic Vladimir Stasov – even more influential than Cui, and more favourably disposed to Tchaikovsky's music – suggested he compose a musical fantasy based on Shakespeare's *The Tempest*.

Stasov had been present when Tchaikovsky had played the final movement of his Second Symphony on the piano at Rimsky-Korsakov's house. He was convinced Tchaikovsky could go on to greater things. *The Tempest*, he told Tchaikovsky, was ideally suited to the composer's style of writing.

Tchaikovsky not only rose to the bait, but such was his respect for Stasov that he asked the critic for his advice. Stasov laid out a plan, stressing that the storm should begin 'suddenly, at full strength, in violent turmoil', in a way no composer had depicted a storm before, and how the various characters should be brought in.

Taking himself off to Shilovsky's estate in Ukraine – Shilovsky was away, allowing him total calm – Tchaikovsky sketched out the entire piece in less than two weeks, 'with no effort at all'.

Conditions were ideal. Although prone to complain of feeling lonely, Tchaikovsky liked no one's company better than his own. He would write in a later letter about this sojourn in Usovo:

> I was in an exalted, ecstatic frame of mind, wandering alone through the woods by day, over the boundless steppes in the evening, and sitting by night at an open window, listening to the solemn silence of this remotest of places.

Then Shilovsky returned and ruined everything:

> All the charms of my intimate communion with nature immediately disappeared. My little corner of Paradise turned back into a commonplace country estate.[8]

Shilovsky really had fallen out of favour, quite possibly having been displaced by Eduard Zak. Still, Tchaikovsky returned to Moscow in an altogether better frame of mind. The quiet and tranquillity of Usovo had allowed him to compose swiftly and easily, something he was not used to.

Back in his new, larger apartment, he put the finishing touches to *The Tempest*. He was well satisfied with his work. The premiere in Moscow was scheduled for 7 December. A month before that he received news of Eduard Zak's suicide.

The news was a hammer blow to Tchaikovsky, all the more so since – given the secrecy of the relationship, necessitated by the law and public opinion – he had to grieve in private, or at least within a very small circle of friends.

One can imagine his frame of mind at the premiere of *The Tempest*. Braced as he always was for negative reviews, he must have felt particularly vulnerable. In the event, he had reason to be both pleased and disappointed, in both cases from somewhat unexpected directions.

César Cui, who had previously been so predictably critical, was entirely won over: 'Such passion, such talent, so exquisitely sonorous a score!'[9]

Meanwhile Tchaikovsky's great supporter Stasov, the inspiration behind the piece, damned with faint praise:

> What an incomparable work! The storm itself is of course trite and unoriginal, Prospero very ordinary, and near the end there is a very banal cadence straight out of some awful Italian opera finale – but these are minor quibbles. All the rest is wonder piled on wonder! . . . What languor, what passion!"[10]

Yet it was Laroche, who this time had entirely changed his tune, who stung most, accusing Tchaikovsky of composing unoriginal music, openly stealing from Glinka, Schumann and Litolff.

"Such passion, such talent, so exquisitely sonorous a score!"

César Cui on *The Tempest*

Above

Stage design for
the prologue of *The
Snow Maiden*.

Tchaikovsky was furious. This was an accusation he was in no mood to hear:

> *I don't care whether he likes* The Tempest *or not . . . I didn't really expect him to . . . But what does gall me beyond belief is his insinuation that I have stolen from every living composer.*[11]

Tchaikovsky was now giving back as good as he got. Zak's death had stiffened the sinews in him. Evidence that he was no longer prepared to be quite so wounded by criticism is the fact that – unusually for him – he did not alter a note of either *The Snow Maiden* or *The Tempest*.

It remains a fact, though, that neither piece is today regarded as being among his best, and neither has found a permanent place in the concert repertoire.

Tchaikovsky retreated into himself after Zak's death. He responded to his misery in the only way he could – by composing. For the second time, he decided to write for that most intimate form of ensemble: the string quartet.

Three years earlier he had composed his first string quartet. It was, by and large, a carefree work. The second movement, in particular, which he marked *Andante cantabile*, was destined to become one of the best-loved pieces of music he would ever write.

He said the inspiration for it came from a builder, a servant or simply a peasant, depending on the telling, whistling a melody he heard through the open window of his attic room at his sister's estate in Kamenka.

It was instantly memorable, mesmerising the first audience that heard it, and it continues to captivate to this day. Tchaikovsky, however, came rather to despise it, or at least to regret the fact that audiences would love it more than pieces he believed deserved more attention.[*] Although some time later he did recount with pride how he had sat next to none other than the greatest living Russian novelist Leo Tolstoy at a performance, and was stunned to see the great man reduced to tears by the *Andante cantabile*.

The Second String Quartet, composed in the aftermath of Zak's suicide, is a different work altogether – more personal, more intense, and considerably darker. It has been described as a conscious attempt by Tchaikovsky to emulate the great composers of the German-Austrian school, at the pinnacle of which stands Beethoven.

David Brown sees an echo in the first two bars of the slow introduction to the first movement of 'the most famous musical moment in all post-Beethoven nineteenth-century music': the opening bars of Wagner's *Tristan und Isolde*, containing the hitherto unheard harmonies of the 'Tristan chord', composed a decade and a half earlier.

The slow movement, in Brown's view, is 'a most naked exposure of [Tchaikovsky's] stress-filled personality, less brutally emotional than some that were to come later, perhaps, but the most self-declaring piece he had yet composed'.[12]

The String Quartet was given an informal performance in early February 1874, just three months after Zak's death. Kashkin, who was there, reported that the audience was in ecstasy – with one exception.

The exception was Tchaikovsky's old mentor turned adversary from the St Petersburg Conservatory, Anton Rubinstein, who had come down to Moscow to hear the work. He was merciless in his criticism. He declared in front of everyone that the work was not in the chamber style, that he did not understand it at all, and that it was devoid of merit.

---

[*] Echoes of Beethoven's disdain for his WoO (*Werke ohne Opuszahl*; works without opus numbers) 57 for piano, which became so popular that he nicknamed it *Andante favori*.

Tchaikovsky was hurt, but defiant. It was the final straw for his relationship with Anton Rubinstein. Tchaikovsky would never again seek his advice or listen to his criticisms.

What Tchaikovsky did not expect was that, in a very short time, he would react in exactly the same way towards Anton's younger brother Nikolay, with whom relations had always been positive and whose criticism, as well as his praise, he had generally appreciated.

Before that, though, there was the premiere of *The Oprichnik* to weather. It took place in St Petersburg on 12 April 1874. It was – César Cui predictably excepted, who found it barren of ideas and without a single outstanding passage – a triumph.

It played for fourteen sold-out performances, with productions later in the year in Odessa and Kiev, and remained popular throughout Tchaikovsky's lifetime. He, however – and not for the last time – found himself in agreement with Cui. He disliked his own opera intensely. He wrote to Modest:

> The Oprichnik *torments me. This opera is so poor that at all the rehearsals . . . I ran away so as not to hear a single note, while at the performance I wanted to sink into the earth.*[13]

Posterity, it seems, has tended to agree with him. Popular *The Oprichnik* might have been, but it has failed to remain in the repertoire. Perhaps the most that can be said for it is that in the pacing of the plot, and the handling of certain dramatic moments, it contains seeds of what would become one of only two truly successful operas Tchaikovsky would ever write, and the only one that can without question be called a work of genius: *Eugene Onegin*.

But that is to come. For the moment, Tchaikovsky needed a break.

13

BENDING THE RULES

*I*n late November 1875, one cold afternoon when there were no classes at the Moscow Conservatory, two dancers took to the stage to perform a little ballet entitled *Pygmalion and Galatea*.

The two danced their parts with great feeling. Pygmalion, the sculptor, showed his rapture for the statue he had carved and fallen in love with, performing carefully executed moves. The statue, Galatea, embodying female beauty, revelled in being the object of her creator's desire.

The two dancers were perhaps a little old, their moves not quite as fluent as they might have been a few years before. But both entered fully into the drama of love declared and love received.

There was only a single witness to one of the most extraordinary spectacles in nineteenth-century musical history, and that was Nikolay Rubinstein, who provided the music at the piano. But Modest recounts the occasion with relish in his memoirs, revealing that his thirty-five-year-old brother Pyotr danced the part of Pygmalion, while the celebrated French composer Camille Saint-Saëns, aged forty and on a visit to Moscow, danced the part of Galatea 'most conscientiously'.[1]

Modest recounts – as his brother must have told him – how instantly the two composers became friends. Saint-Saëns he describes as 'short, lively', fascinating Tchaikovsky with his wit and original ideas, as well as his masterly knowledge of his art. He quotes his brother as saying that Saint-Saëns knew how to combine 'the grace and charm of the French school with the depth and earnestness of the great German masters'.[2]

Modest does not spell it out but Tchaikovsky and Saint-Saëns had much in common. They were both homosexual, both frequently cross-dressed, and both had a fondness for imitating female dancers.

Friendship between the two musicians flourished briefly. Saint-Saëns promised Tchaikovsky he would introduce the Fantasy Overture: *Romeo and Juliet* to a French audience the following year. To that end Tchaikovsky sent Saint-Saëns a photograph of himself, with an accompanying letter reminding him of their ballet escapade.

Saint-Saëns failed to keep his promise, the relationship cooled, and the two became distant. There must, though, have been shared mirth and whispered reminiscences, when the two met again twenty years later as world-famous composers to be awarded honorary degrees at the University of Cambridge.

Despite its short-lived nature, their friendship perhaps provided Tchaikovsky with much needed diversion after a difficult eighteen months.

It began with yet another attempt – his fourth – to write an opera that would satisfy his own exacting standards, as well as those of the critics.

It is worth pausing for a moment to examine this compulsion. It was as if to compose an opera represented the pinnacle of musical achievement, something to which all composers aspired though few achieved. To write for a combination of instruments and voices, orchestra, soloists, chorus, duets, trios, quartets, and more, while maintaining dramatic impact and telling a story, was within the range of truly only the greatest.

In a sense it had begun with Mozart, acknowledged to have created so many operas of genius at such a young age. But the German school that followed him failed to continue what he had started.[*] Beethoven struggled to produce just one opera, refusing to repeat the experience;[†] Schubert, Mendelssohn and Schumann all tried their hand at it, without any great success.

Only a single German composer after Mozart and before Tchaikovsky made a true impact in the world of opera: Richard Wagner. Of Austrian composers, Joseph Haydn might have written a dozen or so operas but

---

[*] Mozart was German, Salzburg, the city of his birth, being an independent city state that was technically part of the Holy Roman Empire of the German Nation. See John Suchet, *Mozart: The Man Revealed.*

[†] When Beethoven heard sounds in his head, he said, it was the sound of instruments, not voices.

none of them have remained in the repertoire, and he is not known as a composer of opera. Bruckner – no operas; Mahler, after several attempts, one unfinished opera. Even Johann Strauss II, famous for his operettas, tried several times to write a serious opera without success.

Italy instead emerged as the natural home of opera, with such names as Cherubini, Bellini, Donizetti. Then along came Giuseppe Verdi, and after him Puccini. But it is worth noting that none of these celebrated composers of opera wrote successfully in other genres. There is not a well-known symphony or concerto, and hardly a string quartet, between them. Conversely the same can be said of the only successful post-Mozartian German operatic composer, Wagner.

Were it not for the phenomenal genius of Mozart, who could create effortlessly in any genre, perhaps so many of them would not have striven so hard to compose an opera. That is certainly true of Pyotr Tchaikovsky. His musical idol was Mozart; all his life he tried to emulate him, aware that the task was impossible.

And so his desire to compose an opera did not leave him after the failure – in his eyes – of *The Oprichnik*. Just a couple of months after its premiere, the perfect opportunity presented itself to try again. This was not a new opportunity; Tchaikovsky had known about it for some little while. Now he decided to act on it: what ensued was a combination of farce and, yet again, failure.

The Russian Musical Society was running a competition to write an opera set to an existing libretto by the poet Yakov Polonsky, based on Gogol's comic fantasy *Christmas Eve*.

Not only did Tchaikovsky know about it, he had even been involved in deciding on the terms of the competition, making it clear to the organisers he had no intention of entering himself. In late spring 1874 he changed his mind. He would compose an opera based on the libretto and submit it.

What changed his mind? Perhaps the prospect of prize money of 1,500 roubles, with guarantee of publication and a production at the Mariinsky

Theatre in St Petersburg. It was the perfect opportunity to establish his operatic credentials once and for all, with minimal organisational effort.

Conscious that the deadline for entry was the end of the year, Tchaikovsky immediately left for the familiar estate of Kondratyev at Nizy in Ukraine, taking with him just his servant Aleksey for company.

He did not have to worry about a lack of inspiration. Composition came more easily to him now than perhaps it had ever done in the past. Despite working for only three hours a day, from noon until three in the afternoon, alongside many card games, swims and bucolic walks, he composed at a frenetic pace.

After six weeks in Nizy, from mid-June until the end of July, he moved to Shilovsky's equally familiar estate at Usovo. There the same pattern continued, and by 21 August, more than four months before the deadline and conveniently ahead of the start of the new academic year, he completed the scoring of his new opera, which he entitled *Vakula the Smith*.

He was in buoyant mood. The summer air in Ukraine always refreshed him, there seemed to be little or no creative struggle, and the company was genial. 'Aleksey is the dearest and most obliging creature,' he wrote of his young servant, now fifteen years of age.[3]

His enthusiasm for his new creation knew no bounds. He felt it was like a child to him. He wrote to Modest:

> *All my thoughts and feelings are now bound up in my beloved child* Vakula *. . . You cannot conceive how much I love him! I'm sure I will go completely mad if he does not prove a success.*[4]

Back in Moscow he submitted his new opera anonymously, as the rules he had helped to draw up required. But in an uncharacteristic show of vanity, at the top of the title page he wrote '*Ars longa, vita brevis est*', knowing full well his handwriting would instantly be recognised. If this gave the judges the impression that Tchaikovsky fully expected to win the competition, they would not have been wrong.

The composer was in for an unpleasant surprise, though; he had mistaken the deadline. It was not the end of the year, but the following August. That meant he had a full year to wait before knowing if *Vakula the Smith* had won the competition.

Tchaikovsky's impatience got the better of him. He was so enthused by his new opera that he wanted it staged, and he wanted it staged now. In what was nothing less than a deliberate flouting of the rules of the competition, he wrote to the director of productions at the Mariinsky, asking for permission to cancel his submission of *Vakula* and whether he would consider it independently of the competition.

He had chosen the wrong man. This official forwarded Tchaikovsky's request to one of the judges, who in turn referred it to the very top – the president of the Russian Musical Society, Grand Duke Konstantin.

The Grand Duke would have none of it. He ordered the judge, Eduard Nápravník, to write Tchaikovsky a strongly worded letter accusing him not only of acting foolishly, but in effect of trying to circumvent the rules.

Nápravník, a conductor, was a good friend of Tchaikovsky, and had conducted the first performance of *The Oprichnik*. Outraged, Tchaikovsky went on the attack. He slated Nápravník for passing what was intended as private correspondence to the Grand Duke. All he was asking was whether his opera could be accepted outside the competition. With just a hint of *mea culpa*, he wrote:

> *Now I see that this was a blunder on my part because the text of the opera is not in my control. But you are unjust in writing to me . . . to tell me that I am very foolish, and moreover you are unjust in suspecting me of some crafty designs: such were not in my head. I beg you very much to put this out of your mind, and equally to disabuse the Grand Duke who, Rubinstein says, was very displeased with my action.*[5]

Despite his mollifying words, Tchaikovsky had no intention of backing down; in fact he went further, completely flouting the competition rules and disregarding the requirement of anonymity. First he arranged for the overture to *Vakula* to be performed on 4 December. And who was conducting? None other than Nikolay Rubinstein, who happened to be one of the competition judges and therefore should have had nothing to do with it. Then, in the first half of 1875 he openly negotiated with publishers about printing the score to *Vakula*. And in May he went so far as to play the opera through to a certain Rimsky-Korsakov, who was another of the judges.

We cannot know why Rimsky-Korsakov so completely took Tchaikovsky's side in the matter. But a fortnight before the judging was due to take place, he wrote to Tchaikovsky expressing his views on *Vakula*, saying, 'I don't doubt for a moment that your opera will get the prize.'[6]

Despite the multiple and outrageous flouting of the rules, both Rubinstein and Rimsky-Korsakov kept their positions on the judging panel, and Tchaikovsky remained in the competition. He appeared to have the full musical establishment behind him.

The result was announced on 28 October. In a decision that cannot have come as a surprise to anyone, and with an absurd attempt to stick to the rules of anonymity, it was announced that the opera with the motto '*Ars longa, vita brevis est*' was not only deemed worthy of the prize, but was '*the only one* that measures up to the artistic demands of the competition'.[7]

Above

Stage design for *Vakula the Smith*.

Tchaikovsky had seen his 'beloved child' take the honours, earning him 1,500 roubles and guaranteed production at the Mariinsky Theatre.

In fact it would be fourteen months before the opera was finally performed, and when at last it was staged the audience was underwhelmed. But not as underwhelmed as Tchaikovsky was himself.

His old enemy self-doubt set in immediately, and he could see nothing but faults. The opera was rerun in each of the following three seasons, but each time Tchaikovsky saw further flaws.

Surprisingly, though, Tchaikovsky did not fall out of love with *Vakula*, as he had with his earlier efforts at opera. A full decade later he completely revised it, rewriting the libretto and even going so far as to give it a new name, *Cherevichki*.*

Finally convinced he had created the opera he was always destined to write, Tchaikovsky himself conducted the new version at the Bolshoy Theatre in Moscow. Once again the reception was lukewarm.

Tellingly, he wrote to his brother after the third performance:

---

*The name given to high-heeled leather boots worn by Ukrainian women. There is no single equivalent word in English.

For the moment the opera arouses interest rather than affection . . . I think that [it] will be performed without much audience clamour – but that, little by little, people will come to love the opera.[8]

He was right about the first part, wrong about the second. The revised opera was performed only five times. It was due to return for two performances the following season but they were cancelled, and it quietly dropped out of the repertoire and never re-entered it. Tchaikovsky did not live to see the piece performed again, and it has been rarely heard since. A successful opera still eluded him.

Perhaps the most surprising aspect of the whole sorry story, though, is that in the months when he was wrangling with the competition judges over his entry, he was in fact embarking on a new composition. This was a work in a new form for Tchaikovsky.

Given the strains he was under – entirely self-inflicted though they were – this new work might have been expected to reflect his habitual depression, now aggravated by anger and frustration. Instead the opposite was the case. The composition would become one of his best-loved works and stand at the pinnacle as one of the greatest of its kind – if not *the* greatest – any composer would ever write.

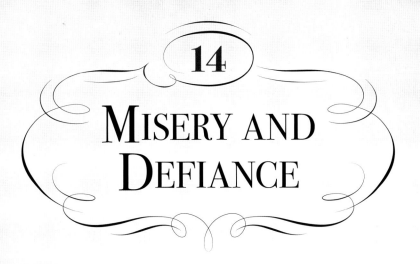

14

MISERY AND DEFIANCE

It was a depressed and restless Tchaikovsky who, at the end of summer 1874, moved apartment yet again. With his two servants in residence, and a steady stream of musical friends paying him visits, not to mention a piano, he needed more space. It was not a major move, just further down the same street, but it did nothing to improve his spirits.

Autumn was a time of year he never looked forward to, because it was a harbinger of the season he disliked most. Winter in Moscow was brutal, the extreme cold made even more uncomfortable by the raggedness of the old city, the haphazardness of narrow streets clogged with ice; it compared unfavourably to St Petersburg, with its relative modernity, broader, carefully laid-out boulevards and the salty air of the Baltic making the bitterly cold temperatures more bearable.

To add to his perpetual homesickness for St Petersburg, Tchaikovsky was confronted every day by the inescapable fact that, as a musician, he was still failing to make any great impact – or, in his view, just still failing. True, he had enjoyed a certain amount of success with symphonies and string quartets, piano pieces and individual works, some of which were receiving performances. But for every one of his admirers he had many more detractors, and the ranks of those critical of him had been swelled by his blatant manoeuvring to win the opera prize for *Vakula*.

As autumn moved into winter, Tchaikovsky's thoughts turned, as they tended to each year at this time, to getting out of the city, possibly to his sister's estate in Kamenka, or to warmer spots on the Mediterranean. Yet instead he sat at the piano, manuscript paper and pencils on a table beside him, and began a brief but intense period of composition.

What brought on this sudden burst of creativity is not known. More significantly, exactly what made him decide to write a piece of music for piano and orchestra is not known either – particularly since it was a form he had, in the past, dismissed as unworkable.

Within little more than seven weeks Tchaikovsky had completed his First Piano Concerto. The work that would bring such joy to so many millions of people over the succeeding decades and centuries was about to bring more misery to its composer than he could ever have thought possible.

The first person he told about it was Nikolay Rubinstein, for the very good reason that he admired Rubinstein greatly as a pianist, and the less good reason that he did not rate his own talent as a pianist particularly highly. (In fact, Tchaikovsky was every bit as accomplished a pianist as Rubinstein.) He wanted to know what Rubinstein thought about it from a pianist's point of view. Had he written anything impractical, ineffective, too difficult technically? He was also considering asking Rubinstein to give the work its first public performance.

Even if Tchaikovsky was too modest to acknowledge his own ability, he had other doubts about his decision, as he admitted in a letter to his brother:

> *I must mention the fact that some inward voice warned me against the choice of Nikolay Rubinstein as a judge of the technical side of my composition. However, as he was not only the best pianist in Moscow, but also a first-rate all-round musician, and knowing that he would be deeply offended if he heard I had taken my concerto to anyone else, I decided to ask him to hear the work and give me his opinion upon the solo parts.*[1]

There was the truth of it. So sensitive was Tchaikovsky that he was scared, above all else, of offending Rubinstein. In the event he should have heeded that 'inward voice'.

It so happened that both Tchaikovsky and Rubinstein were invited to a party at the home of one of the Conservatory professors and his wife on Christmas Eve 1874. Rubinstein suggested that they meet beforehand at the Conservatory and that Tchaikovsky should play through the piece.

Tchaikovsky arrived first and set up his manuscript on a piano in one of the classrooms. After a little while Rubinstein arrived with two other Conservatory professors, both good friends of Tchaikovsky, Nikolay Kashkin – he of the shaved beard – and Nikolay Hubert.

What follows has gone down as one of the most extraordinary scenes in musical history. Tchaikovsky sat at the keyboard and played through the first movement. The final chord, and then – silence. Not a word, not a single remark or comment, had Rubinstein uttered during the whole movement, and not a single word did he utter now. The other two, clearly taking their lead from Rubinstein, said nothing either.

Tchaikovsky did not suspect for a moment that Rubinstein was too awestruck to speak. He knew the opposite was the case. He described the feeling later:

> Do you know the awkward and ridiculous sensation of putting before a friend a meal which you have cooked yourself, which he eats – and holds his tongue?[2]

Tchaikovsky knew already the verdict was grim but, as he put it in his letter, just a single word would have done, 'friendly abuse' even – 'anything to break the silence'. But not a word was said. He knew what was coming:

> [Rubinstein] was preparing his thunderbolt, and [Hubert] was waiting to see which way the wind would blow. I did not require a judgement of my work from the artistic side; simply from the technical point of view. Rubinstein's silence was eloquent. 'My dear friend,' he seemed to be saying to himself, 'how can I speak of the details, when the work itself goes entirely against the grain?'

Tchaikovsky is, of course, speaking after the event, but there was no doubt he was receiving the message loud and clear, and it was not looking good.

Nevertheless, he refused to let the silence intimidate him; he gathered himself together and played through the rest of the concerto. At the end, he turned questioningly to Rubinstein. Even in his darkest moments, he could not have been prepared for what he heard:

> Then a torrent broke from Rubinstein's lips . . . My concerto was worthless, absolutely unplayable; the passages so broken, so disconnected, so unskilfully written, that they could not even be improved; the work itself was bad, trivial, common; here and there I had stolen from other people; only one or two pages were worth anything; all the rest had better be destroyed, or entirely rewritten.[3]

Now it was Tchaikovsky's turn to be stunned into silence. He was shocked and hurt beyond words. Rubinstein had even included the most wounding criticism possible, one he knew would hurt the most: the claim that Tchaikovsky was stealing from other composers. This accusation had been levelled at Tchaikovsky before, and it had stung more bitterly than any other.

As Tchaikovsky stood there, rooted to the spot and unable to find words to defend himself, Rubinstein added insult to injury by sitting at the piano himself and parodying certain passages in the concerto: 'For instance *that*? . . . And what meaning is there in *this*? . . . And look there! Is it possible that anyone could [write *that*]?'

In case he was not adequately conveying Rubinstein's verbal demolition, Tchaikovsky added:

> But the chief thing I cannot reproduce: the tone *in which all this was said. An independent witness of this scene must have concluded I was a talentless maniac, a scribbler with no notion of composing, who had ventured to lay his rubbish before a famous man.*[4]

He went on to say that friendly criticism was one thing, and was something he welcomed, but this was delivered in such a way that it cut him to the quick. He looked to the other two for support. Hubert made some attempt to soften the criticism, but broadly agreed with it. Kashkin remained silent, conspicuously failing to come to his friend's defence. Rubinstein was not a man to challenge.

Tchaikovsky was, literally, speechless. He ran upstairs and sequestered himself in a room. Minutes later he heard footsteps on the stairs and Rubinstein entered. He saw how upset Tchaikovsky was and ushered him into another room. If Tchaikovsky was expecting a mollified or contrite Rubinstein, he was in for a shock.

One can almost imagine Rubinstein jabbing his finger at Tchaikovsky as he repeated his view that the concerto was 'impossible'; in several places it needed to be completely revised. Then, uttering what he must have thought was an inducement, he promised Tchaikovsky that if he reworked the piece along the lines he suggested, he would have it performed at one of his concerts.

The normally mild-mannered Tchaikovsky had heard enough:

> *'I shall not alter a single note,' I replied. 'I shall publish the work precisely as it stands.' This intention I actually carried out.*[5]

One would like to imagine Tchaikovsky jabbing his finger back at the arrogant Rubinstein and standing his ground, but that would not have been in character. That he was mortified can be in no doubt. At the very least Rubinstein had been highly insensitive to talk in such a way to the notoriously thin-skinned Tchaikovsky. It was almost as if he was setting out to wound the man as much as provide a critique of the music.

It is impossible to know why Rubinstein should launch such a scathing attack on a composition that is appreciated today as being close to perfection. Perhaps it was jealousy because he knew he could never compose anything remotely as good. Maybe he was just in an unusually bad mood that day and decided to throw his weight around.

What is certain is that Tchaikovsky never viewed their relationship in quite the same light again. Nikolay Rubinstein was soon to make amends, but the two never rekindled their former closeness.

For the time being Tchaikovsky was determined not to let Rubinstein anywhere near his piano concerto. In the first place Rubinstein was not to receive the dedication, even if that had been Tchaikovsky's first intention. Instead it went, initially at least, to a student of piano and composition at the Moscow Conservatory, Sergey Taneyev, whom Tchaikovsky greatly admired, and who was about to win a gold medal for both disciplines, the first in the history of the Conservatory to do so.[*]

Above

Hans von Bülow.

In the event, Tchaikovsky removed the dedication to Taneyev and gave it instead to the German pianist and conductor Hans von Bülow,[†] who had in the past publicly praised his works. He chose von Bülow because Tchaikovsky decided he should give the first public performance of the work – in Boston in the United States, where von Bülow was about to embark on a tour.

Why did Tchaikovsky choose to have his First Piano Concerto premiered on the other side of the Atlantic? Almost certainly to forestall any more wounding criticism from the Moscow musical elite.

On 13 October 1875 the most popular piano concerto ever written, Tchaikovsky's Piano Concerto No. 1 in B flat minor, Op. 23, was heard for the first time. Von Bülow was at the keyboard, the American Benjamin Johnson brought in at short notice to conduct, the pianist having fallen out with the original choice.

It would be satisfying to be able to report an unqualified success. Success it was, certainly: von Bülow reported to Tchaikovsky that the concerto

---

[*] And whose elder brother Vladimir had so graphically chronicled the public floggings at the School of Jurisprudence.

[†] Von Bülow was renowned as a conductor of Wagner operas. His wife Cosima, Liszt's daughter, had seven years earlier left him for Wagner.

Right

From left to right:
Modest Tchaikovsky,
N. D. Kondratyev,
Anatoly Tchaikovsky
and Pyotr Ilyich
Tchaikovsky, c. 1875.

was so well received that the finale had to be repeated, causing Tchaikovsky to note sourly to Rimsky-Korsakov, 'That never happens here!'[6]

The critics were less impressed though. One wrote that the work was never destined to become 'classical', and the American composer George Whitefield Chadwick, who was in the audience, reported that the trombones made a wrong entrance in the first movement, causing von Bülow to sing out in a perfectly audible voice, 'The brass may go to hell.'[7]

One month later the work received its first Russian performance in St Petersburg at a concert put on by the Russian Musical Society, with two relatively unknown names as soloist and conductor. Tchaikovsky was there and was very disappointed. Likewise the critics, who were lukewarm.

Three weeks later, though, at another RMS concert, at the keyboard was the work's original dedicatee, Sergey Taneyev, and on the podium none other than . . . Nikolay Rubinstein.

The sequence of events that led to the concerto's most vituperative critic conducting it before a Moscow audience is not known, nor Tchaikovsky's reaction when the decision was made, but it seems there must have been changes of heart.

The performance was an outstanding success with audience and critics alike. Once again Tchaikovsky was in the audience, and it is a measure of his forgiving nature that he was unstinting in his praise of a man who had treated him like the least talented of students:

> *[I] could not wish to hear a better performance of the piece than this one, for which [I am] indebted to the sympathetic talent of Mr Taneyev and Mr Rubinstein's mastery as a conductor.*[8]

Three years later Rubinstein was to admit openly the error of his first judgement. He proceeded to learn the solo part, performing the concerto as often as possible and becoming one of its most vocal champions. Tchaikovsky, though, never quite forgave him.

As always, Tchaikovsky was not quite finished with the work. He incorporated several revisions when the complete score was published, and a full fourteen years later he made a striking alteration to the opening chords on the piano, redistributing the notes to give the famous opening so familiar today.

Is it any surprise that throughout the compositional process and first performances of his supremely popular First Piano Concerto, Tchaikovsky was once more wrestling internally with his own nature, struggling to reconcile his public and private personas?

A matter of weeks after the blistering encounter with Rubinstein in that piano room at the Conservatory, he wrote to his younger, heterosexual, brother Anatoly:

I am very, very alone here, and if it weren't for my constant work, I should simply succumb to melancholia. It's a fact that [my homosexuality]* constitutes an unbridgeable chasm between me and the majority of people. It imparts to my character an aloofness, a fear of people, a timidity, an excessive shyness, a distrustfulness – in a word, a thousand traits which are making me more and more unsociable.[9]

If Tchaikovsky is here giving us a perfect thumbnail sketch of his personality, with words such as 'timidity' and 'shyness', a letter he wrote a couple of months later to Anatoly's twin, the homosexual Modest, shows us another side to his character:

It makes me angry that you possess every single one of my shortcomings; that's a fact. I should like to find in you the absence of just one of my bad personality traits – and I simply can't. You are too like me, and when I am angry with you I am, in effect, angry with myself, for you eternally act as a mirror in which I see reflected all my weaknesses.[10]

This is a Tchaikovsky not known to history, to the countless admirers of his music down the centuries – and not known to most of those around him either, with the exception of a close few.

As for the shortcomings to which he refers, the bad personality traits, the weaknesses, his use of the plural seems a little disingenuous. He is clearly referring to one 'fault' in particular, which he is now convinced – and will remain so – that he inflicted on Modest.

The time is fast approaching when he will decide to do something about it, once and for all.

---

* David Brown suggests the missing words may be 'my abnormality'. Poznansky proposes 'my aberration'. I have instead gone for the more direct 'my homosexuality'.

15
SWAN LAKE – AND FAILURE

efore that life-changing moment arrives, however, there is music, and more music. The Piano Concerto No. 1 wasn't the only piece Tchaikovsky was working on that summer. In what appears to have been a burst of creativity, he also wrote the wistful *Sérénade mélancolique* – his first piece for violin and orchestra and a clear precursor of the future Violin Concerto.

This was followed by no fewer than eighteen songs gathered together in three sets. Then, in less than two months – an almost impossibly short space of time – he sketched out his Third Symphony. This was all the more remarkable since it was to contain five movements, his only symphony to do so. He was unenthusiastic about its prospects: 'As far as I can see this symphony presents no particularly successful ideas, but in workmanship it's a step forward,' he wrote to Rimsky-Korsakov.[1]

For once the characteristically pessimistic Tchaikovsky afforded himself more praise than either the critics or posterity. After a handful of performances the work was to drop largely out of the repertoire, where it remains, perhaps its most memorable feature being the name, the 'Polish', given to it by the English conductor Sir August Manns for no other reason than Tchaikovsky's directive *Tempo di Polacca* at the head of the final movement, a sobriquet that has stuck.

On returning to Moscow, his creative streak continued. In little more than a month he completed the Third String Quartet, and if it was true that he never again repeated the popular success of the *Andante cantabile* of the String Quartet No. 1, nevertheless this new string quartet was very well received.

Not that Tchaikovsky derived much joy from that. To Modest he wrote after the first performance:

I think I've rather written myself out. I'm beginning to repeat myself, and cannot conceive anything new. Have I really sung my swan song, and have nowhere further to go? It's terribly sad. However, I'll endeavour to write nothing for a bit, but try to recoup my strength.[2]

Typical Tchaikovsky, and wrong on so many counts! He had not written himself out; nor was he repeating himself. Most importantly, he did not follow his own intention of writing nothing for a while. It would be a little glib to extract a single word from those three sentences, particularly since he did not intend it to carry any particular weight. But when one considers what work he actually turned to now – or *re*turned to, to be strictly accurate – that word leaps off the page.

But before that, at the start of 1876, Tchaikovsky had a musical experience that would profoundly affect him. In Paris with his brother Modest, on 8 January the two went to the Opéra-Comique to see Bizet's opera *Carmen*.

Modest wrote later that he had 'rarely seen [his] brother so moved by an evening in the theatre'. This was largely due to the 'stunning performance' of the French mezzo-soprano Célestine Galli-Marié in the title role. She expressed vitality 'shrouded in a certain indescribable magic web of burning, unbridled passion and mystic fatalism', in Modest's graphic depiction.[3]

There was a legend attached to this opera, and Modest states that his brother was not only familiar with it but had told it to him in graphic detail. Bizet – in one of the great tragedies of musical history – had died only three months after the first performance, which had been mauled by the critics. To compound matters, he died believing his opera to have failed.

Before that, at the thirty-third performance of *Carmen*, on 2 June 1875, with Bizet seriously ill but with recovery still believed possible, Galli-Marié turned up all spades during the fortune-telling scene with the Tarot cards. She had a sudden premonition of Bizet's death, and when she left the stage she fainted. She could not go back on to finish the act.

Her premonition was fulfilled. Bizet died that night. The following day the performance was cancelled. In subsequent performances Galli-Marié was so moved by his sad fate that her interpretation of the role, it was said, became ever more moving and emotional.

The impact of *Carmen* remained with Tchaikovsky. At the end of the following year he wrote:

> *This music has no pretensions to profundity, but it is so charming in its simplicity, so vigorous, not contrived but instead sincere, that I learned all of it from beginning to end almost by heart.*[4]

And again, nearly three years later on 18 July 1880, he wrote with extraordinary prescience:

> *Yesterday evening . . . I played through Bizet's* Carmen *from cover to cover. I consider it a* chef d'œuvre *[masterpiece] in the fullest sense of the*

word: one of those rare compositions which seems to reflect most strongly in itself the musical tendencies of a whole generation . . . I am convinced that ten years hence Carmen *will be the most popular opera in the world.*[5]

After seeing that performance in Paris, Tchaikovsky bought a picture of Bizet and wrote on it the date of what was for him an unforgettable experience. We can fully believe Modest that it was seeing *Carmen* that convinced Tchaikovsky that his next opera would be on a real-life subject from recent times. *Eugene Onegin* was less than a year and a half away.

What, then, of that single word that Tchaikovsky included in the letter to his brother after the first performance of the Third String Quartet? Tchaikovsky had experienced that extraordinary burst of creativity in the summer of 1875, culminating in the Third Symphony. His spirits had been lifted by seeing his favourite pupil, Sergey Taneyev, graduate. But something else also contributed to his more positive mood. Just before leaving Moscow, he received a commission from the Imperial Theatres to write a ballet.

The idea appealed to him, not least because there was a payment of 800 roubles attached to it, but also because this was a musical form he had not yet attempted. Operas, symphonies, quartets, songs, piano pieces and much more, but not yet a ballet.

We know how much Tchaikovsky enjoyed dance. He frequently performed, particularly in female roles, for a friendly audience; he had accompanied Saint-Saëns in that impromptu performance at an empty Moscow Conservatory. And back in the summer of 1871, had he not composed and choreographed a miniature ballet for his sister's children, *The Lake of the Swans*?

Maybe the memory of that ballet had stayed in his mind; maybe the idea had emerged in conversation with Shilovsky's stepfather Vladimir Begichev, who developed the storyline; maybe his use of the word 'swansong' in that letter had been a subconscious acknowledgement of what was going through his mind.

The exact origins of the most popular ballet ever written, Tchaikovsky's *Swan Lake*, are shrouded in mystery. But we certainly do know what happened once the composer turned his mind to it, and taken in its entirety the experience does not make for comfortable reading.

No sooner had Tchaikovsky completed his Third Symphony than he turned his attention to the ballet. As with the symphony, he worked hard because he wanted to, and once again found that inspiration was not in short supply.

Above

Page from the
Swan Lake score
in Tchaikovsky's
own hand.

Within just a fortnight, he had sketched the first two acts of the ballet. Satisfied with what he had achieved, he decided a pause was in order. He wrote to Taneyev back in Moscow, outlining the work he had done, and his decision to allow himself a little breathing space:

> *You see, I haven't been idle! However, I am now experiencing some fatigue, and as from yesterday I'm giving myself a real holiday until I'm back in Moscow. I don't want even to think about music until then.*[6]

Once back in Moscow, after supervising performances of his Third Symphony, he returned to *Swan Lake*. He clearly enjoyed this new musical discipline. Modest was able to report that his brother was in uncharacteristically good mood, the only interruptions to his schedule being when his pet dog Bishka from time to time presented him with litters of six puppies, a habit he attributed to his own tendency to write romances or piano pieces in groups of six.[7]

It is not often that something could bring a smile to Tchaikovsky's face. Bishka managed to achieve it, and rather more importantly, so did early rehearsals for *Swan Lake*.

Even while Tchaikovsky was still composing, the dancers were beginning rehearsals for the first act. Tchaikovsky went along to see how

it was going, and found the whole thing vastly amusing. To keep costs down, the music was provided by a solo violinist, and Tchaikovsky told his brother how comical he found it to watch male dancers and ballerinas leaping and whirling about to 'one little violin', casting smiles at an imaginary audience.

His account ended with an uncharacteristic shuffling off of any doubt or modesty: 'Everyone at the theatre raves about my music.'[8]

Under pressure to complete the score as swiftly as possible, Tchaikovsky once again sought sanctuary in Ukraine, finishing the ballet in late March, and returning to Moscow in early April.

It was a full year before *Swan Lake* received its premiere, which took place in Moscow on 20 February 1877. If Tchaikovsky's mood had been good while composing the ballet – there is no doubt he had clearly enjoyed the process of composition, perhaps more so than for any work hitherto – that was soon to change.

The premiere, if not an outright disaster, was far from being a success. Modest wrote in his memoirs:

> *The composer was not to be blamed for the very moderate success of* [Swan Lake]. *The scenery and costumes were poor, while the orchestra was conducted by a semi-amateur, who had never before been confronted with so complicated a score.*[9]

Tchaikovsky, reverting to type, professed himself unsurprised. He told his brother the work was mediocre, and did not deserve anything better. The critics agreed with him. 'Tchaikovsky's music contains many beautiful moments and, as music for a ballet, it is perhaps even too good; but it would be a mistake to rank it with the same composer's other works,' wrote one. Another confessed to boredom, declaring it 'interesting, perhaps, only to musicians'. Perhaps the most scathing pointed to 'Mr Tchaikovsky's usual shortcoming: a poverty of creative fantasy and, in consequence of this, thematic and melodic monotony'.[10]

One can imagine Tchaikovsky agreeing with the critics. There is no evidence of the composer doing anything to stop subsequent productions being adapted, altered, new music substituted, some scenes taken away, others added, so that over the following years what the ballet audiences saw bore little resemblance to what Tchaikovsky originally wrote.[*]

---

[*] Soviet censors in the 1930s ruled that the ballet should have a happy ending, with the lovers united and the Black Swan dead – it is said on the direct orders of Stalin.

Left

Anna Pavlova in *Swan Lake*.

It was not until after Tchaikovsky's death that conductors and choreographers went back to the original, emphasising – as Tchaikovsky had clearly wished – the central theme of doomed young love, and the haunting, glorious melodies that accompanied it.

It took time to put a final end to productions that allowed the lovers to escape death in the final scene, and the ballet that is performed today is faithful to Tchaikovsky's intentions. Yet it is surely a supreme irony that Tchaikovsky shared a cruel fate with the composer whose work he admired so much.

Just as with Bizet and *Carmen*, Tchaikovsky would never know that *Swan Lake* was destined to become the best-loved ballet ever written.

IN LOVE –
AND ALONE

That intense period of creativity, which had led to the composition of so many works, finally took its toll on Tchaikovsky. The difficult and complex process of staging a ballet – a new experience for him – was the final straw. He fell ill, seriously ill, and his doctor feared he had contracted typhus.

He had long planned to travel to Bayreuth in Bavaria to see Wagner's *Ring* cycle in the first summer festival there. This his doctor allowed but insisted he take a summer break in Vichy first, where he could rest and take the waters.

Tchaikovsky agreed – and not just for reasons of health. He needed to get away. All through this period of hard work, his old demons were haunting him once more. His fame as a musician was growing, even if he himself doubted his talents. This inevitably led to interest in his private life. His easy, friendly nature and his legendary kindness did nothing to discourage this. Unfortunately for him, people were beginning to talk.

There is no question that his homosexuality was general knowledge at the Conservatory. For one thing, he stood out among professors who openly pursued female students. It was noticed that he clearly favoured male students over females, and he was known to be liberal with invitations to male students to visit him for private tuition at home.

What began as rumour was soon confirmed as fact, and Tchaikovsky was aware of it. He resented it, believing Nikolay Rubinstein – who knew

he was homosexual – was using the situation to put undue pressure on him. He wrote to Anatoly:

> *[Rubinstein] continues to think that I am maintained [at the Conservatory] by his benefactions alone. Do you know what I see at the root of all this? Still the same thing. Blackmail! He is saying that with my shameful reputation I should thank my lucky stars that he still keeps me on.*[1]

Note his use of the word 'shameful'.

If it was generally known within the walls of the Conservatory that he was homosexual, this was not – yet – the case across society at large. Certainly there were those who knew, and others who suspected, but in the circles in which Tchaikovsky moved there was a desire to allow him his privacy, particularly since so many aristocrats were themselves homosexual.

What Tchaikovsky feared most was that his private life would become public knowledge, and with his music becoming better known, and audiences more varied, there was a risk of this happening sooner or later. Homosexuality was officially illegal, punishable by imprisonment and regarded with opprobrium by the populace at large; he was naturally keen to avoid public scrutiny at all costs.

Despite himself, he was once again finding himself irresistibly drawn to young men, and to one young man in particular. Tchaikovsky's hitherto favourite student, Sergey Taneyev, was beginning to fall out of favour. The young man who had performed the First Piano Concerto to acclaim would stay on good terms with Tchaikovsky, but his tendency to speak his mind about Tchaikovsky's compositions – not always in complimentary terms – would cause a certain alienation in years to come. It is also possible Tchaikovsky attempted to seduce Taneyev, without success.[*]

Meanwhile another student, Iosif Kotek, fifteen years younger than Tchaikovsky, enrolled at the Moscow Conservatory just short of his sixteenth birthday. He studied violin, as well as composition and music theory under Tchaikovsky.

Tchaikovsky spotted his talent from his first day in class, nurturing him throughout his five years at the Conservatory. He called him 'Kotik' – Russian for 'tomcat' – and there is no doubt he was physically attracted to the teenager. As time went on the attraction became mutual. In a letter to Modest in the year Kotek graduated, Tchaikovsky described his feelings in graphic detail:

> When he caresses me with his hand, when he lies with his head inclined on my breast, and I run my hand through his hair and secretly kiss it . . . passion rages within me with such unimaginable strength . . .

It seemed, though, that the friendship – at this stage, at least – had not yet developed into a full-blown physical relationship:

> Yet I am far from the desire for a physical bond. I feel that if this happened, I would cool towards him. It would be unpleasant for me if this marvellous youth debased himself to copulation with an ageing and fat-bellied man.[2]

A typical piece of Tchaikovsky self-deprecation.

---

[*] Much later in life, after Tchaikovsky's death, Taneyev came to know the great novelist Leo Tolstoy, whose wife Sofia developed a strong attraction to him, causing her husband to be jealous. Contemporaries reported that Taneyev was totally unaware of her feelings.

In the future Kotek would come to play a far larger part than Tchaikovsky could ever have imagined at this stage. But now, Tchaikovsky needed to get away – from the pressures of work, and from the compulsion of temptation.

As his doctor had recommended, he travelled to Vichy in France to rest and take the waters. It was a disaster. He hated every minute. He described the average day in detail to Modest: a bath in the warm springs and some mineral water to start the morning, at 8 a.m. a visit to a café to read the papers, a long breakfast at ten, between breakfast and three in the afternoon more reading and a wander through the park, at five another long meal, perhaps the theatre in the evening, and bed not later than ten.

Worst of all, there were Russians everywhere, and thus the constant risk of being recognised or engaged in conversation; at breakfast a thoroughly unpleasant Russian alongside him, another Russian opposite him, very nice but fat. In a letter to brother Anatoly, he did not hold back:

> . . . accursed, loathsome, revolting Vichy! Here everything has conspired to make my stay intolerable . . . the bustle, the crush for every glass of water at the spring . . . the complete absence of any natural beauties, but most of all the loneliness – all this deeply poisons each minute of my life. Such a melancholy has fallen upon me that I shall scarcely be able to last out the entire course . . . O accursed, accursed, accursed Vichy![3]

That word 'loneliness' is perhaps the most striking word in this outpouring. If Tchaikovsky was on the lookout for any kind of human connection, he was not finding it.

There was a solution, however. He could leave Vichy early, rather than staying for the full three weeks the doctor had prescribed, and travel to nearby Lyons, where Modest was staying with a young boy he had been engaged to tutor.

The doctor was in no position to stop him, and so Tchaikovsky was pleased to get out of Vichy and join his brother – and the boy – in Lyons. He was stepping out of the frying pan of Moscow and Kotek, into the fire of Lyons and Kolya.

Kolya Konradi was seven years old and a deaf mute. Modest had been employed to take Kolya to Lyons, where there was an institution that specialised in educating deaf-mute children. Tchaikovsky had met Kolya briefly on an earlier occasion, and had much admired the young boy's beauty.

Also in Lyons was Kolya's governess, Sofya Ershova, with whom the Tchaikovsky brothers established a cordial relationship. Within a couple of days of Tchaikovsky's arrival in Lyons, the four travelled down to the coast to enjoy some sun and sea bathing.

Their choice of resort – Palavas-les-flots, on a spit of land in the Mediterranean south of Montpellier – proved to be disappointing. The small town was dreary and boring (Vichy, by comparison, was paradise, a disgruntled Tchaikovsky later said), the bathing was poor and, judging by the faces in a photograph taken while they were there, the weather, food and just about everything else was similarly mediocre.

Worse than that, everyone except Tchaikovsky drank the local water and became ill. Tchaikovsky had brought some bottles of Vichy water with him and thus avoided the poisoning.

With Modest and Sofya out of action, it fell to Tchaikovsky to care for Kolya, the boy he was growing to love. This brought out an unexpectedly paternal quality in Tchaikovsky that he had not exhibited before, and it was not unnoticed by his brother.

Given Tchaikovsky's depression and Kolya's disabilities, the result could have been disastrous. The opposite was the case, as Modest noted:

> *Generally nervy, irritable moreover after his incarceration at Vichy, upset by the vestiges of the attack of depression that had overcome him while there, he was attentiveness, patience, gentleness itself in his handling of this deaf and dumb boy who was himself nervy, fidgety, and able only with great difficulty to express himself to those around him. The mutual adoration of two friends, which had already before this established itself, became even stronger.*

The next sentence written by Modest shows us a Tchaikovsky we have not encountered before:

> *I can truly say that this relationship with a boy who at that moment was entirely dependent upon him, this role as head of the family which for a short time had fallen to his lot, showed Pyotr Ilyich a way out of the melancholy that was tormenting him, out of the 'loneliness' of his recent years.*[4]

This time 'loneliness' is placed in inverted commas by Modest. Is he hiding something with his laudatory language? Was his brother's fondness for the boy purely paternal or was it something else, and if so did Modest know about it? Certainly Tchaikovsky does not mince words about his feelings for Kolya in a letter he wrote to Modest shortly after the trip:

Modya, kiss this divine boy's little hand, his little foot, but especially his wonderful sweet little eyes! You don't know how much I adore him. Not a minute goes by that I don't think of him.[5]

From France, Tchaikovsky made his planned trip to Bayreuth, where he heard the first full performance of Wagner's *Ring* cycle. He went to pay a visit on the German composer, but Wagner was not at home to receive him, much to Tchaikovsky's disappointment. He did, though, meet Wagner's father-in-law, Franz Liszt.

Once back in Moscow, those demons were rearing their head again. He was again in close contact with Iosif Kotek, very close contact indeed. He wrote to Modest:

My only need is for him to know I love him endlessly . . . It is impossible for me to hide my feelings for him, although I tried hard to do so at first. I saw that he noticed everything and understood me. But then can you imagine how artful I am in hiding my feelings? . . . Yesterday I gave myself away completely . . . burst. I made a total confession of love, *begging him not to be angry, not feel constrained . . . All of these confessions were met with a thousand various small caresses, strokes on the shoulder,* cheeks, *and strokes across my head. I am incapable of expressing to you the full degree of bliss that I experienced by completely giving myself away.*[6]

Clearly Tchaikovsky's attraction to Kotek was reciprocated, though the young student was not exclusively homosexual, which Tchaikovsky was soon to learn. At the same time, it appears Tchaikovsky was seriously thinking of setting up house with Modest and Kolya. But even he realised this might lead to unacceptable gossip:

I do not want evil tongues to wound an innocent child, about whom they would inevitably say that I am preparing him to be my own lover, moreover, a mute one.[7]

In the autumn of 1876, at the age of thirty-five, Tchaikovsky announced a new course of action. Perhaps the tenderness he felt towards Kolya in the south of France had brought out a hitherto hidden desire to start a family. Perhaps his periodic self-loathing finally overwhelmed him.

It was time to take the single most important decision of his life. He would get married. The single most important decision, and also the worst.

17
A WOMAN ENTERS HIS LIFE

The first person Tchaikovsky told of his dramatic decision was, unsurprisingly, his brother Modest. Rather than take full responsibility, he ascribes the necessity for his plan to his siblings, as if it is their fault that he is having to take such drastic action. At the same time, he offers a brotherly word of advice to Modest to 'do as I am going to do': the only way, as Tchaikovsky saw it, to avoid inevitable scandal – and perhaps also, to some extent, to assuage the guilt of his brother following in his footsteps:

> *I am now living through a very critical moment in my life. When an opportunity occurs I'll write to you about it in rather more detail, but meanwhile I'll simply say:* I have decided to marry. *I cannot avoid this. I have to do it – and not just for my own sake, but also for* you, *and for Tolya, and for Sasha, and for all those I love. And you, Modya, need to think seriously about this.*[1]

To call this disingenuous is an understatement. One suspects that he was pre-empting what he knew he would hear back from his brother. He was not wrong. Modest was appalled. His lengthy reply to his elder brother is lost – probably destroyed by Tchaikovsky – but it is clear from Tchaikovsky's reply what Modest has said. Not only is he outraged, but so is Sasha. She must have known of her elder brother's homosexuality, having either deduced it herself or heard the truth from Modest.

Tchaikovsky's riposte to Modest, written on 19 August 1876, is, in my opinion, one of the most remarkable letters he ever wrote. It alternates between a *cri de cœur*, a shout of defiance, and an open acknowledgement of his sexuality. He admits candidly that the sole reason he wishes to marry is to still wagging tongues.

If ever a letter presents Tchaikovsky, the man, in all his complexity, his emotional instability, his strengths and weaknesses, his defiance of social norms and his deep-rooted feelings of guilt – even his back-and-forth reasoning that marriage will stop the gossip but why should he be ashamed and why should he not be able to pursue happiness on his own terms . . . this is it.

For all these reasons it is worth quoting at some length:

> I've lost your letter, and I cannot reply point by point to your arguments against marriage. I remember that many of them are unsound; many, on the other hand, coincide completely with my own thoughts. You say that one shouldn't give a damn for what people say. This is true only up to a certain point. There are people who cannot despise me for my vices simply because they began to love me when they still didn't suspect that I was, in fact, a man of lost reputation.
>
> For instance, this applies to Sasha. I know that she guesses everything and forgives everything. Many other people whom I love or respect regard me in the same way.

And here comes the defiance. It is easy to imagine him clenching his jaw when writing it, mouthing the words angrily under his breath:

> Do you really believe that the consciousness that they pity and forgive me is not painful to me when, at bottom, I am guilty of nothing! And is it not a terrible thought that people who love me can sometimes be ashamed of me! But, you know, this has happened a hundred times, and it will happen a hundred times more.

Then the obvious solution:

> In a word, I should like by marriage, or by a generally open liaison with a woman, to stop the mouths of various contemptible creatures whose opinion I do not in the least respect, but who could cause distress to people close to me.

But wait. Having announced that he is determined to enter into marriage, it suddenly seems as though his mind is not in fact made up. The thrill of his true desires is simply too great to resist, something Modest has evidently warned him about:

In any case, do not fear for me, dear Modest. The fulfilment of my plans is not nearly as close as you think. My habits have become so hardened that it's impossible to discard them like an old glove. And besides, I am far from possessed of an iron character, and . . . I have already three times given way to the force of natural inclinations. Thus you are completely right in saying in your letter that, despite all one's vows, it is not possible to restrain oneself from one's weaknesses.

Note the word 'weaknesses'. However defiant he may be, his desires are still, to him, a weakness. Finally there comes determination – provided he can find the right kind of woman, someone who will not prevent him from indulging in those 'natural inclinations':

All the same, I am standing by my intentions, and you may be sure that, one way or another, I shall carry them through. But I shall not do this suddenly or hastily. In any case I do not intend to take a yoke upon me. I shall only enter a legal or an extramarital union with a woman if I can fully guarantee my peace and freedom.[2]

'Convoluted' does not begin to describe it. Will he marry, or won't he? Will it be marriage or a union of convenience, nothing more? Will it be soon, to still those annoying voices, or will he wait a little while? Will it 'cure' his homosexuality or merely conceal it – and what might any woman involved make of it all?

We shall put all these questions aside for a short while, as Tchaikovsky himself did, to concentrate on the more pressing subject of music. While he agonised over the question of marriage, his creative juices were in full flow.

The compositions poured from him. Only three days before writing that tortuous letter, he was commissioned – by Nikolay Rubinstein, no less, showing that Tchaikovsky was clearly back in favour with the Conservatory head – to write an orchestral piece for a charity concert in aid of victims of the war that had broken out between Turkey and Russia's fellow Slavs in Serbia.

Borrowing folk tunes and patriotic themes, in the extraordinarily swift period of five days Tchaikovsky composed the *Slavonic March*, or *Marche slave*, orchestrating it as well. The premiere was an absolute triumph. A member of the audience reported:

The rumpus and roar that broke out beggars description. The whole audience rose to its feet. Many jumped on to their seats: cries of bravo and hurrah were mingled together. The march had to be repeated, after which the same storm broke out afresh. Many in the hall were weeping.[3]

"Despite all one's vows, it is not possible to restrain oneself from one's weaknesses."

Tchaikovsky

Above

The Death of Francesca da Rimini and Paolo Malatesta by Alexandre Cabanel.

Immediately after composing *Marche slave*, he set about writing an orchestral piece based on the tragedy of Francesca da Rimini, as related in Dante's *La Divina Commedia*. The original suggestion had come from Modest some months earlier. Tchaikovsky must have been ruminating over it since then as, in the space of just three weeks, he completed it. Another triumphant premiere followed, which further cemented his position as Russia's most popular composer.

Next, in complete contrast to the tragedy and pathos of *Francesca da Rimini*, Tchaikovsky composed his *Variations on a Rococo Theme* for cello and orchestra, the closest he would ever come to writing a cello concerto. Consisting of a theme and eight contrasting variations, it took its cue from Tchaikovsky's avowed musical hero, Mozart. Again composition was swift, taking just a month.

Tchaikovsky was at the height of his creative powers, which makes it all the more extraordinary that, in the midst of this, not only did he write that tortured and tortuous letter, but shortly after that he was to be distracted in a most singular and unexpected way. Towards the end of 1876, a woman entered Tchaikovsky's life. Given his resolve to marry, we might expect this to be the beginning of a relationship, particularly since over the ensuing years Tchaikovsky came closer to this woman than he ever would to any other person, revealing more intimate details of his life to her than to anybody else, including his brother Modest.

Yet although the two were in intimate contact for nearly fourteen years, not only was there never any question of romance but during all that time they never met in person. The intimate relationship between them existed only in letters, more than twelve hundred of them.

It would become one of the most extraordinary relationships – indeed *the* most extraordinary relationship of its kind – in all classical music.

Nadezhda Filaretovna Frolovskaya, almost ten years older than the composer with whom she would become so closely associated, was born in the village of Znamenskoe near Smolensk in western Russia. Her family was wealthy, owning several landed estates, and could afford to give Nadezhda Filaretovna a rounded education, including a solid grounding in music.

By her middle teenage years she was a capable pianist with a good knowledge of the classical repertoire. She was also well versed in literature, history and philosophy, as well as being competent in foreign languages.

The young girl was thus highly eligible, and at the age of seventeen she was married to one Karl Otto von Meck, ten years older than her and an engineer from Riga on the Baltic. Together they would have no fewer than thirteen children, eleven of whom survived into adulthood.

Nadezhda von Meck, the name under which she would secure her place in musical history, grew – by her own admission – into a difficult and imperious woman. She was used to getting her own way, and was intolerant of those who dared to disagree with her.

This was no doubt the result of the early years of married life, which saw her endure strains and hardship. Driven by ambition herself, she was disappointed by her husband's lack of it. Karl von Meck had a poorly paid job as a government official and, unlike his wife, seemed content with his lot.

When she urged him to try for better-paid employment, he assured her that, with a growing family, it was safer for him to stay where he was than to risk changing course and failing.

She meanwhile had enough energy for both of them. With children arriving on a regular basis, she found herself having to fill the roles of mother, governess, nurse, dressmaker and housekeeper. Yet as well as her domestic duties, she kept abreast of political and social trends.

With a keen eye to future advancements, she spotted that Russia was lagging behind western Europe in transport and communication. She saw too that the country's lumbering industry was beginning to wake up to this deficiency and the need to do something about it.

Nadezhda Filaretovna decided that the future lay in railways, and she urged her husband to extricate himself from the position of a poorly paid cog in a government machine – his income was a mere 20 kopeks a day – and put his engineering qualifications to use in the railway industry. She encouraged him to find a partner with capital and enter what she saw as a burgeoning industry.

She did not just urge him; she harangued him to such an extent that, no doubt with considerable trepidation, he resigned his position with the government and threw his lot in with the railways.

Within just a few years Karl von Meck was a multi-millionaire. In 1860 there were a hundred miles of railway track in Russia; twenty years later, there were over fifteen thousand miles of laid track.

Karl von Meck was responsible for hundreds of miles of railway, from Kursk just outside Ukraine to its capital Kiev, as well as the highly profitable line from Moscow to Ryazan, a hundred and twenty miles to the south-east, with its near monopoly of the transport of grain. He was responsible for several other lines as well. Meck had found his calling, and he had his far-sighted and determined wife to thank for it.

Almost literally overnight, the burgeoning von Meck family found itself among the newly rich. They were not just comfortable; they were very wealthy. Their lives had changed for ever, and over the ensuing years their fortune was steadily enhanced, as the Russian railway system reached ever further to distant locations, making the vast country feel, for the first time, like a homogeneous whole.

Then, in 1876, twenty-eight years into the marriage, everything changed. Karl von Meck died suddenly at the age of fifty-five.

Nadezhda von Meck, now forty-five years old, found herself a wealthy widow, with no material concerns whatsoever. Furthermore, with her eleven surviving children now moving into adulthood, she could absolve herself from the need to play much part in supporting them.

In fact, she involved herself more not less in their lives. Exhibiting the same steely determination that she had with her husband, she withdrew almost totally from social life and set about devoting herself to the task of controlling every aspect of her children's lives. She arranged their marriages, bought homes for them, even chose the furniture for their houses.

This devotion, though, was narrow and damaging to those closest to her. She declined any invitation to meet the families of the spouses of her children, or even to attend any of their weddings. She never paid visits to her married children, instead summoning them to see her.

If her behaviour caused resentment, she was happy to accept it. She was perfectly aware of how she appeared to others, and was her own worst critic, while not stinting in her criticism of others.

'I am very unsympathetic in my personal relations,' she wrote in a letter,

> because I do not possess any femininity whatever; second, I do not know how to be tender, and this characteristic has passed on to my entire family. All of us are afraid to be affected or sentimental, and therefore the general nature of our family relationships is comradely, or masculine, so to speak.[4]

As for her marriage to von Meck, though there is no direct evidence – she does not refer to it a single time in any of her voluminous correspondence – it seems unlikely to have been very happy. It is probable that she resented deeply the fact that society's values cast her, the wife, as inferior to her husband, despite the undoubted fact that she was the driving force behind their relationship. She was effectively a feminist before the term existed.

Although for her marriage was the only acceptable place for sexual relations, and therefore necessary in order to start a family, she did not view the institution in a favourable light, writing in a letter to Tchaikovsky: 'You may think that I am a great admirer of marriages . . . but I shall tell you that I am, on the contrary, an irreconcilable enemy of marriages',[5] and in a separate letter stating: 'The distribution of rights and obligations as determined by societal laws I find speculative and immoral.'[6]

She was not alone in her views. Contemporary Russian radical thinkers were publishing similar opinions, which were equally favourable to both sexes, but the authors were all men. For a woman to hold such views – and express them – was practically unheard of.

Here, then, is an extremely wealthy widow not afraid to speak her mind. She also enjoyed being a patron of the art she loved most, music. Even before her husband's death she was supporting musicians and musical establishments.

In later years, in both Russia and Europe, she employed Claude Debussy to accompany her at the piano, and also to teach her children. Debussy actually fell in love with one of the von Meck daughters and wanted to marry her; Madame von Meck forbade it.[*]

"For a woman to hold such views – and express them – was practically unheard of."

---

[*] In September 1880 she sent Debussy's *Danse bohémienne* to Tchaikovsky to ask his opinion; a month later Tchaikovsky wrote back to her, 'It is a very pretty piece, but it is much too short. Not a single idea is expressed fully, the form is terribly shrivelled, and it lacks wholeness.' Debussy did not publish the piece, and the manuscript remained in the von Meck family until 1932. (Poznansky, p. 375; *CNvM*.)

One of her beneficiaries was the Russian Musical Society, through which she became acquainted with the head of the Moscow Conservatory, Nikolay Rubinstein. As so often, from centuries long gone up to today, when patrons make money available to artists, they expect their views and requests to be accepted and acted on.

The sole exception to Madame von Meck's decision to retire entirely from public life was her attendance at concerts put on by the Russian Musical Society, which she always attended incognito, sitting alone in the balcony.

As a consequence she donated large sums to the organisation, in return for which Rubinstein had to accept her strongly expressed opinions regarding performers and repertoires. He was, by all accounts, uncomfortable when she expressed opinions contrary to his own, but was obliged to acquiesce in order not to risk losing her donations. Theirs was a relationship conducted on a strictly professional level; anything even close to friendship between patron and music director was out of the question.

Rubinstein was therefore the obvious choice for von Meck to turn to when she decided she wanted to employ a violinist to accompany her on the piano, and to travel with her and her family; in effect a resident musician, to whom she would pay a handsome salary.

Such a musician would, of necessity, be fairly young and unmarried, allowing him to travel at his employer's whim for unspecified amounts of time. Given the salary and the chance to see something of Europe's cultural high spots, it was an attractive proposition.

There was an obvious choice, and Rubinstein made it. The offer was put to young Iosif Kotek, impecunious and recently graduated from the Conservatory, and a great friend of Tchaikovsky with whom he was – judging by the intensity of Tchaikovsky's letter quoted above – amorously involved.

Kotek accepted, and entered the employ of Madame von Meck. From her point of view, it was a fortuitous choice. Given her interest in music, and frequent attendances at RMS concerts, she had inevitably heard plenty of music by the city's – the country's – most celebrated composer, Pyotr Ilyich Tchaikovsky, and she liked what she had heard.

She quickly established that Kotek had been taught by none other than Tchaikovsky himself, leading her to ask him whether he thought the composer might be prepared to make arrangements of some of his own music for violin and piano, so that she and Kotek could play them together. Using Kotek as an intermediary, von Meck made a very substantial financial offer to Tchaikovsky to arrange some of his pieces for violin and piano.

Tchaikovsky, perennially short of money, was hardly likely to refuse such a wealthy benefactor. He fulfilled the commission in rapid time, almost as an aside while working on his *Rococo Variations*. Madame von Meck was

enormously pleased with the result. Towards the end of December 1876, she wrote to him in effusive terms, using self-deprecating language, which seems to contradict her notoriously autocratic reputation:

> *Permit me to convey to you my sincerest gratitude for such a swift execution of my request. To tell you how much delight your compositions afford me I consider out of place because you have not been used to that kind of praise, and the worship of a being, in music as insignificant as I, might appear to you only ridiculous, and my enjoyment is so dear to me that I do not wish it to be ridiculed. Therefore I will only say, and I ask you to believe this literally, that with your music I live more lightly and more pleasantly.*
>
> *Accept my sincerest respect and sincerest devotion.*
> *Nadezhda von Meck.*[7]

Tchaikovsky's musical prowess has tamed this 'difficult' woman, without him ever having met her. But if she genuinely believed that Tchaikovsky would 'ridicule' her for her lack of musical expertise, she had misjudged her man. Here was a human being who could match her self-deprecation word for word.

He replied to her the following day, with a blend of formality and deference matching hers:

> I am sincerely grateful for all the kind and flattering things you have been so good as to write to me. On my side I will say that, for a musician amid failures and obstacles of every kind, it is comforting to think that there is a small minority of people, to which you also belong, who love our art so sincerely and warmly.
>> Sincerely devoted to you and esteeming you,
>> P. Tchaikovsky[8]

With these two brief, formal, almost over-modest notes, there began the correspondence that, it is not an exaggeration to say, is unmatched in the history of music. Well over a thousand letters over a period of more than thirteen years, reaching a level of intimacy – at least in words – neither of them had enjoyed with anyone else before.

The formality of that opening exchange was soon brushed aside. Within just a few weeks, von Meck wrote again, this time altogether more intimately:

> There is much, much that I would wish to write to you, when the opportunity occurs, of my imaginary relationship with you, but I am afraid of trespassing upon your so limited free time. I will say only that this relationship, however abstract it may be, is precious to me as the best, the highest of all feelings of which human nature is capable.[9]

One could easily forgive Tchaikovsky if he took fright at this, an unknown woman declaring quite openly that she desires a relationship with him, even if 'imaginary'. Exactly the opposite happened. Tchaikovsky replied in kind, quite content to escalate the relationship:

> Why do you hesitate to tell me all your thoughts? I assure you I should have been most interested and pleased, as I in turn feel deeply sympathetic toward you. These are not mere words. Perhaps I know you better than you imagine. If, some happy day, you will do me the honour of writing to me what you have so far withheld, I shall be very grateful.[10]

Clearly von Meck felt emboldened by his response. She sent him a long and rambling letter by return, beginning somewhat meekly but quickly taking a

"*Tchaikovsky's musical prowess has tamed this 'difficult' woman, without him ever having met her.*"

more dramatic turn as she professed her love for him – a man she had never met. It ends with the extraordinary proposition that gives this relationship its quality of uniqueness – that the two should never meet.

The opening, asking him for a photograph, could, with more contemporary language, have been written today from a fan to a rock star:

> *Your generous reply to my letter filled me with joy deeper than I have long known, but you know this common failing of human nature: the more kindness you receive, the more you want . . . I cannot stop myself asking you an enormous favour which you may find unwelcome and inappropriate . . . I am not sure how you will respond to this, Pyotr Ilyich, but from all I know of you I suspect that you of all people will be slow to condemn me for asking – if I am wrong, then I humbly beg you to tell me so directly and bluntly, and turn down my request – which is that you give me your photograph . . . I possess two already, but I want to have one from you. I want to search your face for clues as to those sources of inspiration, those feelings which inspire you to compose music which transports me into a realm of sensations, aspirations and desires that life itself can never satisfy . . .*[11]

She has two photographs already! She wants to search his face! And, of course, it was all for love of his music: flattery was certainly something Tchaikovsky was susceptible to, having taken his fair share of its opposite.

She goes on to praise his Symphonic Fantasia: *The Tempest*, which had attracted its share of criticism. Not from von Meck, though. It had left her 'completely delirious, beyond any hope of salvation'.[12] It awakened a desire in her to find out everything she could about its composer, hoping to find similarities that could allow her to identify as closely as possible with him – 'a similarity of outlook, a shared capacity for depth of feeling, and a common range of sympathies, so that it becomes possible to be close although far distant'.[13]

And then, the surprising revelation, at least to us, if not to Tchaikovsky himself:

> *I am so intent on knowing everything about you that at any time you care to name I can tell where you are and, as often as not, what you are doing . . . There was a time when I was desperate to meet you. But now, the more enamoured I become of you, the more an acquaintanceship frightens me – I am sure I would be in no fit state to make sense if we began a conversation – though if we were to meet by chance, face to face, I would be unable to treat you as a stranger, and I would hold out my hand to yours, if only to press it, without a word being spoken. In short,*

I prefer to think of you from a distance, to hear you in your music, and
to feel at one with you in your work . . .[14]

Once again Tchaikovsky replies in a similar fashion, expressing a desire to be close to her, as she has to him. He, too, has been drawn to her as a person who clearly has so much in common with him. A degree of scepticism is in order here, since the two have never met. Both have formed intimate opinions of each other solely by talking with other people.

Then he echoes her desire that they should never meet, believing he understands her motive, though she did not express it as he is about to:

You will believe me when I say that I quite understand why, loving my
music as you do, you do not wish to make the personal acquaintance
of its creator. You are worried that you will not discover in me those
attributes with which your imagination has endowed me. And you are
absolutely right. I am quite sure that, on closer acquaintance, you would
not find that balance, that perfect harmony between the musician and
the man, of which your imagination dreams.[15]

She was no doubt filled with joy that Tchaikovsky sent her not only a photograph, but a piece of music too.

She responded at once, sending him a photograph of herself – 'not expecting it to give you any pleasure, merely to express to some extent the depths of the feelings I hold for you'.[16]

Here are two people, a musician and his female admirer, expressing an affection for each other that is clearly close to love, at least on her part. If hers is an infatuation born of the music, what can we say about his?

Is he to some extent liberated by engaging with a woman he knows he will never have to meet in person? Perhaps, although we cannot rule out a financial motive either. She is very wealthy, and has already advanced him a considerable sum of money, over and above the musical commission. He obviously would not want to jeopardise that.

His burgeoning relationship with Madame von Meck was not the only distraction he had to contend with. Another woman approached him out of the blue. Once again, she wanted intimate contact.

This time, the result would be very different.

18

'SHE IS REPULSIVE TO ME'

Tchaikovsky wrote that startling letter to his brother about his decision to marry on 19 August 1876. By total coincidence, just seven months later he received a letter from a woman declaring that she was in love with him, and had been so for years.

Once he was over the initial shock, Tchaikovsky must have thought – at least to begin with – that providence was smiling on him. If this letter was to be taken seriously, half the battle was perhaps already won. He would have no need to look for a wife; it appeared she had come to him.

Antonina Milyukova was eight years younger than Tchaikovsky – twenty-nine when she wrote that letter – and had been a piano student for just a single academic year at the Moscow Conservatory. Tchaikovsky would later claim he had no memory of her existence.

According to Antonina, she had first met Tchaikovsky at the home of her brother in May 1872, just before she enrolled at the Conservatory.[*] For her it was love at first sight.

At the Conservatory it seems she continued to love him from a distance, impressed more by his good looks and gentle demeanour than by

---

[*] Other accounts put the meeting seven years earlier at the home of a singer who was a friend of Tchaikovsky, but given that Antonina would have been only seventeen at the time, the 1872 date seems more likely.

his musical prowess. It appears there was no meeting between the two, with Antonina continuing to love him 'secretly', as she was to put it much later in her memoirs.

Then, out of the blue, came that letter professing her long-lasting and undying love. Why she chose to write it at that particular moment is not known. If indeed Tchaikovsky did view her confession as providential, he certainly did not give that impression at first.

Antonina's letter to him, and his reply, have sadly disappeared, but there can be no doubt from what followed that Tchaikovsky set out to disabuse her of any notion of a relationship, and used unequivocally strong words. He also, true to character, listed his shortcomings, making it clear to Antonina that he did not wish to hear from her again. She was not put off; in fact his words served only to redouble her love for him.

In response she wrote two letters in a single day, with an ever increasing intensity of emotion. The first is a straightforward declaration of love. 'Wherever I may be, I shall not be able to forget you or lose my love for you,' she wrote. 'What I liked in you [when I first came to know you] I can no longer find in any other man; indeed, and in a word, I do not want to look at any other man after you.'

Perhaps to make Tchaikovsky jealous, she relates how she had to listen to a man she had known from his student days declaring his love for her, which she found 'distressing'.[1]

Later that day she sat down at her writing desk for a second time, and this time she discarded all inhibitions, her fervour spilling out on the page. So desperate was she that towards the end the letter contains an overt threat of suicide:

> . . . will you really break off this correspondence with me, not having seen me even once? No, I am convinced you will not be so cruel. Do you, maybe, take me for a frivolous person or a gullible girl . . . ? How can I prove to you that my words are genuine . . . ? After your last letter I loved you twice as much again, and your shortcomings mean absolutely nothing to me . . .
>
> I am dying of longing, and I burn with a desire to see you, to sit with you and talk with you, though I also fear that at first I shan't be in a state to utter a word. There is no failing that might cause me to fall out of love with you . . .
>
> I sit at home all day, pace the room from corner to corner like a crazy thing, thinking only of that moment when I shall see you. I shall be ready to throw myself on your neck, to smother you with kisses . . .
>
> My first kiss will be given to you and no one else in the world. Farewell, my dear one. Do not try to disillusion me further about yourself,

because you are only wasting your time. I cannot live without you, and so maybe soon I shall kill myself. So let me see you and kiss you so that I may remember that kiss in the other world . . .

If you knew how I suffer, then probably out of pity alone you would grant my request.[2]

History has been unkind to Antonina, and the disparaging accounts of her date from this letter. Even if she and Tchaikovsky had known each other well, or Antonina had been a teenage girl, the letter could still be seen as emotionally immature. The fact, though, that they had never properly met – even Antonina's account of that first meeting makes it clear that no contact, verbal or otherwise, took place – and that Antonina is a woman approaching thirty years of age, puts it in a different league.

Tchaikovsky's biographers liberally use words such as 'hysterical', 'emotionally fragile', even 'unbalanced' to describe Antonina. 'Unhinged' is used too – always in the context of her inexplicably bizarre behaviour having a deleterious affect on the genius of the great composer.

We shall see from the life that Antonina went on to lead that these words might not be too much of an exaggeration, but to put all the blame on her for the events that followed is unwarranted. Tchaikovsky must bear a large degree of responsibility. The way he treated her was appalling.

It was at this point, having received that long, emotionally fraught letter, that Tchaikovsky decided Fate had intervened in his deliberations about marriage. He agreed to meet Antonina.

That meeting took place on 20 May in the house in Moscow in which Antonina was renting a room. There are no details of what took place at the meeting, or of what was said. Nor is it entirely clear which of them initiated the meeting. Antonina in later correspondence said it was Tchaikovsky; he said it was at her request.

What is known, however, is that – surprisingly – the two met for a second time only three days later, in the evening. It can therefore be surmised that the first meeting had gone well.

In fact it must have gone extremely well, because at the second meeting Tchaikovsky made a formal proposal of marriage. Antonina's joy must, however, have been tempered somewhat by the caveats Tchaikovsky attached to his offer.

He told her openly that he did not love her, but that in all circumstances he would be 'a staunch and grateful friend'. He described to her in detail 'my character – my irritability, volatile temperament, my unsociability – finally, my circumstances'.[3]

"To put all the blame on Antonina is unwarranted. Tchaikovsky must bear a large degree of responsibility."

What does he mean by 'my circumstances'? Could it be that he is telling her he is homosexual, even that he wants to be able to continue his homosexual lifestyle after marriage, as he had intimated in that letter to his brother Modest? Given what we know of what was to follow, it seems unlikely.

It is entirely possible, given the mores of the day, not only that she did not know her husband was homosexual but that she might never have known – even that she might not have known what homosexuality was.

Antonina, unsurprisingly, was not deterred by his warnings, and was swift to accept his proposal of marriage. For her, an impossible dream had come true. His attitude was rather different:

> *Having lived thirty-seven years with an innate aversion to marriage, it is very distressing to be drawn through force of circumstances into the position of a bridegroom who, moreover, is not in the least attracted to his bride . . . In a day or two my marriage with her will take place. What will happen after that I do not know . . . If I am marrying*

without love, it is because circumstances conspired to make it impossible for me to do otherwise.[4]

These are searing words; he is condemning his marriage to failure even before it has begun. He is not attracted to his bride, he does not love her, and as for those final words, they are disingenuous to say the least. Circumstances have not in any way made it impossible for him to do otherwise: he made the proposal after all. He evaded her to begin with; he could have continued to do so.

How do we know all this? To whom did Tchaikovsky write these words? Not, as we might expect, to his brother Modest, to whom he was accustomed to pouring out his innermost feelings, particularly with regard to amorous encounters, but to the one person who might be expected to react with absolute horror to his impending marriage: the other woman who had professed an irresistible attraction to him, even if she had not overtly used the word 'love'. Nadezhda von Meck.

He wrote these words to von Meck on 3 July, nearly six weeks after that second meeting with Antonina at which he had proposed marriage. He had therefore had plenty of time to think about it; time that he actually used well.

He went, once again, to stay with his old friend Shilovsky, the man with whom he had holidayed on the French Riviera, whose country estate had welcomed him on many lengthy visits, with whom he had certainly enjoyed a homosexual relationship – and who had recently married.

No details are known about this particularly stay, other than that Tchaikovsky had spacious quarters to himself, and alternated between composition and long walks in the countryside. He was working on two new compositions more or less simultaneously: his opera *Eugene Onegin*, and his Symphony No. 4. These would become two of his finest compositions. He would never again write an opera as good; the symphony would be equalled, but never bettered.

He made good progress on both. It is possible he was encouraged by observing Shilovsky's newly acquired domestic contentment. Perhaps that encouraged him to go ahead with his own marriage.

What it did not do, though, was convince him that he was making the right decision. Those defeatist words were written to von Meck on his return to Moscow. Lest there should be any doubt, two days later he wrote to his sister Sasha and, once again, the letter makes for depressing reading:

I shall . . . refrain from describing my bride's qualities since, except that she is a thoroughly respectable girl and loves me very much, I still know very little about her. Only when we have lived together for some time will the facets of her character reveal themselves to me with complete clarity . . . I shan't bring her to see you at Kamenka until I'm no longer shocked by the thought that my nieces will call her auntie. *At the moment, although I love my bride, it still seems to me a little impertinent on her part to have become aunt to your children, whom I love more than any other children in the world.*

I have spent a month not far from here in the country at the Shilovskys'. I needed to stay there, first to begin my opera, secondly to acclimatise myself to the thought that I'm getting married. The proof that I'm taking this important step not frivolously but with deliberation is shown by the fact that I spent this month very calmly and composed a whole two-thirds of the opera.[5]

It is no exaggeration to claim that Tchaikovsky is embarrassed by the woman he has decided to marry. He has already established, both in reports from friends and his own encounters with her, that her education is limited; that she has difficulty in engaging in conversation on intellectual matters, with a limited knowledge of literature, and even of music. This Tchaikovsky attributes to her parents's marriage breaking up when she was just three years of age, resulting in a difficult childhood.

And yet, despite all these misgivings, he does not reverse his decision. Events now unfolded with startling rapidity. Three days after he wrote to von Meck, and the very day after his letter to Sasha, Tchaikovsky married Antonina.

The wedding took place on 6 July at the church of St George on Malaya Nikitskaya Street in Moscow. The ceremony was conducted by one Dmitri Razumovsky, a professor of church music and one of Tchaikovsky's colleagues at the Conservatory.

There were just two witnesses, and they are interesting choices. One was the only member of the Tchaikovsky family to be present, the groom's younger (heterosexual) brother Anatoly. The other was the young violinist Iosif Kotek.

The ceremony progressed along well-established lines, although Tchaikovsky professed later that he felt like a bystander, as if it were all happening to someone else. Then came the moment when Razumovsky told Tchaikovsky he could kiss his bride.

Then a kind of pain gripped my heart, and I was suddenly seized with such emotion that, it seems, I wept. But I tried quickly to regain control of myself, and to assume an appearance of calm. However, Anatoly noticed my condition, for he began to say something reassuring to me.[6]

It can be safely deduced that the emotion Tchaikovsky was feeling was not joy. If the omens for this marriage had not been good, the reality was soon to get a lot worse. After the wedding breakfast, bride and groom took the train to St Petersburg so that Tchaikovsky could introduce his wife to his family, in particular his father, who was now eighty-two years old.

The train journey was traumatic. We know about it in great detail from a letter he wrote to Anatoly two days later. Tchaikovsky sat in the carriage with Antonina, trying his best to engage her in conversation as far as Klin, north-west of Moscow, by which time it would be dark and he would be absolved of any further effort and be able to sleep.

At the second station, the door of the carriage was flung open and who should bound in but his old friend Prince Meshchersky, the aristocrat whose flamboyant homosexuality was considered to be so shocking, even by fellow homosexuals, that he was christened 'Prince of Sodom and citizen of Gomorrah'.

Tchaikovsky gave his friend such a despairing look that Meshchersky, to Tchaikovsky's relief, invited him out into the corridor of the train. Before any words could be exchanged, Tchaikovsky broke down in tears.

> Meshchersky showed [me] much tender sympathy, and did a lot to prop up my fallen spirit. When, after Klin, I returned to my wife, I was much calmer.[7]

This was Tchaikovsky's description of how Meshchersky helped him, as written in his letter to Anatoly. Has he left anything out? Most of the biopics that have been made of Tchaikovsky's life indicate that there was much more to it than that. The encounter is depicted as a full and passionate one, after which Meshchersky delivers a calmer, sated Tchaikovsky back to his wife.

Lurid imaginings or a more accurate portrayal of events? Perhaps Meshchersky really did simply offer reassuring words to his friend, which had the desired effect of lifting his spirits and calming him. Or perhaps more happened than that.

The newly wedded couple stayed at the Hotel Europa in St Petersburg for what was in effect their honeymoon, and it can be deduced with some confidence that on the wedding night the marriage was not consummated. In a letter to Anatoly, Tchaikovsky describes how his wife agreed to everything he suggested, and after he took a strong sedative, he prevailed on his 'discomfited wife not to be discomfited', before falling asleep 'like a log'.[8]

Why else would she be 'discomfited', other than by his evasion of any sexual activity? It can also be assumed that the marriage remained unconsummated, since, while still technically on honeymoon, Tchaikovsky wrote

"A kind of pain gripped my heart, and I was suddenly seized with such emotion that, it seems, I wept."

Tchaikovsky, when told he could kiss his bride.

to Anatoly that, 'in the physical respect, my wife has become *absolutely repulsive* to me'.[9]

In St Petersburg he introduced his wife to his father and stepmother. He noted that his father seemed to be very taken with her but that while his stepmother was perfectly courteous, she frequently had tears in her eyes. Did she sense the torture Tchaikovsky was putting himself through?

It was with relief that he returned to Moscow with Antonina. There, at least, he could resume what to him was a relatively normal life, avoiding his wife as much as possible.

After inviting a male friend to dinner, he contrived to spend the whole of the next day in the friend's company, rather than with Antonina. When walking with her, if he bumped into someone he knew, he was embarrassed to acknowledge her as his wife.

In conversation with friends and colleagues, Kashkin noticed how carefully Tchaikovsky would attend to what she was saying, frequently interrupting her, fearing that otherwise she would embarrass herself with her ignorance.

Tchaikovsky received little encouragement from these close friends and colleagues. Kashkin reported that at a meeting in Rubinstein's office in the Conservatory, Antonina was discussed. It was agreed the general impression she gave was 'favourable, if rather colourless'.

Rubinstein delivered a withering verdict: 'She's certainly pretty, and well enough behaved, but she's not particularly *likeable*. It's as if she were not quite a real person, more some sort of synthetic confection.'[10]

A photograph of the newly married couple shows two unsmiling faces, heads far apart, eyes looking in different directions, hands not touching. Their faces give nothing away. Interestingly, they gave vividly contrasting accounts of their life together elsewhere.

Antonina was clearly basking in the warm glow of having secured as husband the man she fell in love with all those years ago. She would later reflect:

> I would look at him surreptitiously, so he didn't notice, and admire him enormously, especially during morning tea. So handsome, with kindly eyes which melted my heart, he breathed such freshness into my life! I would just sit there looking at him, and think, 'Thank God he belongs to me and no one else! Now he is my husband, no one can take him away from me.'[11]

If she had known how Tchaikovsky himself saw their relationship, she might have been forgiven for believing it was not her husband talking but someone entirely different:

> During the day I tried to get on with my work, but in the evenings I found her company intolerable. Not daring to visit a friend, or even the

"I stand so far above this one, I am so superior to her that at least I shall never be frightened of her."

Tchaikovsky on his wife

theatre, I would set off each evening for a walk, and wander for hours through the far-flung, little-known streets of obscure Moscow.[12]

The more Tchaikovsky came to know her, the more he came to despise her, and that is not too strong a word. To his astonishment, he discovered that she had never been to a single concert at the Russian Musical Society. To add considerable insult to injury, although she had loved Tchaikovsky for some years, by her own admission she was not at all familiar with his music.

To say that Tchaikovsky knew from the moment he married Antonina that he had made a mistake misses the point. He knew *before* he married her. Everything that happened thereafter served only to emphasise his folly.

To make matters worse, he had to admit to himself that it was wrong to blame her:

> *She is positively agreeable to everything, and will never want more. All she needs is to cherish and care for me . . .*
>
> *There is no point in deceiving myself. She is a very limited person, but this is even a good thing. An intelligent woman might instil fear of herself in me. I stand so far above this one, I am so superior to her that at least I shall never be frightened of her.*[13]

After a brief pause in Moscow, another duty had to be fulfilled; it was time for the composer to meet his wife's family, or at least her mother and siblings, her father having died. He managed to keep the meeting brief, and hated every moment:

> *[Antonina's]* family environment *I liked very little. I have now passed three days in the country at her mother's, and it convinced me that everything that does not completely please me in my wife stems from the fact that she belongs to a very weird family, where the mother was always at odds with the father and now, after his death, is not ashamed to revile him in every possible way, where this same mother* hates!!! *some of her own children, where the sisters exchange catty remarks with one another, where the only son quarrels with his mother and all his sisters,* and so on, and so on.[14]

Things got inexorably worse. Tchaikovsky unburdens himself, again, in a letter to his patron Nadezhda von Meck. His words are full of pain and anguish:

> *. . . as soon as I found myself alone with my wife with the consciousness that it was now our fate to live with each other inseparably, I suddenly felt that not only did she not inspire me with even a simple feeling of friendship, but that she was* hateful *to me in the fullest sense of that word.*[15]

Even if we allow a degree of exaggeration given Tchaikovsky was writing to his (female) patron, and particularly since he has asked her to advance him some much needed money, we have evidence in other letters that his words were not in any sense exaggerating how he felt. That, deep down, he knew Antonina was simply doing her best to please him can have served only to deepen his wretchedness.

He left for a short break, first alone to a spa town in the Caucasus, then to his sister Sasha in Kamenka. He kept delaying his return to Moscow, as if trying to put off the inevitable. On finally returning he re-entered the same nightmare. Nothing had changed; nothing was going to change.

Tchaikovsky, tortured at the best of times, was now more angst-ridden than ever, and we, a century and a half later, want to shout at him that he must have seen this coming, he must have known he was making a dreadful mistake. Indeed, we *know* he knew, from his outpourings before the marriage itself.

So here he is, just a matter of weeks after his marriage, now convinced beyond any doubt that there is no escape from the disaster for which he is entirely responsible, unable to escape. Or *almost* unable. There is one way out of it: suicide.

Late one cold winter's night, walking around the city, struggling to find a method of taking his own life that would look like an accident in order to spare his family pain, he decided upon a plan.

Without hesitating, he stepped into the icy Moskva river. He stood there, submerged up to his waist, until his body was numb with cold before staggering home, in the desperate hope he would contract pneumonia.

Remaining bed-bound the following day, he explained to a concerned wife and his manservant Aleksey – whose relationship with his master by this time had become one of close friend – that he had been persuaded to join a late-night fishing party, and had accidentally fallen into the river.

Some biographers have doubted that this incident occurred but as Anthony Holden points out, the friend to whom he relayed this account, Kashkin, was a reliable correspondent, and the incident accurately mirrors his frame of mind. In another letter he wrote to von Meck, 'I fell into despair and sought death,' and on the manuscript of his Fourth Symphony he wrote, 'In the event of my death, deliver this to Mme von Meck.'[16]

Contrary to his expectations, he did not even suffer a sniffle. But his desperate action made him realise he must end his marriage. To achieve this he came up with a plan more devious, though less dramatic, than wading into the Moskva. He cabled Anatoly in St Petersburg, asking him to send a

telegram in the name of the conductor at the Imperial Theatres regarding the planned revival of his opera *Vakula the Smith*, which meant he would need to travel to St Petersburg straight away.

Anatoly, who seems to have replaced his twin Modest as Tchaikovsky's chief confidant, complied immediately. On 25 September 1877 a relieved Tchaikovsky left Moscow for the capital.

Relieved, but in a state of intense nervous exhaustion. Anatoly was shocked by his brother's much-changed appearance when he met him at the station. He was in such a weakened condition that he had to be physically supported into the Hotel Dagmar. Once inside the room he was first greatly distressed and then, utterly exhausted, collapsed into a deep sleep.

A psychiatrist was summoned, examined Tchaikovsky, and delivered the verdict that was music to Tchaikovsky's ears. He was ordered to take a complete break away from the city. For his own health it was imperative he should separate from his wife. In fact, if possible, he should never see her again. Whether the doctor received any inducement to make such a drastic order, we do not know. In any case, both brothers were very satisfied with the doctor's recommendations.

Leaving Tchaikovsky cloistered in the hotel, Anatoly left for Moscow to break the news to Antonina. First he called on Nikolay Rubinstein to explain the situation. Anatoly was clearly somewhat distressed by the whole affair and, fearing that Anatoly might not be firm enough with the wronged wife, Rubinstein insisted on accompanying him to see Antonina.

The meeting that then took place left both men nonplussed. Rubinstein explained the position in such a direct manner, it made Anatoly go 'hot and cold'. Antonina, though, reacted in a way that both men found utterly bewildering. She listened without a word, then indicated she was happy to do whatever her 'darling Peti' wanted. Then she served tea.[17]

Having delivered the *coup de grâce* to the Tchaikovskys' marriage and partaken of a surprisingly gracious cup of tea, Rubinstein departed, leaving Anatoly to work out the details.

Having expected some sort of dramatic scene, Anatoly simply could not fathom her response to the entire encounter. No tears, no hysterics, no protestations; instead, returning from showing Rubinstein out, Antonina beamed at him and remarked, 'Well, who'd have thought I would entertain the famous Rubinstein to tea at my home today!'[18] Then she enquired what Anatoly would like for dinner.

He made his excuses and left as soon as it was polite to do so. Returning to St Petersburg he was able to reassure his brother that his short-lived marriage of three months – during which he had spent only a matter of weeks with his wife – was at an end.

That is not to say that their relationship was finished. Divorce was some way off, and Tchaikovsky would find that his wife would frustrate his attempts to bring the marriage to a formal end several times, always hoping for some sort of reconciliation.

But this separation marked a turning point in Tchaikovsky's life, both physically and emotionally. In the first place he never again returned to live in Moscow, a city he had never liked.

Of more significance to his wellbeing, his failed marriage had taught him an important lesson. He had learned, finally, that his homosexuality was not a curse to be cured; it was rather an essential part of his make-up, and he should accept it.

He wrote as much in a letter to Anatoly only months after leaving his wife:

Only now, especially after the tale of my marriage, have I finally begun to understand that there is nothing more fruitless than not wanting to be that which I am by nature.[19]

There is not a single document from the rest of Tchaikovsky's life that can be interpreted as any kind of expression of self-torment about his sexuality. Yet this was no fleeting thought. As far as it was possible for such a deeply emotional, highly strung and easily wounded man, Pyotr Ilyich Tchaikovsky was finally, at the age of thirty-seven, at peace with himself.

19

FATE

Looking back today, it is difficult to understand how Tchaikovsky could ever have imagined that marriage was a sensible course of action. On 28 September 1876, only six months before receiving the first letter from Antonina, he wrote to Modest:

> I am so set in my habits and tastes that it is not possible to cast them aside all at once like an old glove. And besides, I am far from possessing a will of iron, and since my last letters to you I have already surrendered some three times to the force of my natural tendencies. Would you imagine! One of these days I even went to Bulatov's* country estate, and his house is nothing but a pederastic bordello. As if it were not enough that I had been there, I fell in love *as a cat with his own coachman!!!* So you are perfectly right when you say in your letter that it is not possible to restrain oneself, despite all vows, from one's weaknesses.[1]

'*I am so set in my habits and tastes . . .*' and yet he thought marriage could alter that. Behind the attempt at humour is a man ill at ease with himself, afflicted by 'weaknesses' he confesses he is unable to control. His apparent disapproval of the 'pederastic bordello' is in fact anything but. This is sex

---

* Classmate of Tchaikovsky at the School of Jurisprudence and fellow homosexual.

with boys. His words imply he knows it is wrong but that he simply cannot help himself.

Only two months into married life, he fled from his wife to the safety of his sister's estate in Kamenka. There – and Sasha must have been aware of it – he surrendered to those 'tendencies' again. The object of his desire this time was one of the estate's servants, Evstafy.

He pours out his desires in unrelenting detail, once again, in a letter to Modest:

> *As regards my source of delight, about whom I cannot even think without being sexually aroused and whose* boots I would feel happy to clean all my life long, *whose chamber pots I would take out and I am generally ready to lower myself anyhow, provided that I could kiss, even if only rarely his hands and feet.*[2]

Throughout his life, from being a young man struggling to get his music heard and appreciated to being the most famous composer in Russia and arguably the best known in Europe, Tchaikovsky was a regular visitor to male prostitutes. It was, it seems, the only way he could guarantee satisfaction without consequences. Yet, even while describing the joy this brought him, he acknowledges the sordidness he believes is inherent in what he is doing.

This is an extract from a letter to Modest dated 26 February 1879, less than two years after his marriage, when he is thirty-eight and living in Paris:

> *A bed, a pitiful little trunk, a dirty little table with a candle-end, a few shabby trousers and a jacket, a huge crystal glass, won in a lottery – those make the room's only decorations. Yet it did seem to me at that moment that this miserable cell is the centrepiece of the entire human happiness . . . There occurred all kinds of* calinerie *[tenderness] as he put it, and then I turned frantic because of amorous happiness and experienced incredible pleasure. And I can say in confidence, that not only for a long time but almost never have I felt so happy in this sense as yesterday.*

The next morning the guilt has set in. He writes:

> *This young man has* much good *at the roof of his soul. But, my God, how pitiable he is, how thoroughly debauched! And instead of helping him to better himself, I only contributed to his further going down.*[3]

It is telling that Tchaikovsky sees goodness in the male prostitute. It was inherent in his character to see the worth of individuals, often contrasting them with his own lack of such a quality. He extends this, perhaps surprisingly, to the person he has come to loathe, his wife.

In attempting to explain to Nadezhda von Meck the folly of his marriage, he goes out of his way to praise Antonina, when one might have expected the reverse – especially since he is writing to a female benefactor. His description of his wife does him credit:

> *Justice demands that I add the following: [Antonina] strove to please me in every way, she simply fawned on me, not once did she question any of my wishes, any of my thoughts, even if they touched on our everyday domestic life. She genuinely wished to inspire love in me and lavished endearments on me to the point of excess . . . She behaved honestly and sincerely. She mistook her desire to marry me for love.*

That last sentence is perhaps more applicable to someone else. Consider these words to von Meck:

> *. . . you are surely wondering how I could have resolved to join my life to such a strange companion? Even I now find it incomprehensible. Some kind of madness came over me. I fancied that I might inevitably be moved by her love for me, in which I then believed, and that I might inevitably, in my turn, fall in love with her.*[4]

In other words, he was deceiving himself about his reasons for marrying, just as he accused Antonina of doing.

If he had any concern that his marriage would in any way alienate his benefactor, he need not have worried. Von Meck was entirely on his side over the whole sorry business. She could see clearly where the fault lay, and it was not with her musical idol.

> *It pains me greatly, Pyotr Ilyich, that you accuse yourself so and worry yourself with compassion for your wife . . . She is one of those happy natures . . . who cannot grieve strongly and lastingly because they are unable to feel anything deeply; they live an objective, even purely material, life, and you have undertaken to provide for this; consequently, the ideal way of life for such natures – to eat well and to sleep even better – is being fulfilled by you for your wife, and you are entitled to nothing but gratitude from her.*[5]

As for Tchaikovsky, he, like von Meck herself, inhabited an entirely different realm of deep emotions which, by their very nature, were sure to lead to disappointment when attempting to consort with lesser individuals:

> *How are those who are capable of feeling as deeply as you and I to be happy: for if life is called an ocean, then society is . . . a shallow stream in which only those who skim the surface come off well . . . Yet, you and*

I, with our inability to treat anything whatsoever superficially, to amuse ourselves with trifles . . . we, with our need for profound emotions, broad interests, must beat our breasts, our heads, and our hearts against the stony bottom of that stream, and . . . must die without achieving that happiness which you know exists, which you see clearly before you, but which the shallow swimmers will not allow you to reach. They are not to blame, these flat-bottomed vessels, because they are fine as they are, but still how difficult it is for those who row deeply![6]

This is quite extraordinary language, poetic and descriptive.

If Nadezhda von Meck had known Tchaikovsky and Antonina for years, become close to them, understood them, we might be inclined to give some value to her character assessments. But let us not forget that she had never for a single moment met either of them!

Not that this would have troubled Tchaikovsky. All that mattered was that he had not in any way alienated his patron by his marriage. If anything it appeared to have increased her admiration for him. After all, if he had made a grave mistake, had he not successfully extricated himself? He deserved nothing but plaudits. Von Meck, by tying her emotions with his, by declaring their similarities, was in effect saying that the love she had for him existed on an altogether higher plane.

Her admiration for him also manifested itself in practical terms, for which he had good cause to be grateful. Within a month of ending his marriage, he began to receive a regular allowance from Nadezhda von Meck, an annual subsidy of 6,000 roubles, paid monthly, which at last gave him financial independence.

Some time earlier, during his stay at Shilovsky's country estate, Tchaikovsky had begun work on two new compositions. It is surprising that he was able to do any composing at all, given the turmoil of his private life. That these two works would be two of his greatest is a truly extraordinary achievement.

Indeed, the two works are *products* of his emotional turmoil. Both reflect that turmoil. Does this mean that without it he might never have written them? It does not. In the mind of a creative genius life itself is a stimulus.

He began work on the new symphony first. Within weeks of making early sketches, he received that first letter from Antonina. Coincidentally, shortly after that he paid a visit to a friend and her husband in Moscow. That friend, Elizaveta Lavrovskaya, happened to be an opera singer.

In casual conversation, the subject of a possible opera was discussed. Elizaveta asked Tchaikovsky if had any plans to compose a new opera, and her husband suggested a number of possible plots – plays and novels – that he might consider suitable.

Tchaikovsky was in no mood to turn his attention to an opera – the new symphony was his priority – and he rejected every suggestion. But Elizaveta clearly knew her man. She dropped the name of the Russian writer Tchaikovsky admired above all others into the conversation.

Had he considered Alexander Pushkin's verse novel *Eugene Onegin*? Her opinion was that it would make an ideal opera. It had all the necessary ingredients – a woman's love for a man being rejected, then later the same man's love for the woman being rejected in turn. Why, there is even a duel to heighten the drama.* Was it not perfect?

Tchaikovsky was initially unpersuaded. He later wrote to Modest that the idea seemed to him to be wild, to the extent that he did not even answer Elizaveta. But she had planted a seed.

A few days later he was having dinner alone in a restaurant, and began thinking of *Onegin*. Ideas began to take shape. By the end of the meal he had made up his mind. He dashed off to find a copy of the work, read it in one sitting, was unable to sleep at all that night, and by the morning had the entire scenario worked out in his head.

That was how he explained it to his brother. Even allowing for a certain amount of exaggeration, it is clear that Tchaikovsky had reached a speedy decision. He would set Pushkin's verse novel to music.

This is where events in his life come into play. There is a crucial moment early in the story when the heroine, Tatyana, sits at her desk and writes a long letter to a man whom she has met and with whom she has fallen hopelessly in love.

After receiving the letter, Onegin decides the kindest course of action is to come and see Tatyana and explain to her why she should put any thought of love out of her head. He explains to her that he does not love easily, and for that reason considers himself unsuited to marriage. The best he can offer her is brotherly affection, and he counsels her to be less open with her emotions in the future.

Substitute the names, and is this not exactly what happened between Antonina and Tchaikovsky? Did she not write him a long letter openly expressing her love for him, and did he not – at first at least – make strenuous efforts to persuade her of her folly?

"It is surprising that Tchaikovsky was able to do any composing at all, given the turmoil of his private life."

---

* Ironically, Pushkin himself was killed in a duel.

Tchaikovsky began composition immediately, and it is no surprise that the first passage he began to compose was the letter-writing scene. Art was imitating life – and life was also now beginning to imitate art.

Tchaikovsky (conveniently) explained it all in a letter to Modest, and we can see clearly just how close the parallels were in his mind:

> *Having received a second letter from Miss Milyukova, I was ashamed, and even became indignant with myself for my attitude towards her. In her second letter she complained bitterly that she had received no reply, adding that if her second letter suffered the same fate as the first, then the only thing that would remain for her would be to put an end to herself.*
>
> *In my mind all this tied up with the idea of Tatyana, and it seemed to me that I had myself acted incomparably more basely than Onegin, and I became really furious with myself for my heartless attitude to this girl who was in love with me.*[7]

It would seem that at least part of the reason why Tchaikovsky agreed to meet Antonina, which subsequently led to marriage, was his immersion in the plot of Pushkin's *Eugene Onegin*. What is beyond doubt is that the opera he created was his greatest, and the letter scene the most emotionally powerful of any he would write.

Just as *Eugene Onegin* was unlike any previous opera Tchaikovsky had written, so the new symphony took his compositional powers to new heights. It is simply in an entirely different league to the previous three, and once again this can be attributed in large measure to what was occurring in his life. In fact one modern biographer has called the Fourth Symphony 'a true piece of emotional autobiography'.[8]

From the opening notes we are in a different realm, a sound world that Tchaikovsky has not inhabited before.

We know exactly what was going through Tchaikovsky's mind, what he was trying to achieve while composing the new symphony, because he explained it in great detail in a lengthy letter to von Meck.

The 'seed' (his word) of the whole symphony is that dramatic opening, the strident call in triplets on French horns, augmented by bassoons. This is 'Fate' (again his word), and the influence of Beethoven's Fifth Symphony, with its famous opening bars (individual quavers, not triplets as here), is obvious. If that was Beethoven's translation of Fate into music, this is Tchaikovsky's.

There is no gainsaying Fate, no fighting it. You can do no more than reconcile yourself to it. That is the message of the first movement. There is a sense of abandonment to it, of allowing Fate to determine the course of your existence.

But in a perfect mirror of Tchaikovsky's own life, all is not gloom. A

gently syncopated theme brings light. Here he uses the key of C flat, which has no fewer than seven flats. This progresses into an even lighter theme, for which he writes in the key of B major, which uses five sharps. The two keys are in theory the same: C flat = B. But Tchaikovsky is sending a message to conductor and players: notes written as sharps should sound just slightly brighter than the same notes written as flats.

The brightness cannot last, however, and the Fate theme cuts back in again, as if awakening the listener from a daydream – Tchaikovsky's own description.

The second movement at first offers no respite, a mournful oboe playing a melancholy theme. Yet there is no gloom here; it is more akin to nostalgia for a time long ago, building to a climax that could almost be called joyful, before descending again. Tchaikovsky himself described it to von Meck as like sitting alone in the evening, weary from your labour, taking a book,

Above

Stage design for 'Garden at the Larin's country estate', Act I, of *Eugene Onegin*.

but it falls from your hand. 'It is both sad that so much is *past and gone*, yet pleasant to recall your youth', in his words.[9]

The opening theme returns in the strings, but a flute dances above, as if to prevent too much sadness. When a lone bassoon takes up the theme, there is almost a jauntiness to it, despite the instrument's naturally dark tone. The movement ends rather surprisingly with a musical question mark.

If the listener wonders why, the third movement provides the answer. Tchaikovsky had never written anything like this before. The clouds have lifted entirely. Plucked strings set a tone that is carefree and abandoned, 'elusive images which rush past in the imagination when you have drunk a little wine and experience the first stage of intoxication', as Tchaikovsky wrote to von Meck.[10]

Suddenly an oboe cuts in, followed by a piercing piccolo – 'drunken peasants and a street song . . . disjointed images which rush past in your head when you have fallen asleep. They have nothing in common with reality; they are strange, wild, and disjointed.'

The sense of abandonment continues in the blazing opening of the final movement, which Tchaikovsky describes as a 'festive merriment of the people'. Going among the people and allowing yourself 'to be carried away by the spectacle of others' joys' causes you 'to forget yourself' and any troubles you may have.

But just as you achieve this blissful state, 'irrepressible *fate* again appears and reminds you of yourself'. You realise that not a single person has turned to look at you, or even glance at you, and they have not noticed that in fact, despite your brief happiness, you are 'solitary and sad'.

They may be happy, but that is because their feelings are 'simple and direct. You have only yourself to blame.'[11] This is pure Tchaikovsky; the composer translating his emotions into music, and always an element of self-doubt, of guilt. But he had never hitherto written music with such searing honesty.

Is all lost? No. The horns again, not this time with the Fate motive, but a beguiling little march, taken up by strings then wind, swooping questions posed and answered, and then the music becomes unstoppable. Blazing trombones take the lead with a well-known Russian folk tune, as if to keep the Fate motif at bay. They will not allow it back in.

Tchaikovsky described the ending thus: 'Do not say that everything in this world is sad. There are simple but strong joys. Rejoice in others' rejoicing. To live is still possible.'[12]

Musically, this is a new Tchaikovsky, totally in control of his material. To read his own descriptions of his creation is illuminating and revelatory. I cannot think of many other composers who have written down their thoughts about a symphonic work in such detail.

Yet, this being Tchaikovsky, even his own explanations do not satisfy him. At the moment he was about to send the letter, he adds a postscript:

> *Just now, as I was about to place this letter in its envelope, I re-read it and was horrified by the vagueness and inadequacy of the programme which I am sending you. For the first time in my life I have had to put into words and phrases musical thoughts and musical images. I have not succeeded in saying this as I ought. I was terribly depressed last winter when I was composing this symphony, and it serves as a true echo of what I was going through at that time. But it is merely* an echo. *How can it be translated into clear and defined verbal forms? I am not able to, I do not know how to.*[13]

He is being a touch disingenuous here. Few composers enjoy trying to explain their music in words; in fact Tchaikovsky makes a very good job of it, and we have reason to be grateful.

It is telling that the person he chose to illuminate was Nadezhda von Meck, rather than one of his brothers or a musical colleague. In fact he leaves her in no doubt the symphony is for her. The letter begins with the words: 'In *our* symphony . . .' before going on to say she is the only person to whom he can explain the meaning of it.

In fact Tchaikovsky wants to dedicate the symphony to his benefactor, and despite her usual reluctance to accept dedications he expresses the hope that she will make an exception. But if she should find it disagreeable to have her name on the title page, he would understand.

In her reply she shamelessly tested the depths of his attachment to her:

Permit me to ask you one question, namely: do you consider me your friend? Because of my liking for you, my opinion of you, my concern for you, and my boundless desire that everything should be for your good, I have grounds for calling myself your friend. But because you *have never yet once called me by that name, I do not know whether* you *acknowledge me as your friend, and regard me as such. If, in answer to my question, you can say* yes, *then it would be extremely agreeable to me if you would set down on your symphony that you dedicate it* to your friend, *mentioning no name.*[14]

This is about as close to a declaration of love as it is possible to get, without actually using the word. Given his continuing troubles with Antonina, we might expect Tchaikovsky to take fright and run in the opposite direction.

But there are two factors to consider. The first is that she is paying him a generous allowance; the second, probably just as important if not more so, is her stipulation that the two should never meet, however deep her feelings for him might be. She cannot pose a challenge to his way of life.

Tchaikovsky decided to leave his benefactor in no doubt. He wrote across the title page of the manuscript: 'Dedicated to my best friend.'

Tchaikovsky, thirty-seven years of age as the year 1878 dawned, was exhausted, emotionally and physically. It is sobering, even today, to consider what the preceding nine months had held for him. He had met a woman, married her and left her, all in the space of four months. He never fully recovered from the experience.

He had been working feverishly, composing two new works, an opera and a symphony, on a scale he had never undertaken before. Small wonder his family and close friends feared for his health and wellbeing.

They decided that he needed to get away – away from Russia, away from Antonina. In trying to persuade him of this, they were pushing at an open door. He was more than willing to be taken in hand and led away from the trauma at home.

The prospect of travel into western Europe also held a clear attraction for him: he would be in exclusively male company.

20

'IT STINKS TO THE EAR'

Paris, **Florence, Rome,** Venice, Vienna, Berlin, Florence again, before finally settling in a small pension on the shores of Lake Geneva. Tchaikovsky was restless, his mental state fragile. Antonina had been packed off to Odessa with a financial settlement, but this had not bought her silence, as Tchaikovsky had hoped it would. She dashed off letter after letter to her itinerant husband, in Tchaikovsky's tortured mind somehow seeming to know where he was stopping next even before he did.

Sasha, worried on behalf of her brother, hurried down to Odessa and brought Antonina back with her to the safe confines of Kamenka, where she hoped to be able to control and calm her. It was some comfort to Tchaikovsky, at least, to know his sister could keep an eye on her, and at least attempt to rein her in.

In fact, unknown to him, Modest and Sasha were secretly plotting to effect some kind of reconciliation. To them, if Tchaikovsky could just be persuaded to live with Antonina as man and wife, as was his initial plan, his problems would evaporate. He would not only be free to compose as he wished, but his standing in society and musical circles would be immeasurably enhanced.

Once Tchaikovsky, still on his travels, got wind of this, he was furious. It was obvious Antonina was talking to Sasha and beginning to win her round. Did they not understand? How much more explaining did he need to do?

He wrote an angry letter to his sister:

Now with threats, reproaches, and accusations of dishonourable behaviour – now, conversely with expressions of love and tenderness (such as today) [Antonina] is trying vainly to get somewhere. For God's sake let's drop forever the question of our reconciliation. I'm not in dispute with her. She didn't wish to do me ill, and I'm not accusing her of anything. Even if you're right that she is good-hearted, even if I'm guilty all round because I've not known how to appreciate her, even if it's true she loves me – yet live with her I cannot, cannot, cannot.

He is clearly emotionally fraught, working himself into something of a frenzy. It appears there is nothing, absolutely nothing, he will stop at to get rid of her:

Demand of me whatever satisfaction you will for her: when I return to Russia I'll give her two-thirds of my earnings, I'll hide myself in any backwood you like, I'm prepared to become a beggar – in a word, anything you like – but for God's sake never hint to me that I should return to A[ntonina] I[vanovna]. Very likely I've got an illness – but it's an incurable illness. In a word, in the fullest sense of the expression, I do not love her![1]

Note those words 'incurable illness'. There again is that deep guilt over his sexuality. He still cannot bring himself to spell it out clearly to his sister, but he must have left her in no doubt. His marriage to Antonina had failed. He was the way he was, they needed to understand that, and there was nothing more he was prepared to do to try to change it.

At least his family was a long way off, back in Russia, and in no position to influence his behaviour. His travels gave him the perfect opportunity to indulge himself, in Italy particularly.

He visited Florence twice. On the first occasion he had encountered a young boy, aged about eleven, singing in the street, accompanying himself on guitar.[*] Immediately interested aesthetically as well as musically, he enquired after the boy and established that his name was Vittorio.

Vittorio made a deep impression on Tchaikovsky. In a letter to von Meck, he described the boy: 'His voice was marvellously rich, with a finish and warmth that one rarely encounters in professional artists'.[2] So deep was the impression he made, that Tchaikovsky decided to return to Florence

---

[*] Italy, as a country, was unrivalled in this form of street entertainment. In Rome another boy singer, Amici, also captured Tchaikovsky's attention.

with the sole aim of finding him again – in Tchaikovsky's own words, 'To meet and once more to hear the singing of that divine boy has become my life's goal in Florence.'[3]

At first he had no luck; despite encountering other talented street singers, none was his Vittorio. Finally, however, he encountered a group who knew the boy and promised Tchaikovsky the boy would be on the Lungarno,* by the bridge, at nine o'clock.

Cancelling his previous engagement, at nine o'clock Tchaikovsky returned to the bridge, and there he was! Despite the fact the boy had grown considerably in the two months since he had first seen him, Tchaikovsky knew it was him as soon as he heard his voice. And when Vittorio started to sing, Tchaikovsky confessed himself enraptured.

> It is impossible to describe . . . I wept, I broke down, I languished with delight.[4]

---

* The broad avenue that runs alongside the River Arno.

It is by no means certain that Tchaikovsky had a physical relationship with the boy, but from the evidence of his letters it is clear that he was as much attracted to Vittorio physically as he was by his voice. The fact that the censor also intervened in his letters reinforces the probability that something happened between them.

Some days later Vittorio came to Tchaikovsky's hotel and sang for him again. Only now, Tchaikovsky claimed, did he realise how 'positively beautiful' the boy was.

He took the boy to a studio and had his photograph taken. The photograph, which has survived, shows a strong but sensitive face, abundant hair parted in the middle. The eyes are half closed, with telling bags underneath, suggesting a hard life singing on the street late into the night. In fact Tchaikovsky suspects Vittorio is being 'exploited by his father, his uncles, and various relatives'. Tchaikovsky arranged to meet Vittorio again but the boy failed to show, sending word that he had a sore throat.[5]

Without Vittorio, Tchaikovsky's dislike of Florence – a mass of people moving through narrow streets – led to the decision to move on again. Craving fresh mountain air and more solitude than he was able to enjoy in a crowded city, he settled into a small lakeside pension in Clarens, a small town on the north bank of Lake Geneva.

It was not long before even that began to grate. He wrote to a colleague back in Moscow:

> Mountains are very fine, but it's very difficult for a Russian to stand their overwhelming grandeur for long. I'm dying for a plain, for a boundless, distant prospect, for an expanse of open country, and for wide horizons.[6]

It seems there was no pleasing him.

To add to his gloom he had heard that his half-sister Zinaida, his father's daughter by his first marriage, had died at the age of forty-nine. He had never been particularly close to Zinaida, but he knew the effect her death would have on his ageing father, who was now eighty-two.

Most disturbingly his depressed mood was affecting his work. Once settled in Clarens, he made the decision to compose a piano sonata, the only time in his life he attempted this particular genre. Work was a struggle and he soon discarded the piece, considering it of inferior quality.[*]

His mood was to change, though, and quite dramatically, for the better. He was joined in Clarens by his brother Modest, along with his young pupil Kolya, as well as his faithful servant Aleksey, now aged twenty-nine,

---

[*] An opinion with which musicologists unanimously agree.

although 'Alyosha', as Tchaikovsky affectionately called him, managed to get on the wrong side of his master pretty quickly, with his enthusiastic seduction of the landlady's maid, Marie, in the adjoining room.

Tchaikovsky wrote to one of his other brothers: 'Henceforth he will be nothing more than a servant to me. The over-spiced affections of old are no more.' This view was reinforced when the seduction resulted in a birth nine months later.[7] Nevertheless Tchaikovsky remained unswervingly loyal to his servant, who returned that loyalty fully for the rest of his employer's life.

Tchaikovsky's disposition was improved further with the arrival of his former lover Iosif Kotek, the Conservatory student with whom Tchaikovsky had been so impressed, and who had been one of only two witnesses at his marriage ceremony.

Tchaikovsky was once more with those he felt most at ease with and he revelled in reviving old habits. To the delight of Kotek and young Kolya, in a particularly good mood one day he relived a moment he had not experienced since indulging himself with Saint-Saëns some years earlier. Tchaikovsky and Modest danced a grand *pas de deux*, 'which was favoured with loud approval of the spectators'.[8]

Tchaikovsky's disposition might have improved with Kotek's arrival, but the relationship was not uncomplicated. Kotek's fortunes had undergone a dramatic reversal. Employed by Nadezhda von Meck – the original conduit through which von Meck and Tchaikovsky had first established their relationship – Kotek had managed to offend the lady with his persistent womanising among the members of her circle.

Perhaps surprisingly, Tchaikovsky was not unduly concerned about his homosexual friends indulging in heterosexual relationships – his servant Aleksey being an example – almost as though he wanted them to experience the full range of experiences on offer, even if he would not do so himself.

But Kotek, in Tchaikovsky's view, had taken matters too far. 'He has become a desperate womaniser, and nothing but this subject interests him,' he wrote to his brother.[9] Kotek, in his turn, was just as displeased as Tchaikovsky. It appears he had contracted syphilis and he accused Tchaikovsky of spreading malicious gossip about him, ruining his reputation and being the cause of his losing his position in Nadezhda von Meck's household.[10]

His dismissal meant an end to his earnings, and Kotek asked Tchaikovsky to subsidise him, since it was Tchaikovsky – in his view – who had caused him to lose his job.

Tchaikovsky was not best pleased, but found it impossible to resist. He still felt a strong affection for the young man, as he articulated in a letter to Anatoly:

[I do not] wish to upset him. In short, there are moments when I am angry at myself and angry at him and the result of all this has been the sulks. But do not pay attention to this, and do not think that he is a burden to me. In the first place, I enjoy making music with him; in the second he is essential for my violin concerto; in the third I love him very, very much. He has the kindest and most tender of hearts, and his character is extremely comforting and pleasant.[11]

This is a particularly revealing passage. Not only does he declare that his love for Kotek is still very much alive, despite the womanising, but he also refers – for the first time – to a new composition, a violin concerto.

Extraordinary though it may seem, within days of jettisoning the piano sonata, Tchaikovsky began work on – for him – another entirely new form of composition. Rather than taking refuge in a tried and tested genre, such as a symphony or a piano concerto, he moved in a new direction.

Undoubtedly it was Kotek, a highly accomplished violinist, who provided the initial inspiration. He had arrived with his violin under his arm, and a bag full of piano-duet pieces and other arrangements for piano and violin.

Tchaikovsky immediately delighted in accompanying Kotek at the piano. One of the pieces they played – possibly on the very first day after Kotek's arrival – was Édouard Lalo's *Symphonie espagnole*, in effect a violin concerto in five movements.

Tchaikovsky professed himself captivated by the piece, which he had not known before. He wrote to von Meck that what impressed him most was the way Lalo was not striving for profundity, that he was more concerned about musical beauty than observing established traditions. This he had in common not only with fellow French composers Delibes and Bizet, but also the Germans. One senses a sideways swipe by Tchaikovsky at his fellow Russian composers!

It is easy to imagine Tchaikovsky, his creativity sparked anew as he sat at the keyboard playing through piece after piece, the young man he admired and loved by his side matching his skill on the violin.

Within days of Kotek's arrival, Tchaikovsky said he wanted to write a violin concerto, and he would welcome Kotek's guidance on what the instrument was capable of – how to show it off to best advantage, and what pitfalls to avoid. To Tchaikovsky's delight, Kotek responded enthusiastically.

The piano sonata forgotten, Tchaikovsky set to work. He completed the first movement in just five days, and the finale in only three. The middle movement, the slow movement, proved problematic. Tchaikovsky was not happy, considering it too slight for a concerto, and when Modest concurred, Tchaikovsky wrote an entirely new movement in the incredible space of twenty-four hours.[*]

Within a month the concerto was complete and orchestrated, which, given its substantial length – anything from thirty-five to forty-five minutes, making it one of the most substantial in the repertoire – is truly impressive.

Tchaikovsky, fully aware of his achievement, modestly attributed much of the credit to young Kotek. He wrote to his brother Anatoly:

> *How lovingly he is busying himself with my concerto! It goes without saying that I would have been able to do nothing without him. He plays it marvellously!*[12]

Which is, of course, far too generous. Kotek, just twenty-two years of age, freshly graduated from the Conservatory and with no experience of composition himself, can have been at best only of limited value to Tchaikovsky. But it is typical of the man that when he loves, he also lauds.

The obvious dedicatee of the Violin Concerto was Iosif Kotek, since he had played such a large part – in Tchaikovsky's eyes – in its creation. But he knew the potential scandal that would cause. There was bound to be gossip about the nature of his relationship with the younger man, who was sixteen years his junior. He knew rumours had circulated before; a dedication would only intensify them.

Having had such a miraculously painless birth, the concerto was now to experience a less idyllic early life. Instead of Kotek, Tchaikovsky offered the dedication to Leopold Auer, a Hungarian violinist and professor at the St Petersburg Conservatory, and to whom Tchaikovsky had three years earlier dedicated his *Sérénade mélancolique* for violin and orchestra.

The premiere was planned for March the following year, 1879, but Auer declared the composition inferior to Tchaikovsky's other works, and some passages unsuited to the violin, and he refused to perform it.

Tchaikovsky, his skin as thin as ever, was deeply hurt by Auer's rejection. He turned to the Russian violinist Adolph Brodsky, a professor at the Moscow Conservatory, who agreed to take it on.

Brodsky premiered the Violin Concerto in Vienna on 4 December 1881. In gratitude, Tchaikovsky gave Brodsky the dedication.

Tchaikovsky was left bruised on both a personal and a musical level by the whole experience, however. In between Auer's rejection and Brodsky's

"Rather than taking refuge in a tried and tested genre, such as a symphony or a piano concerto, he moved in a new direction."

---

[*] He did not discard the original slow movement. It became *Méditation*, the first of three pieces for violin and piano entitled – significantly – *Souvenir d'un lieu cher* ('Memory of a dear place').

acceptance, he had asked his dear young friend Iosif, who knew the work more intimately than anybody else, to perform it in public. To Tchaikovsky's inestimable hurt, Kotek refused, believing it would be poorly received and would damage his budding career.

When it was finally given its first performance by Brodsky, the critics were merciless. In what one biographer calls 'one of the most notorious verdicts in the history of music journalism', Eduard Hanslick, one of the most famed and influential critics of his time, declared that the concerto 'brought us face to face with the revolting thought that music can exist which stinks to the ear'.[13]

Even today I have seen Tchaikovsky's Violin Concerto described as one of his less sophisticated works. But if it is not as ground-breaking in form as his Piano Concerto No. 1, it is no less seductive. Full of melody – typical of Tchaikovsky – from the opening bars, it is instantly beguiling. Just because the motifs are instantly memorable makes them no less worthwhile.

The second and third movements are intensely Russian, redolent with themes of home that Tchaikovsky carried in his head. It is unsurprising that he set them down on paper while, in effect, in self-imposed exile from his homeland. The second movement in particular, which Tchaikovsky completed in just twenty-four hours, is the most consistently melodic movement he had composed since the *Andante cantabile* of his First String Quartet.

The work that was dismissed as causing 'a stink to the ear' is now, and will remain, one of the best-loved violin concertos ever written.

The self-imposed exile had now lasted for the best part of six months. Tchaikovsky could delay his return to Russia no longer. For one thing he could not continue to remain absent from the Moscow Conservatory. He held a paid professorship, and he needed to resume his duties.

He was dreading returning to teaching. He disliked it, and he knew that everybody staring at him across the classroom would know about the debacle of his marriage. Now that he had an independent source of income from Nadezhda von Meck, he wanted to devote his time to composition. Sooner or later, he knew he would leave the Conservatory, but a deep-seated financial insecurity prevented him from doing so just yet.

It was May. The new term at the Conservatory would begin in September. If he returned now, he would have time to acclimatise once more to his home surroundings. He knew he had an open invitation to stay with his sister at Kamenka. As always, the thought of summer in the Ukraine held a real attraction for him. Not least because there was one other matter on his mind at this point, something that needed to be sorted out. Being with his family, having support around him, would be essential. He wanted to divorce Antonina.

21

A Sort of Freedom

With a return to his homeland imminent, Tchaikovsky was filled with patriotic longing. His love for Russia was boundless. At home he would find plenty to complain about, but each time he travelled abroad he could not conceal his desire to return to Mother Russia.

One can imagine him approaching the border post wreathed in smiles, relishing the chance to converse with strangers in his own tongue. He was rudely disabused. He described in a letter to von Meck how the gendarme was 'rough and drunken',[1] and took for ever to establish whether the number of passports matched the number of people travelling. The gendarme then eyed Tchaikovsky suspiciously and looked him up and down before finally giving him back his passport.

The customs official was no better. He rummaged through their luggage and demanded fourteen gold roubles from Tchaikovsky for a dress he had bought for his sister. Then there was a long train journey in dirty carriages with unappealing company: a long and boring conversation with a gentleman who insisted there was nothing more humane than England's politics.

There was 'a mass of dirty Yids with that poisonous atmosphere which accompanies them everywhere'.* In one station they saw a hospital train

---

* Like many of his compatriots, Tchaikovsky had an anti-Semitic streak. This comment was redacted in early editions of his correspondence.

filled with typhoid victims. At each station young army recruits, on their way to join the war against Turkey, boarded the train, which led to repeated fare-wells with mothers and wives. 'All this poisoned for me the pleasure of seeing my own passionately loved native land!' an exasperated Tchaikovsky wrote.[2]

Kamenka (with Antonina no longer there) provided welcome relief. Sasha and her family swept Tchaikovsky up, along with Modest and Kolya, who had decided to stay, much to Tchaikovsky's delight. He was even more pleased when Anatoly joined them after a few days.

Sasha gave her elder brother a small peasant cottage to himself, set in the grounds away from the main house. It had just two rooms and a kitch-en, which was perfectly adequate for his needs. He had a lovely view down onto the village and the river meandering in the distance. The garden was thick with sweet peas and mignonettes, and he looked forward to them soon being in flower and giving off a wonderful scent.

Best of all, Tchaikovsky reported to Madame von Meck, Sasha had had a piano put in the little room alongside the bedroom. Tchaikovsky was looking forward to composing again. Everything was right. He was relaxed, comfortable in the bosom of his family, in idyllic surroundings.

Compose he did. He took up again the piano sonata he had discarded, completed a set of Twelve Pieces for piano he had begun in Clarens, and composed several pieces for children (no doubt written for his nieces and nephews) as well a patriotic march to support the volunteer fleet in the war effort, all proceeds to go to the fund for building cruisers.

It would be pleasing to report that, in the wake of the brilliant Violin Concerto, Tchaikovsky's compositional genius was in full flow. The oppo-site was the case. Musicologists are unanimous in their assessment that the works Tchaikovsky produced in Kamenka in the summer of 1878, when he was thirty-eight years old and at the height of his powers, are almost totally devoid of merit. In fact one biographer, David Brown, calls the Piano Sona-ta 'a strong candidate as the dullest piece of music Tchaikovsky ever wrote'.[3]

We can get an inkling of just why this might have been the case by look-ing at what else was going on in Kamenka. Anatoly had taken it on himself to arrange a divorce settlement for his brother, the main inducement for Antonina being a large lump-sum payment, which Tchaikovsky had es-tablished Nadezhda von Meck was prepared to subsidise, on condition her involvement was kept secret.

The brothers were confident Antonina would consent, given that there was a large sum of money at stake. They were mistaken; she adamantly re-fused their offer. Strangely, for the moment at least, Tchaikovsky was quite phlegmatic, confident it would all work out and seemingly unconcerned if it did not. He ended his letter to Anatoly with an explicit turn of phrase:

"Despite the fact Tchaikovsky stated that he accepted full responsibility, there was not an ounce of regret or remorse in him for the breakdown of the marriage."

'One can live without [the divorce]. She, to be sure, will later repent, the bitch, but it will be too late.'[4]

His coolness did not last, his aggressive tone perhaps a portent of what was to come. After several sleepless nights, he sat down to respond to his wife. He made it clear to Antonina that she must officially apply for a divorce and, in the most direct language he could muster, stated once more that there was no chance that the marriage could be salvaged.

Despite the fact Tchaikovsky stated on several occasions that he accepted full responsibility, there was not an ounce of regret or remorse in him for the breakdown of the marriage he had willingly entered into and had wilfully ended, and this would not change in the years ahead. In writing of Antonina he is cruel, his depiction more than tinged with misogyny:

> *I now have all too obvious proof of the extent to which she is bereft of the aggregate of those human qualities which are called the soul. She cannot, and never will, know moral suffering. In her, all that can suffer is the most pitiful pride of a creature of the female sex obsessed by a monomania that consists in the fact that all creatures of the male sex, myself included, appear to her to be in love with her.*[5]

Antonina's response, when it came, was as emotional as Tchaikovsky's had been heartless, accusing him of thinking only of himself, oblivious to the grief and embarrassment he was making her endure. She claimed that a divorce would mark her with an 'indelible stain'. Poznansky points out this was untrue, since it was Tchaikovsky who was admitting guilt for the breakdown of the marriage, by concocting an adultery, and that therefore any social stigma would fall on him. But it is not unreasonable to think that she might have felt humiliated over the whole affair, and perhaps concerned for her reputation. Even given her irrational behaviour, perhaps Antonina deserves more sympathy than biographers of her husband are inclined to afford her.

Tchaikovsky, himself not always reacting with total rationality, interpreted Antonina's letter, in which she did finally accept the offered sum, as a capitulation, a sign that she had finally agreed to a divorce. He was ecstatic. At last she had agreed, he wrote excitedly to von Meck:

> *Upon reading [her letter], I went mad with joy and ran about the garden for an hour and a half to suppress with physical exhaustion the joyous excitement that it had caused me.*[6]

Given Tchaikovsky's excitable nature, this is unlikely to be an exaggeration. But his joy was premature.

As one relationship disintegrated, another intensified. Almost as soon as he arrived in Kamenka, Tchaikovsky received an invitation from Madame von Meck to spend some time at her estate at Brailov in Ukraine, which her husband had bequeathed to her in his will.

So that he would be under no illusion, she assured him she would be absent in Moscow, and he would have the run of the place. He was welcome to bring his personal servant Aleksey with him, and she would put the entire staff at the estate at his disposal. She assured him she would not tell them who her invited guest was.

Tchaikovsky needed little encouragement. He loved being in Ukraine, the beautiful countryside and warm weather calming his often fraught nerves. Brailov was only a day's carriage ride west of Kamenka, and so it would be simple to travel there from his sister's estate.

If he expected luxury, he was not to be disappointed. He might have been used to staying at the country estates of some of his wealthy friends, but it was always in company, with an endless round of dinners and entertainment. Here he was alone in magnificent surroundings.

He described his impressions in a letter to his sister Sasha at Kamenka:

I am living in clover here . . . I live in a palace in the literal sense of the word, the furnishings are luxurious, apart from polite and affectionately obliging servants I see no human figures and no one comes to make my acquaintance, the strolls are charming, and at my disposal I have carriages, horses, a library, several pianos, a harmonium, a mass of sheet music – in a word, what could be better.[7]

In these congenial surroundings Tchaikovsky was once again able to compose. As a gift for his benefactor he put together three pieces for violin and piano, and gave them a title inspired by his surroundings, *Souvenir d'un lieu cher* ('Memory of a dear place'). The first piece was in fact a transcription of the rejected slow movement of the Violin Concerto, to which he gave the title *Méditation*.

He also composed a set of six songs, but in a non-musical sense the most important work he composed in Brailov was for the Russian Orthodox Church: the *Liturgy of St John Chrysostum*.

Composing music for the Church was strictly the monopoly of the St Petersburg Court Chapel, known as the Imperial Chapel, but Tchaikovsky wanted to challenge this, and in his publisher, Pyotr Jurgenson, he had a willing accomplice.

Tchaikovsky composed the *Liturgy* and Jurgenson published it. Predictably all copies were seized by the Director of the Imperial Chapel. A legal challenge followed, and two years later – in a firm break with tradition –

the judgment went in favour of Jurgenson. Tchaikovsky's composition thus altered the history of Church music in Russia.

In Jurgenson Tchaikovsky had found more than a publisher. In his early years Jurgenson had lent him money, now he handled the composer's business affairs and, perhaps most helpfully of all, he acted as an intermediary in Tchaikovsky's convoluted divorce proceedings.

Despite Jurgenson's best efforts, however, Tchaikovsky had to return to Moscow. Despite his optimism, Antonina was clearly not getting the divorce under way; Tchaikovsky would have to do it himself.

Reluctantly he left Brailov and returned with Aleksey to the capital. There he entered a world of which he knew little, and was utterly appalled. The Diocesan Court of the Orthodox Church, which handled divorce cases, was thoroughly corrupt.

He wrote to von Meck that everything was done by bribes, with absolutely no shame. Every step in the process required a payment, basically a bribe, and every bribe was at once divided among officials, clerks, and priests.

Furthermore, the procedure on which he had to embark was so complicated, and so time-consuming, requiring proof of the husband's adultery (which of course had not happened), statements from witnesses, interrogation of husband and wife, as well as of witnesses, and most important of all an application from the wife to the archbishop for the dissolution of the marriage – something Antonina was hardly likely to agree to – that Tchaikovsky decided he had no choice but to put the whole thing off.

It had become clear that, at the very least, the process would require his presence in Moscow for weeks, possibly months, and he simply could not face the ordeal. To complicate matters still further, Antonina had disappeared. Jurgenson set off in pursuit. While he was searching for her, Tchaikovsky left Moscow once again for the peace of Kamenka.

He received word from Jurgenson some days later. He had found Antonina, who was still in Moscow, and she was insistent that she would speak to no one but her husband. She was also adamant that she could not support the story about her husband's supposed adultery.

Tchaikovsky was beside himself. To von Meck he wrote that Antonina was obsessed with the belief that he was in love with her, which to him demonstrated only her 'phenomenal and total stupidity'.[8]

To Modest he was even more scathing: 'It is clear that she has completely lost her mind.' He ended his letter to his brother with a sentence that, had he but known it, was to prove prophetic: 'I am beginning to worry that she will never leave me alone.'[9]

With the divorce proceedings postponed, Tchaikovsky spent as long as he could in Kamenka, followed by another short stay at Brailov. The summer was drawing to an end. Soon he would have to face the inevitable start of the new academic year.

Tchaikovsky was still dreading returning to the Moscow Conservatory in September. He hated teaching more than ever. He hated the hours he had to keep, the lessons he had to give.

Words cannot express my aversion to everything to do with the Conservatory: to its walls, its people, its professors, its students . . . I escaped from the place as from some loathsome, stinking, stifling dungeon.[10]

He wanted his freedom. He wanted to be able to travel where he liked, and be free to compose. He just needed to find the confidence to resign his professorship.

He could not have known it but the opportunity he so wanted was about to present itself, though in the most painful of ways. He was actually on the train to Kiev, on the first leg of his return journey north, when by pure chance he happened to pick up a copy of the newspaper *New Times* at one of the stations.

What he read shocked, disgusted, and hurt him. He described it in a letter to Modest as 'dirty, base, vile, slander-filled'. The newspaper had published an article attacking the Moscow Conservatory in the most vitriolic terms.

At first it seemed to Tchaikovsky that the attack was on the institution itself, and the internal tensions and rivalries in which it abounded. But a segment comprised a direct personal assault on the teaching staff, and in particular on their amorous adventures. He quoted it to Modest:

> There is almost nothing there about me personally, and it is even mentioned that I am occupied only with music, taking no part in the intrigues and squabbles. But one part of the article talks about the amours of the professors with the girls, and at the end is added: 'There are at the Conservatory also amours of a different kind, but about them, for a very obvious reason, I shall not speak,' etc. It is clear what this is an allusion to . . . [So] my reputation falls upon the whole Conservatory, and for this I feel even more ashamed and more wretched.[11]

He could not escape from the ignominy that attached to his sexuality and now – if this article was to be believed – it had also damaged the institution that employed him.

On the journey he had time to reflect, and he was able to see how he might be able to turn matters to his advantage. In light of the article, it would better for the Conservatory, as well as for him, if he were to leave.

In fact, he wrote to Modest, he was of half a mind to resign at once and not even return to Moscow. But he had an apartment rented and his employers were counting on him; he could not let them down.

He was, though, determined to leave, and he had a plan:

> I have made up my mind to endure until December, then leave for Kamenka for the holidays and from there to write that I am sick, having naturally informed Rubinstein secretly beforehand so that he might look for another professor.[12]

In the event, he did not need to claim ill health. In October he told Rubinstein he had decided to leave. Rubinstein had just returned from Paris, where he had performed Tchaikovsky's Piano Concerto No. 1 in the hall of the Trocadéro as part of the International Exposition. It had been triumphantly received.

At a dinner at the Conservatory in his honour on his return, Rubinstein made a speech praising Tchaikovsky to the hilt and saying how fortunate the Conservatory was to have such a celebrity on its staff.

The compliment was a poisoned chalice as far as Tchaikovsky was concerned. He feared he would have to put off his departure until the following summer. But Rubinstein was understanding.

The man who had initially torn the Piano Concerto to shreds, and who had just performed it to acclaim in Paris, realised that Tchaikovsky's

"Tchaikovsky's growing fame was taking him beyond the confines of the Conservatory."

growing fame across Europe was taking him beyond the confines of the Conservatory. He had no choice but to let him go.

The two men agreed Tchaikovsky would leave in December. But then Tchaikovsky heard from Nadezhda von Meck, to whom he had written informing her of his desire to leave and at the same time asking her to increase her financial support. She was unhesitatingly in favour of his plans, and assured him he had no cause to worry about money.

Emboldened, Tchaikovsky informed Rubinstein he intended leaving in October, just a matter of weeks after the new academic year began. Rubinstein was in no position to stop him.

Tchaikovsky took his last class on 7 October 1878. The following day he had a farewell lunch with old friends. These were mostly musical colleagues with whom he had once been on an equal footing. Now he had surpassed them all.

The following day he wrote to von Meck:

Despite all my joy at my longed-for freedom, I experienced some sadness at parting from people among whom I have lived for more than twelve years. They all seemed very grieved, and this touched me.[13]

There was more sadness when he arrived back in St Petersburg the following day and paid a visit on his elderly father. He found Ilya to be cheerful and in good health, but there was a coldness from his father he had not known before.

Even if his relationship with his father had never been particularly close, Ilya had swelled with pride at his son's achievements, having wished nothing more for him than a 'normal' happy married life.

Tchaikovsky knew full well his father's coldness was due to the sorry saga of his abortive marriage. But this alone was not enough to cloud Tchaikovsky's happiness at his freedom.

'I am a *free* man,'[14] he wrote to von Meck, and he intended to take full advantage of that. His immediate plan was to return to Clarens in Switzerland, a location where he had spent many a happy hour and where he wished to base himself again.

But he would not stay long. In fact he would not stay long anywhere. As 1879 dawned, Tchaikovsky became something of an itinerant. For the next decade he would have no fixed abode.

The 1880s have been called by some biographers Tchaikovsky's wilderness years, but that is to paint too bleak a picture. This was what he wanted – the ability to move on at a moment's notice, whether to escape pressures of work or home, or simply because he wanted a change of scene.

He was, at last, free.

22
THE BOULEVARDIER

The return to Clarens was put on hold. Nadezhda von Meck had other plans for Tchaikovsky. She was herself in Florence, and she suggested to him that it would please her greatly if, before heading for Clarens, he would stay awhile in Florence.

It was at this point that Tchaikovsky's relationship with his patron, or more accurately hers with him, deepened quite significantly.

In her letters encouraging him to come, she used more intimate language than she had done before. 'My dear'; 'Oh, how dear you are to me'; 'What a wonderful person you are, what a matchless heart you have'; 'How I love you'.[1]

If we today find her attitude somewhat controlling, there is evidence Tchaikovsky did so too – particularly when he read in her letters how she intended to take care of every detail of his stay in Florence. She would choose an apartment for him, and make sure it contained everything he needed.

His worries were compounded when she wrote to tell him that she had found the perfect apartment for him, just 'two steps' from the villa where she herself was staying. He wrote to Anatoly that although the apartment was in a lovely spot with a marvellous view of the city, it would constrain him to be so close to his patron. The possibility of them accidentally meeting concerned him deeply.

He need not have worried. On arrival in Florence on 20 November 1878 he found a letter in the apartment in which – although he did not go into details in relaying this to Anatoly – she had made adequate arrangements to ensure there would be no meetings at all.

But still he had cause for concern. Every day he saw her walk past his apartment building, slow her pace, and peer towards his windows as if to try to steal a glimpse of him. He did not know how to react to this: '[Should I] go to the window and bow? But, in that case, why not also shout from the window, "Good morning"?'[2]

His ultimate fear was that sooner or later she would try to engineer a meeting, accidentally or otherwise; that she would try to entice him to her. He was aware she now saw him, for the first time, as someone unencumbered by marital ties, just as she was.

He thought his worst fear had been realised when von Meck dropped him a note inviting him to visit her villa while she was out, so that his presence in the place where she lived might bring her a greater understanding of his lifestyle. He politely declined.

Not that his concerns prevented him from enjoying his stay in Italy's most cultured city, richer in art than any other, centre of the Renaissance, home to Raphael, Michelangelo, and Leonardo da Vinci.

He might not have enjoyed the narrow streets and teeming crowds the last time he was in Florence, but this time he was living in real comfort, with none of the strains of renting in a foreign city.

In letters he referred to his stay in Florence as an 'idyll'. It is not entirely clear what caused him to use such a lyrical word. There is no evidence he rekindled his relationship with Vittorio, the boy singer, or if he did, he did not refer to it in letters.

We do know, because he said so in a letter to Modest, that he met a pimp named Napoleon, who it appears had procured for him on his earlier visit. He told Modest he had kept his eyes open so as to steer clear of the man, but inevitably the scoundrel had accosted him one day in the street, and was enticing him back into his old ways.[3]

In the event his stay in Florence was short-lived. By Christmas von Meck had moved on to Vienna, and wrote to him that it was time he left Florence for Clarens, as he had originally intended.

With von Meck paying his rent in Florence, he could hardly refuse her instructions. But he did not intend to do exactly as he was told. He would indeed proceed to Clarens, but he would make a detour to Paris en route.

There was a musical reason for doing this. He was intending to compose another opera, and he had in mind the story of Joan of Arc. He was anxious to track down a copy of the libretto for Auguste Mermet's opera *Jeanne d'Arc*, which he would use as the basis for his own – for which he had the working title of *The Maid of Orleans*.

That was all von Meck needed to know. He certainly did not intend to enlighten her to the fact that he had arranged to meet up with young Kotek in the French capital. His patron had held Kotek in contempt ever since she had dismissed him from her service.

Unfortunately for Tchaikovsky, it was heterosexual interests that Kotek was keen to pursue in the French capital. It was not long before Tchaikovsky grew tired of Kotek's obsessive womanising, for which he found that it was he himself who was paying.

Not that the composer abstained entirely from sexual pursuits. On his visit to Paris two years previously he had seen an actor by the name of Jules Boucher at the Comédie Française, and found himself strongly attracted to him. It lifted his mood inestimably to discover that Boucher was performing during his visit, so Tchaikovsky once more made his way to the Comédie Française to indulge his infatuation.

He wrote to Modest – who had been in Paris with him two years earlier and had been equally attracted to the handsome Boucher – that at the end of the play Boucher had to slap another character across the face. In a remarkably candid comment, no doubt written with a smile on his face, Tchaikovsky wrote:

> *What I wouldn't give to have that same hand . . . give me a hundred slaps in the face! . . . What an enchanting person and what a marvellous actor he is!*[4]

It is not known whether anything developed with Boucher, but any happiness Tchaikovsky might have been enjoying was interrupted by a message from Antonina. Anatoly wrote to Tchaikovsky to inform him that a man named Simonov, who claimed to be Antonina's relative and close adviser, had visited him and imparted the news that Antonina was now prepared to file for divorce and wished to know her husband's terms.

This might have seemed welcome news, but Tchaikovsky panicked. He had never heard of Simonov before and suspected that he was a swindler making a very clumsy attempt at blackmail.

Tchaikovsky was deeply fearful that Antonina would declare in the witness box that her husband was homosexual, and accuse him of sodomy:

> *I can see myself in the dock, outwitting the prosecution in my closing speech, but collapsing beneath the weight of the shameful indictment. I have tried to put a brave face on things, but already I consider myself utterly ruined.*[5]

"Tchaikovsky was intending to compose another opera, and he had in mind the story of Joan of Arc."

Above

Sketched sets for
The Maid of Orleans.

After several days he regained his composure. He wrote to Anatoly that he would deal with it all in his own good time, and that would not be before he had returned to Moscow.

On 30 December Tchaikovsky was once more back at the familiar pension in Clarens, the Villa Richelieu, and its solicitous proprietress Madame Mayor, who surrounded him with care and attention.

Accompanying Tchaikovsky on his travels was his faithful servant Aleksey, who was happy to renew his relationship with Madame Mayor's maid Marie, and reacquaint himself with his illegitimate child.

In congenial surroundings, therefore, Tchaikovsky once more turned to composition, beginning work in earnest on *The Maid of Orleans*. Dissatisfied with Mermet's libretto, Tchaikovsky wrote his own text.

He worked hard in the morning, sometimes carrying on into the afternoon but almost always ending the day with a late afternoon or early evening walk. He wrote in some detail about these walks to his brother Modest, but all published editions of his correspondence are heavily redacted, either by the Soviet authorities or by Modest himself. Alexander Poznansky draws what he says is the inevitable conclusion from this censorship: that the composer was obviously enjoying casual encounters with young men, indulging his homosexual proclivities.[6]

Inspiration was once more coming easily to Tchaikovsky. In the extraordinarily brief period of just fourteen days he had sketched out half the opera. He took a few days off, and after five more days' work the opera was three-quarters sketched out. He wrote to Modest that he was generally pleased with progress, but confessed to being a bit tired. Given his varied daily schedule, that is hardly surprising.

His spirits renewed by the speed and success of his work, Tchaikovsky was not overly concerned by a summons from Nadezhda von Meck to 'join' her in Paris – or at least to come and stay in the apartment she had rented for him. In fact the development was rather fortuitous: Tchaikovsky had become dangerously short of money. He would use the visit as a means to extract funds from his patron.

It was a different Tchaikovsky who arrived back in Paris in early February 1889. His confidence restored by the near completion of his opera, he made von Meck aware of his financial predicament, at the same time reassuring her his Muse was once again in full flow. She responded by immediately advancing him a thousand francs.

Tchaikovsky took to the familiar boulevards with something of an uncharacteristic swagger:

> *I walk along the streets in a new grey coat with a most elegant top hat, showing off a silk shirt front with coral studs and lilac-coloured gloves. Passing the mirrored piers in the Rue de la Paix or on the boulevards, I invariably stop and admire myself. In shop windows I also observe the reflection of my elegant person.*[7]

The composer as dandy! It can be deduced from this that he was in good spirits, pleased with the way work had gone on *The Maid of Orleans*, relieved to be once again in funds. But of course this is Tchaikovsky, and so those demons are never far away.

On his own in Paris, with von Meck informing him that attacks of migraine were keeping her housebound, he was free to indulge himself. However hard he tries, he simply cannot resist temptation. It is now that he describes an encounter with a male prostitute.[*]

In between his extra-curricular activities, Tchaikovsky threw himself into completing *The Maid of Orleans*. The work was soon done, leaving just the orchestration to be carried out and the vocal text to be prepared. He would complete both tasks the following summer, while in Kamenka and Brailov.

---

[*] See p. 170.

Tchaikovsky managed to secure a premiere for his new work in St Petersburg in February 1881. It received considerable acclaim on its opening night, although cuts and revisions were made.

In one of those musical twists of fortune, the opera swiftly faded, its initial success evaporating. It was revived in only one more season, never again to be heard in Tchaikovsky's lifetime.

Tchaikovsky finally left Paris for Russia in February 1879. On 24 March, he walked into his brother's St Petersburg apartment to find Antonina waiting for him, having talked her way in past the doorman.

The scene that followed was 'shattering'.[8] We know details of the encounter, because Tchaikovsky chose to write about it in copious detail to Nadezhda von Meck – somewhat surprisingly, since she had so obviously relished the break-up of his marriage.

No sooner had he stepped into the study than Antonina hurled herself at him, kissing him and weeping uncontrollably, insisting that she could not continue in this separation, that he could name any condition if only they could live together again as husband and wife.

Tchaikovsky struggled to maintain his resolve. He told her again it was his fault, but that she must understand that their marriage was unquestionably over.

He suggested she return forthwith to Moscow, and gave her a hundred roubles for the journey. Finally, Antonina seemed to regain a certain amount of composure and agreed to leave. In an extraordinary aside, Tchaikovsky wrote that Antonina listed on her departure all the men she believed were in love with her.[9]

As this is Tchaikovsky's account of events, a certain amount of exaggeration in his description of Antonina's behaviour can be assumed, but there is no doubt that the gist of what he wrote is accurate, given what is known of what followed.

Antonina did not return to Moscow. Instead she lurked in the street outside his apartment, pouncing on him whenever he left the building, protesting that she could not bear to be apart from him.

Four days after their meeting in Tchaikovsky's rooms, she wrote to him in the most pathetic terms, 'If you cannot love me as I love you, at least show me some compassion. Come to me. I am yours, body and soul. Do with me what you wish.'[10]

As I mentioned earlier, biographers of Tchaikovsky tend to be unkind to Antonina. There might be some truth in all those descriptions of her as unstable, even crazed. But no one can accuse her of being inconsistent. She expressed her undying love for Tchaikovsky even before meeting him. And she expressed it to the end.

Tchaikovsky sought sanctuary in Kamenka and Brailov, where he would complete work on *The Maid of Orleans*. But the emotional trauma of Antonina's behaviour had taken its toll. Modest was in Kamenka too, and he and Sasha described their brother as being almost at breaking point.

Tchaikovsky had found a number of times that when he was away from Antonina his resolve hardened. It was so much easier to express toughness and determination in writing than in person. He had promised Antonina that he would write to her and he kept his word, but it was hardly what she was hoping for. He denied every demand she had made, and informed her that all future correspondence from her would be returned unopened.[11]

It was during this stay at Kamenka that Tchaikovsky began to pay particular attention to the child who could perhaps be described as the love of his life. Vladimir Lvovich was born in 1871, Sasha's sixth child and second son. From his very first moments in the world, his parents – and indeed the whole family – noted his resemblance to Uncle Pyotr.

Nicknamed 'Baby', the infant struggled to say the English word, rendering it as 'Bob'. The name stuck; he would be Bob Davydov for life. During the summer of 1879 Tchaikovsky found himself more and more drawn to the boy. He was extremely fond of all his nieces and nephews, but he made no secret of the fact that Bob was his favourite.

The decision to move on from Kamenka to Brailov was made for Tchaikovsky by his patron, and there was no gainsaying her. Once again she made all necessary arrangements in advance, this time giving him a cottage to himself in the grounds of the estate.

Nadezhda von Meck was herself in residence in the main house. Sequestering Tchaikovsky in his own cottage, with his own staff to take care of all his needs, was the perfect solution, particularly since she intended sending him a daily timetable of her movements, in order to avoid any possibility of a chance meeting between them.

So Tchaikovsky took leave of his family, arriving in Brailov on 8 August. The cottage had a well-stocked garden with a river running at the bottom and magnificent views. Fields and copses surrounded the cottage, allowing Tchaikovsky plenty of choice for long walks. The main house lay a considerable – and safe – distance away.

Or so both of them thought. On 14 August the inevitable happened. Tchaikovsky set out for his daily walk slightly earlier than his usual four o'clock. Nadezhda von Meck, who normally dined at four o'clock, was running late and had not yet returned to the house.

"If you cannot love me as I love you, at least show me some compassion."

Antonina Milyukova

When she entered the grounds, there was Tchaikovsky on the path right in front of her. He described the scene to his brother:

I met her nose to nose. It was terribly awkward. We were face to face for only an instant, but all the same, I was dreadfully embarrassed, although I did tip my hat politely. She, it seemed to me, became utterly distracted and did not know what to do.[12]

Tchaikovsky took full responsibility for the unwanted encounter. Immediately on returning to the cottage he wrote her a letter, apologising profusely for miscalculating the time. Her response was entirely unexpected:

I am delighted at this meeting. I cannot convey how sweet and wonderful it was when I realised that we had met you, when I, so to speak, felt the reality of your presence in Brailov. I do not want any personal communications between us, but silently, passively to be near you, to be under the same roof with you . . . to meet you on the same road . . . to feel you not as a myth but as a living person whom I love so and from whom I receive so much good, this gives me extraordinary pleasure. I regard such episodes as extraordinary happiness.[13]

This was exactly what Tchaikovsky did not want to hear, and he must have wondered if perchance she had engineered the 'accidental' meeting. It was never discussed again, and the extraordinary fact remains that this was the sole face-to-face encounter between the two during the whole of their relationship.

As autumn turned to winter in 1879, a few months short of his fortieth birthday and with a newly completed opera under his belt, Tchaikovsky was the most renowned composer in his homeland of Russia and increasingly well known across Europe. And yet so much of his life was dictated by unconventional relationships with two different women.

It was a strange, and quite probably unique, state of affairs for a man who was rapidly becoming a household name.

23

An Impenetrable Secret

Nadezhda von Meck has more than earned her place in musical history.

A curious woman whose actions and character remain difficult to fully comprehend a century and a half on, not only did she give Tchaikovsky the freedom and financial stability he needed to pursue his art, but through the copious correspondence between them we gain an extraordinary insight into his working methods.*

Tchaikovsky wrote more intimately to his patron than to any other person, not excepting his brother Modest. The single subject he does not discuss with her is of course his sexuality, though he hints at it many times. It is, I believe, a reasonable assumption that she was aware of it; only with mutual understanding could their relationship be relied on to remain platonic, and her intensely emotional language should be seen in that context.

Of more importance to musical history is his description to her of his compositional process. It affords us a first-hand account of a composer at

---

* Hundreds of letters passed between them in both directions. To date three volumes have been published, albeit in original Russian only; volumes four and five are due to be published in 2018, with several more still to come. It is quite possible that not all the correspondence has yet come to light.

Above

Sasha and Lev Davidov with their seven children at Kamenka, 1880. Tchaikovsky's favourite nephew, Bob, is sitting in the front row on the left.

work, and I cannot think of another composer of true greatness setting down his working methods in such detail. It is therefore worth examining in some depth.

First, how does the act of composing a piece actually begin?

The seed of a future composition usually reveals itself suddenly, in the most unexpected fashion. If the soil is favourable – that is, if I am in the mood for work – this seed takes root with inconceivable strength and speed, bursts through the soil, puts out roots, leaves, twigs, and finally flowers . . . It would be futile for me to try and express to you in words the boundless bliss of that feeling which envelops you when the main idea has appeared, and when it begins to take definite forms. You forget everything, you are almost insane, everything inside you trembles and writhes, you scarcely manage to set down sketches, one idea presses upon another.[1]

There has never, I believe, been a more explicit description of the white heat of creativity and how it renders the artist incapable of doing anything other than setting it down. So strong can inspiration be, Tchaikovsky says, that if it were to continue unbroken, the artist would be unable to survive – 'the strings would snap and the instrument shatter into smithereens'.

But what exactly is inspiration? Tchaikovsky confesses he does not know. It is a 'supernatural, incomprehensible force which no one has explained'.[2] It can sometimes be wayward: a commissioned piece of music – one that is not the product of inspiration alone – can be successful, while something that springs from the composer's inspiration alone might be less so. It is a mystery.

How does Tchaikovsky actually transfer the ideas that form in his brain onto paper?

> *I write my sketches on the first piece of paper that comes to hand, sometimes on a scrap of music manuscript paper. I write in a very abbreviated form. A melody can never appear in my head without its harmony. Both these musical elements, together with the rhythm, can never be separated from each other. That is, every melodic idea carries its own implicit harmony, and is unfailingly furnished with its own rhythmic structure.*[3]

This is illuminating. Tchaikovsky does not simply hear a tune in his head: he hears the whole harmony. Melody, harmony, rhythm – the three elements of a line of music are created together. No single element can be separated from the other two.

That is not to say that inspiration is of itself sufficient. Sometimes he can tell it is not successful, and then drastic remedial action is required.

> *What was written in the heat of the moment must subsequently be critically scrutinised, amended, supplemented and, in particular, abridged in the light of structural requirements. Sometimes one has to do oneself violence, be merciless and cruel to oneself, that is, cut off completely bits that had been conceived with love and inspiration.*[4]

Here is a composer recognising that the fruits of genius are not by themselves enough. The resulting composition has to fit the required structure, be it symphony, opera, quartet, for whatever combination of instruments. A flight of fancy will not do.

Unsurprisingly, his work is not limited to his time at the composing table:

> *. . . if I am in a normal state of mind, I can say that I am composing every minute of the day, whatever the circumstances. Sometimes I observe with curiosity that unbroken labour which . . . goes on in that region of my head which is given over to music. Sometimes this is some*

preparatory work . . . while on another occasion a completely new independent musical idea appears and I try to retain it in my memory. Whence all this comes is an impenetrable secret.[5]

An impenetrable secret, even to Tchaikovsky.

It would be an exaggeration to say Tchaikovsky was becoming something of a recluse, but there is an element of truth in it. If he socialised, it was with people he already knew, those with whom he could relax and be himself. Even then he was not always happy.

December 1879 saw him in Rome, mixing with familiar faces from the past, such as Prince Golitsyn, at whose estate in Ukraine he had spent the entire summer of 1864. He was not as pleased as he might have been by the arrival of his old friend Nikolay Kondratyev, who had endeared himself to Tchaikovsky some years earlier with his praise of the opera *The Oprichnik.*

Kondratyev was married with a daughter, but was well known for his homosexual activities when away from home. He was a much changed character to the man Tchaikovsky had once known, having become 'a desperate debauchee and libertine' and indulging daily in heavy 'drinking bouts and amorous adventures', as Tchaikovsky wrote in a letter to Anatoly.[6]

In the event things turned out not to be as bad as Tchaikovsky feared. He managed for the most part to avoid being swept up in the general debauchery and drunkenness of the celebrations, keeping largely to himself.

Nor was his mood much lowered when word came from Anatoly in St Petersburg that their father was seriously ill, and that he should return immediately. Tchaikovsky decided to wait a few days to see how serious the situation was.

Two days later a telegram arrived informing him of his father's death the previous day, 9 January 1880. Ilya was eighty-four. Tchaikovsky's letter to Anatoly expressed sadness, but was hardly an outpouring of grief:

Your letter is infinitely sad, and at the same time it is infused with something ineffably radiant . . . I think the soul of our dear departed was illuminating your thoughts when you wrote it.[7]

Significantly, only six months before, he had written to Nadezhda von Meck to tell her it was the twenty-fifth anniversary of his mother's death, and he missed her as much as ever.

The loss of his father did nothing to dampen his creativity. While in Rome he composed his *Italian Capriccio,* a piece redolent of the Italian

folk music and songs that he had picked up on the streets of Rome. There
is a bugle call, echoing one by an Italian cavalry regiment, that he heard
from his hotel room each morning from the neighbouring barracks, and
the piece ends with a lively *tarantella*. Few of his compositions are so bursting with exuberance.

In a now familiar pattern, Tchaikovsky returned to Russia in spring
1880 and prepared to spend the summer at Kamenka and Brailov. It proved
to be a fertile period. He set about composing two radically different pieces.
One was commissioned and the other a product of his own inspiration.

In what seems something of a contradiction of his thoughts in that
letter to von Meck, the commission was unwanted; he did not enjoy ful-
filling it and the composition he produced was, in his own opinion, largely
without artistic merit.

A huge construction project was nearing completion on the northern
bank of the Moskva river. It was to be called the Cathedral of Christ the
Saviour. It had taken more than forty years to build, and would be the tall-
est Orthodox Christian church in the world.

The order to build it had come nearly seven decades earlier from Tsar Alexander I, to pay homage to Divine Providence for saving Russia at a turning point in its history. The event it commemorated was the disastrous invasion of Russia by Napoleon Bonaparte, Emperor of France.

The heroic efforts of mounted Cossacks, the Russian army, and the people of Moscow, who burned their city rather than surrender it to Napoleon, had become folklore. The year in which this occurred, as every adult Russian knew and every school child was taught, was 1812.

Alexander I did not live to see the cathedral completed. Now, sixty-eight years after Moscow had burned, leaving Napoleon with a worthless prize and a Russian winter to contend with, the cathedral – if still not actually complete – was set for a magnificent opening and Tchaikovsky was commissioned to compose a piece of music to mark its consecration.

His old colleague Nikolay Rubinstein suggested to him that he should write a grand commemorative piece, cannily advising him to make it appropriate for other celebratory occasions. It was fortuitous advice.

Yet Tchaikovsky set about the task with little enthusiasm, writing to von Meck that he composed it 'without any warm feelings of love'. In his own words, it was 'very loud and noisy' and without artistic merit.[8] It had taken him a mere six weeks to write it, that fact alone lowering it in his estimation.

When the consecration of the cathedral was postponed, Tchaikovsky rather mischievously offered the piece to a conductor he knew in St Petersburg, hoping for payment. He described it in an accompanying letter as having no serious merits, and he would not be offended if his friend turned it down as being unsuitable for concert performance. The friend politely declined, not because of any misgivings about the piece, but because he was aware of the terms of the original commission.

Sticking firmly to what he had signed up to, Tchaikovsky opened the piece with a plaintive Russian melody of the Eastern Orthodox Church played on small forces – just four cellos and two violas. Further Russian folk melodies portray the distress of the Russian people at the hands of the invading French.

Tchaikovsky used the French national anthem, *La Marseillaise*, to depict the Battle of Borodino, inserting five Russian cannon shots to depict the turning point in the battle. As the *Marseillaise* disintegrates and the French Grande Armée retreats, victory bells ring out and there is a triumphant repetition of 'O Lord, Save Thy People', from which emerges the anthem 'God Save the Tsar', accompanied by more cannonfire.

Tchaikovsky might have considered the piece below his usual standards, but the *1812 Overture*, or to give it its proper title, *The Year 1812, a Festive Overture*, would become the most popular composition he ever wrote. From its first performance, in a tent next to the unfinished cathedral, to the present day, the piece is played on festive occasions throughout the world, often accompanied by cannon and fireworks.

Almost at the same time as composing the *1812*, Tchaikovsky was working on another piece, this one entirely of his own volition, and the contrast between the two could hardly have been greater.

He had originally intended a possible symphony, or a smaller string quartet, but by the time he had completed it, he had produced a four-movement Serenade for Strings. Once again he had worked swiftly, composing the piece in just a few weeks, though this time the speed of composition did not affect his judgement of it.

He created a sumptuous sound for strings alone, using extensive double-stopping in violins and violas to create a towering structure of sound. In contrast to the *1812*, Tchaikovsky professed himself well pleased with the result, saying it was entirely 'heartfelt' and 'not lacking in real qualities'.[9]

This time his impression was accurate. At its St Petersburg premiere in October 1882, the second movement, the *Valse*, received an immediate encore. At its Moscow premiere, it was conducted by his old adversary Anton Rubinstein, who described it as the best thing Tchaikovsky had written. Even he was by now won over.

The Serenade for Strings remains popular to this day, particularly that second movement. But in the *1812 Overture* Tchaikovsky excelled himself in producing exactly what was required, a work of enduring and undying popularity – even if he was unable to recognise it as such himself.

As the remarkably productive year of 1880 came to a close, though, clouds were gathering, and they were of a personal nature.

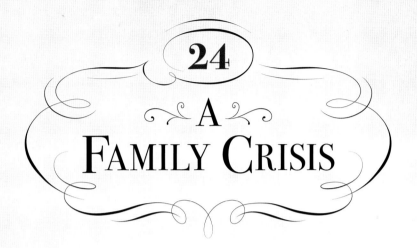

24
A
FAMILY CRISIS

The effort of intense composition, coupled with the strain of staging *The Maid of Orleans*, sent Tchaikovsky off to his familiar European haunts in early 1881, where he hoped the warmth and convivial surroundings would alleviate the depression that threatened regularly to envelop him.

But he could not settle. Vienna, Florence, Rome, Naples, and then France; it was almost as though he was trying to prevent any news from home from finding him. But find him it did. He was in Nice when he heard that his old ally Nikolay Rubinstein had been taken seriously ill in Paris.

The rift caused by Rubinstein's castigation of the First Piano Concerto had long since healed, and the head of the Moscow Conservatory was a firm champion of the music of his old friend and one-time fellow professor.

In the preceding fifteen years or so, Rubinstein had conducted the premieres of almost every orchestral piece Tchaikovsky had written. In return Tchaikovsky had dedicated more of his works to Rubinstein than to any other single person – including a new piano concerto.[*]

---

[*] In fact, on reading through the unfinished score, Rubinstein had once again offered criticism, but it was mild and generally constructive, and Tchaikovsky took no offence. The work is distinguished by solo parts for violin and cello in the second movement, making the movement in places almost a piano trio. Tchaikovsky's Piano Concerto No. 2 remains in the repertoire today, but it has never achieved the popularity of the Piano Concerto No. 1.

As soon as word reached him that Rubinstein was gravely ill, receiving urgent treatment for tuberculosis in Paris, Tchaikovsky immediately headed north for the French capital, but he arrived too late. Rubinstein had died of intestinal tuberculosis at the age of just forty-five.

Tchaikovsky was deeply affected by his old friend's death, writing to von Meck of the heart-wrenching sight at the Gare du Nord of the wooden box containing Rubinstein's body being loaded unceremoniously into the baggage car of a train bound for Moscow.

It had been planned that Rubinstein would perform the premiere of the new work; he had insisted on doing so as atonement for his criticism of the earlier concerto. But it was not to be. The dedication remained, however, and a piano trio Tchaikovsky composed a few months later was dedicated 'to the memory of a great artist'.

Tchaikovsky continued to take sanctuary over the summer months at Sasha and Lev's estate in Kamenka; he still revelled in the company of his nieces and nephews (the eldest Tatyana, known as Tanya, separated from the youngest, Yuri, by fifteen years). His favourite, Bob, was rapidly putting his childhood behind him, and as he grew up his resemblance to his uncle was constantly commented on.

Tchaikovsky wrote to Modest, 'He is so tender and affectionate with me that it constantly moves me, sometimes almost to tears.'[1]

But even in Kamenka all was not well. Tchaikovsky's adored sister Sasha was suffering from bouts of nausea and fatigue, coupled with severe pain in the kidneys.[*]

There was a standard remedy: morphine. Sasha began taking it, and it was not long before she became addicted. The drug came with serious side-effects, affecting her personality and her general health.

There was nothing her husband, or her brother, could do to alleviate this. The need for pain relief meant that Sasha had to continue taking the drug, whatever the impact on her.

Sasha was not the only one suffering. At the age of nineteen, Tanya had fallen in love with an army officer, Vasily Trubetskoy, and become engaged to marry him. After a short visit to Moscow, she had returned to Kamenka distraught, with the news that Trubetskoy had physically attacked her, even attempted to rape her. She had fled back home, the engagement broken off.

She was inconsolable, refusing to eat and rapidly losing weight.[†] In despair, her mother turned to the obvious remedy. Morphine had cured her

---

[*] Probably caused by kidney stones.

[†] Today she might have been labelled anorexic.

pain; perhaps it would do the same for her daughter. Over a period of time Tanya followed her mother into morphine addiction.

Before the morphine took over her life, though, a second tragedy was to befall Tanya – and one that also was to involve her uncle Pyotr. He had noticed a musical talent in his eldest niece, and suggested that she be given music lessons in an attempt to help her recover from the trauma and return her to health.

As it happened, Tchaikovsky knew a graduate of the St Petersburg Conservatory, Stanislav Mikhailovich Blumenfeld, who was currently running a music school in Kiev. Blumenfeld, he thought, would be ideal as her teacher. The suggestion would turn out to have disastrous consequences when the pair fell for each other, causing something of a scandal. Blumenfeld was a lower-middle class Jew; in the eyes of her family, an utterly unsuitable match for Tanya.

Tchaikovsky was himself not free of such prejudice, and soon became outraged by what he saw as shameless behaviour from the couple, flaunting their affection for each other right in front of his eyes, as he complains to Modest:

> I cannot understand the insolence with which they were doing this in my presence. She probably considers me to be so innocent that she is not even afraid . . . To fall so far as to permit oneself without embarrassment things that only prostitutes do. From birth I have always lived among women of irreproachable purity, and it was for that reason that this deed seemed so monstrous to me.[2]

This from a man who was well acquainted with the seamier side of life. His mother might well have been a woman of irreproachable purity, but he knew full well that his wife was capable of an active sexual life away from him. As for Tchaikovsky himself, his own personal life was in stark contrast to any ideal of 'irreproachable purity'. His words have a hollow, hypocritical ring, telling us more about Tchaikovsky than about his niece.

Tchaikovsky's affection for his niece had cooled. He now considered her wilful, difficult and irrational. He had done his best for her, and it had failed. As soon as he could, he escaped to the more congenial surroundings of Paris, where he continued work on a new opera, *Mazeppa*.

Once in the French capital, he slipped back easily into his old life, informing Modest that he had come across a place that catered for gay men.

Late one night, after downing two glasses of 'punch', he took to the boulevards for a nocturnal stroll. Near the Café de la Paix, as he recounted by letter to Modest, who should he spot but a certain Anton, former employee at the Hôtel Richepance where he was staying.

He followed Anton voyeuristically for some time, finally observing him sit down on a bench with a 'Negro' (his word). At this point Tchaikovsky gave himself away, probably on purpose. Anton professed delight to see him, and Tchaikovsky joined them. The Soviet censor has redacted several sentences at this point – which speaks for itself.

After several weeks in Paris, during which he continued with the orchestration of *Mazeppa*, his sojourn was interrupted in March 1883 when Modest wrote to announce he would shortly arrive in the French capital with Tanya, who needed medical treatment for her morphine addiction.

It was just the kind of interruption Tchaikovsky did not want, but he knew, since this involved his family, that he could not avoid it. Little did he know what was to come. Modest arrived with Tanya in tow, and Tchaikovsky was swiftly apprised of the fact that his niece was six months pregnant with Blumenfeld's child.

Modest explained that the distraught Tanya, as soon as she realised she was pregnant, had left Kamenka suddenly for St Petersburg, without telling her parents of her predicament. There, she took refuge with Modest, pleading with him to help her. Tchaikovsky was the only one who could afford to pay for medical treatment for the girl and so Modest proceeded to Paris with her, where medical care was available both for morphine addiction and pregnancy.

Tchaikovsky's kindly instincts were roused and he arranged for medical treatment for Tanya for both conditions. Both he and Modest promised their niece they would keep her secret to themselves.

Tanya's baby, a boy, was born the day after Tchaikovsky turned forty-three, an hour after midnight. All Tchaikovsky's paternal instincts came to the fore. He wrote in glowing terms about the birth to Modest, who had left Paris to return to St Petersburg, and his words do him credit:

> The child lay near her, sleeping peacefully. I was surprised by his size. Ever since yesterday I had begun to feel a kind of tenderness for this child who has caused us so much worry, a desire to be his protector. Now I felt it with tenfold force, and I told Tanya that as long as I am alive, she may rest easy on his account.[3]

Despite developing a deep love for the infant, Tchaikovsky's relationship with his niece would never truly recover after this. He wrote to both Anatoly and von Meck of his desire to cut ties:

> That girl is trouble. I don't believe she will ever be weaned from morphine. Drugs, drink or poison will surely be the end of her . . . I feel sorry for her but I cannot love her . . . My only wish at this moment is to spend the rest of my life as far away from her as possible.[4]

For now, though, the whole incident first had to be concealed. After a swift christening in which he was given the French names Georges-Léon, the baby was given into foster care.

Tchaikovsky was true to his word to Tanya that he would not divulge her secret, but in a letter to Modest he was unsparingly critical. She had not shown the slightest remorse in giving her child up, and seemed to be perfectly at ease living with the 'whirlpool of lies' they had created. 'An unfathomable creature' is how Tchaikovsky described her.[5]

Tchaikovsky needed funds both for medical care and for the family who would bring the child up, and he had no alternative but to ask Nadezhda von Meck for an advance, spinning a tissue of truths and untruths related to Tanya's morphine addiction, overlaid with sufficient ambiguity to prevent any further questioning from his patron. The same tale was told to Sasha and Lev, Tanya's parents.

"Despite developing a deep love for the infant, Tchaikovsky's relationship with his niece would never truly recover."

Sketch of Mazeppa
and Maria, characters
from Tchaikovsky's
opera *Mazeppa*.

As Tchaikovsky had predicted, Tanya returned to the bosom of her family in Kamenka, carrying off the fiction that she had undergone surgery for an ulcer and that, by and large, the treatment for morphine addiction had done its job.

Tanya would never actually beat her addiction, and she died suddenly on 19 January 1887. Her parents never knew of the existence of their illegitimate grandson.

In early 1884 Tchaikovsky attended the premiere of his new opera, *Mazeppa*. Given the traumas he had had to deal with during its composition, it is hardly surprising he wrote that no work had ever given him so much trouble to compose. With his usual pessimism and self-doubt, he wondered if he was losing his powers, though he did also consider whether he was becoming too severe in his self-judgement.

The premiere in Moscow received only lukewarm reviews, causing Tchaikovsky to miss the premiere in St Petersburg four days later, preferring to repair – once again – to Paris, which as usual he found far more congenial.

He had reason to be grateful for his absence. The St Petersburg reviews were awful, a fact Modest was careful to hide from him. When Tchaikovsky finally learned the truth, he wrote to his brother with gratitude, saying that if he had known it might have killed him. The opera soon dropped out of the repertoire, and has not returned.

Mazeppa's failure, compounded by family trauma, deepened Tchaikovsky's habitual depression, which was only briefly alleviated by his being summoned to appear before Tsar Alexander III to receive the Order of Saint Vladimir (4th class).

His depression deepened when, out of the blue, he received word that his young protégé, companion and sometime lover, Iosif Kotek, had contracted tuberculosis and was seriously ill. The violinist, who had done so much to help Tchaikovsky bring his violin concerto to fruition, who had initiated the first correspondence between Tchaikovsky and his patron Nadezhda von Meck, lay in a sanatorium in Davos.

Although relations between them had deteriorated over the saga of the violin concerto, coupled with Kotek's amorous shenanigans, Tchaikovsky

– as would be expected, given his inherently kindly nature – put former feelings to one side and hurried to Davos, hoping he would not arrive too late.

He found Kotek in a pitiful state, with no real prospect of recovery. Again, true to character, Tchaikovsky did what he could to alleviate matters for his friend. He visited Kotek's doctor secretly to ask whether the patient was well enough to be sent to the French Riviera where the warmth might do him good, offering to make funds available to facilitate this.

But he knew in his heart there was nothing that could be done. After six days he felt he had to escape the misery of watching his young friend die, and he returned to the altogether more congenial ambience of the French capital.

From there, after some much needed rest and recuperation in the usual manner – he rekindled his friendship with his old classmate and lover at the School of Jurisprudence, Alexei Apukhtin, who was also in Paris – he returned to Russia.

Arriving in Moscow, he found that word was already waiting for him from Davos: Kotek's tuberculosis had developed into pneumonia, and he was not expected to survive long.

Tchaikovsky agonised over whether to dash back to Davos. He knew he was the only person who was likely to go. If he did not, Kotek would die alone. On the other hand he wondered if he could face the trauma of watching his erstwhile friend in his death throes.

He made the decision not to return, and a week later he learned of Kotek's death. First he received a telegram from Davos, swiftly followed by a consoling letter from Nadezhda von Meck.

It fell to Tchaikovsky, as he relayed in a letter to von Meck, to inform Kotek's parents of their son's death. He was just twenty-nine.

In the aftermath of Kotek's death, Tchaikovsky threw himself into composing. First he revised his opera *Vakula the Smith*, giving it the new title *Cherevichki*.[*] While he was in Davos he had re-read Byron's poem *Manfred*, on which Balakirev had suggested some time before he should base a programmatic composition, as he had done with *Romeo and Juliet*.

At the time Tchaikovsky had rejected the notion, but now on re-reading the poem he judged it suitable. Instead of a single-movement piece, he wrote a full four-movement work. It was published under the title *Manfred Symphony*, his only symphonic work without a number.

Initially considering it to be one of his best works, Tchaikovsky had to be dissuaded from destroying all but the first movement after its mixed

---

[*] See p. 121.

reception. It was soon dropped from the repertoire, and has never really re-entered it.

He then turned his attention to yet another opera, which would be entitled *The Enchantress*. He threw himself into the project, quickly deciding that the libretto with which he had been furnished was far too long. He made extensive cuts, but still produced the longest work he would ever write.

The premiere, at the Mariinksy Theatre in St Petersburg on 20 October 1887, created little impact, and the opera was dropped after a single season. It has seen only occasional revivals since.

Why, despite such industriousness, were the compositions Tchaikovsky was creating at this time not among his best? The answer could well lie once again in his personal life.

His wife Antonina was back in the picture.

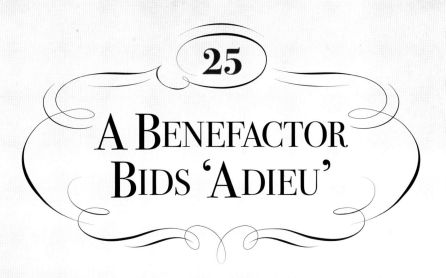

25

A BENEFACTOR BIDS 'ADIEU'

For the first time in his adult life, as he entered his forties, Tchaikovsky was showing signs of a desire to settle down. So many summers spent in the congenial surroundings of Kamenka in Ukraine had increased his love of nature and the countryside. Fields, woods, plants, flowers – they were as essential to him as the books he had accumulated during his life and that he read every night before sleep. Now he felt the need for a more permanent home, to satisfy his bucolic longings and, more practically, to house his belongings.

Whether he liked it or not, his musical life revolved around the two great Russian cities of Moscow and St Petersburg. The former he had always disliked, while the latter was more to his taste, but both harboured less than happy memories for him, whether in the form of unsuccessful performances or of people he had no particular desire to encounter.

Probably the single journey he had undertaken more than any other in his life was the four hundred miles between Moscow and St Petersburg, and it was a journey he knew he would need to take many more times in the years to come. He was familiar with the countryside; he knew the road and the railway. The landscape was largely open and sparsely populated; it made sense for him to situate himself there, close to one or other of the cities and within easy reach of a railway station on the main line between the two.

Moscow offered more attraction, since rail communication with Europe was far better than from St Petersburg, sitting as it did in the north-west corner of the country on the shores of the Baltic. He put it succinctly in a letter to Nadezhda von Meck:

> I have begun to dream of settling down in some stable and permanent home of my own. The nomadic life is beginning to weigh heavily upon me. Whether this will be some place on the outskirts of Moscow or some place farther and more out of the way, I still do not know . . . I must, finally, live in my own place.[1]
>
> My dream to settle down for the rest of my days in the Russian countryside is not a momentary caprice but a true need of my nature.[2]

He found what he was looking for in the village of Maidanovo, around 60 miles north-west of Moscow. For a rent of 1,000 roubles a year, he moved into a small house on the banks of the River Sestra with ponds and lime trees.

He lived to a routine, which he spelled out to his patron, knowing how much she enjoyed learning details of his private life. He got up between seven and eight in the morning, taking morning tea brought to him by Aleksey. He then read, often choosing one of his two favourite English authors, Dickens and Thackeray, as he was trying to improve his English.

A brief walk completed his morning, and then it was composition until one o'clock, when Aleksey brought him lunch. Then another long walk, believing that two hours of walking a day had vital health benefits. Afternoon tea at four o'clock was followed by a glance at the papers, then another two hours of composing, and a final walk before dinner if the weather was fine or a stint at the piano in winter months. After dinner he might play a game of cards with guests or turn to his correspondence.[3]

Tchaikovsky was an inveterate letter writer, which he needed to be, given the volume of correspondence he received. As his fame grew, so did the number of people who wanted to get in touch with him. By this stage in his life, he was beginning to receive letters from all over the world. It was not in his nature to ignore them. As far as he could, if he considered the letter merited it, he would send a reply.

It was while sifting through a pile of letters on the evening of 22 June 1886 that his eyes fell on a large envelope from his publisher Jurgenson. Inside it was another letter. He recognised the writing. For the first time in five years, Antonina was trying to contact him again.

It was now nine years since he had left his wife, and by now – at least in his own head – he had put the whole disastrous experience of his marriage behind him. But she, it seems, had not. In less than a week, a second letter appeared, resorting to her usual entreaties to return to her, professing

" The nomadic life is beginning to weigh heavily upon me."
Tchaikovsky

her love for him while simultaneously boasting of another lover –'She is, I think, quite mad', he wrote to Jurgenson.[4]

His diary entries after the second letter were clearly troubled:

Could eat nothing and all day was not myself. Only towards evening felt better. What's to be done with this madwoman???[5]

Even given Tchaikovsky's thin skin and his predilection for emotional hyperbole, the strain her letters put on him is clear. He tried to draft a reply to her, but the right words simply would not come.

Finally he decided upon his response. Through Jurgenson, he proposed giving her an immediate 600 roubles, but said he was prepared to offer more if she agreed not to contact him again, authorising his publisher to handle any further matters as he saw fit, without needing to consult him.

Antonina accepted the offer. It seemed at last she was satisfied, although the respite was brief. One more letter arrived for him, and it contained extraordinary news. Antonina was the mother of three illegitimate children.

Tchaikovsky had earlier learned that his wife had taken a lover, a lawyer by the name of Alexander Alexandrovich Shlykov – news that had not worried him one bit – and that she had given birth to an illegitimate baby girl five years previously. His fear then was that she might register the baby in his name, since he was still legally her husband. In the event the child, christened Maria Alexandrovna, died at less than one year old.

The following year she gave birth to a son, named Pyotr Petrovich after her husband, and two years after that another daughter followed, whom she named after both herself and Tchaikovsky, Antonina Petrovna.

Little is known of the relationship between Antonina and the father of her children, other than that she lived with him from May 1880, and that he was in constant ill-health. He died in 1888.

She asked her husband for two things: to bring up her children himself, and also to dedicate a piece of music to her. As final proof to Tchaikovsky that she was unhinged, she enclosed an embroidered shirt she had made for him. He wrote to Modest:

A complete and utter madwoman, but behaves like a lamb. Thank God, she has gone after taking a substantial sum from Jurgenson.[6]

All three children had been placed by Antonina in a state orphanage, which Tchaikovsky found distressing, though this was tempered with relief at the fact that surnames were not required in such institutions. But he was adamant there was nothing he could do. To adopt her children would require legal action that risked bringing out into the open details of his private life. It would also make the prospect of divorce even more unlikely.

He was saved by sad circumstance. Pyotr Petrovich died at the age of seven; Antonina Petrovna did not reach her third birthday.

And so, finally, Antonina passed out of her husband's life. She never contacted him again. But we can assume she remained on his mind, as his thoughts continued to turn from time to time to the possibility of divorce. In the event it was never to happen. The legal separation he had longed for never came about; he remained married to Antonina for the rest of his life.

If Tchaikovsky's relationship with one woman who had shared his life had finally reached an end, he was now about to hear from the other, who was also to deliver dramatic and far-reaching news.

In October 1890 Tchaikovsky received a visitor. It was a servant from Nadezhda von Meck's household. He bore a letter from his mistress with 6,000 roubles enclosed – the composer's allowance for an entire year, which she was paying in advance. This was a break with the normal procedure of advancing him funds on a monthly basis. He was mildly surprised and wrote her a short letter of thanks.

Shortly after this Tchaikovsky was in Tiflis in Georgia visiting his lawyer brother Anatoly, who was state prosecutor. He enjoyed the warmth and relaxed atmosphere in the south, renewing several friendships and generally indulging himself.

Two further letters from von Meck found their way to him there. The first was in familiar tones, calling him her 'dear, incomparable friend', and urging him not to forget his 'infinitely loving Nadezhda von Meck'.[7] The only unusual element was that she referred despairingly to the sad fact that her adult children were squandering the inheritance their father had left them, although despite her distress over the situation, there was no suggestion in the letters that her arrangement with Tchaikovsky was in any way at risk. Then, out of nowhere, the bombshell. Just days later a third letter informed Tchaikovsky bluntly that she had gone bankrupt and that she would no longer send him any payments. Von Meck's circumstances had changed dramatically, and she had decided to sever ties with Tchaikovsky. With no prior warning, she brought their entire relationship, financial and otherwise, to an end.

It ended as suddenly as it had begun almost thirteen years earlier. It was all the more surprising given that the two families were now related by marriage. After several years of clandestine match-making on both sides – von Meck being the driving force – her son Nikolay had married Tchaikovsky's niece Anna Davydova, third child of Sasha and Lev Davydov.

In fact the marriage had proved to be not at all what they had hoped for. The strong-willed Anna dominated her weaker husband, frequently

challenging her mother-in-law over family matters. Von Meck, and Tchaikovsky, came to regret that they had worked so hard to unite their two families.

Von Meck's letter has not survived; it is perhaps not an exaggeration to picture Tchaikovsky destroying it in anger and frustration. But we do have his lengthy reply to her, and from it we can deduce the contents of hers.

Tchaikovsky admits that the sudden cessation of funds would affect him (though he was also in receipt of funds from a highly exalted source[*]), but implores her not to worry about him. There is the legendary Tchaikovsky kindness again, for he is clearly downplaying the impact on his own circumstances.

We can ascertain from Tchaikovsky's reply that, despite the curtness of von Meck's letter, at the very end she urged him not to forget her. Again it is characteristic of Tchaikovsky to pick up on this and respond to it:

> . . . my dear friend, rest assured that I will remember your [friendship, compassion, and material assistance] until my last breath, and will bless

[*] See p. 231.

Above

The Tchaikovsky brothers, from left to right: Anatoly, Nikolay, Ippolit, Pyotr and Modest.

"Know once and for all that no one sympathises and shares in all your afflictions more than I."

Tchaikovsky's final written words to Nadezhda

you. I am glad that precisely now, when you can no more share your means with me, I can express with all my might my boundless, ardent, altogether ineffable gratitude. You probably yourself do not suspect the full immensity of your good deed! . . . Without any exaggeration I can say that I have never forgotten you and never will forget you for even a single minute, for my thoughts, whenever I think of myself, always and invariably encounter you. I warmly kiss your hands and beg you to know once and for all that no one sympathises and shares in all your afflictions more than I.[8]

And so the most extraordinary example of patronage in the history of classical music came to an end, suddenly and seemingly without explanation. Why might it have happened?

In the first place, von Meck had belatedly discovered that the fortune her husband had amassed from investing in the railways was considerably smaller than she had believed. She had been a widow for nearly fifteen years. The marriage had not been a meeting of minds: not once, in all the letters von Meck wrote to Tchaikovsky, did she mention her husband.

Then there was pressure from her own family. For some time her eleven children had been embarrassed by the closeness of her relationship with the composer. Increasingly they were hearing gossip about Tchaikovsky and 'La Meck', coupled with scurrilous suggestions as to just how close the relationship might be.

It is possible that the family could have been aware of Tchaikovsky's private life. It is highly likely that, as their mother's closeness to Tchaikovsky intensified over the years, they had made moves to discover what they could about him. Since she had employed Kotek as her resident musician, they might well have unearthed reference to his past relationship with Tchaikovsky. There was always the risk of the disclosure of Tchaikovsky's homosexuality and this, in their eyes, could only harm their mother's reputation.

And then there was the question of money. There was, somewhat understandably, a growing resentment on their part that so much wealth, which inevitably would have been destined for them on their mother's death, was going instead to a musician, a man whom she had never met and had no intention of meeting.

When it was discovered that their father's fortune was not as great as they had imagined, matters came to a head. We can speculate that they presented their mother with an ultimatum: that if she did not break off relations with Tchaikovsky, they would reveal publicly his sexual preferences, which would damage her standing in society irretrievably (not to mention his). Of this, of course, there is no proof.

One other factor should be taken into account. By 1890, Nadezhda von Meck was in the latter stages of tuberculosis. Her right arm had atrophied and she found writing increasingly difficult. Given the nature of her letters to Tchaikovsky, to dictate her words to a third party would have been embarrassing. These were letters that were never intended to be seen by anyone other than the object of her admiration and love.

Today, even if we remain bewildered by the true nature of their friendship, even if it is difficult to rationalise von Meck's behaviour – an infatuation that could exist only by remaining apart – we have reason to be grateful to her.

Nadezhda von Meck ensured that Tchaikovsky was comfortable financially for over a decade, allowing him to travel as he desired, and affording him the conditions he needed in order to compose.

While it would be an exaggeration to say we would not have had the compositions we enjoy today had it not been for her patronage, it certainly is true that the circumstances of their composition would have been very different. Musical posterity owes Nadezhda von Meck a great debt.

If there could be said to be a third woman in Tchaikovsky's life, it was his sister Sasha. Her lovely country estate was permanently at his disposal, and she always looked after him and ensured the ideal conditions in which he could compose. He had found endless joy in the couple's seven children, loving nothing more than to entertain them when they were young, along with Uncle Modest. And with the birth of Vladimir – Bob – he had found someone he could adore as a son.

But life at Kamenka had changed over the years. There was Tanya's addiction to morphine, her illegitimate child and early death. And there was her mother's addiction too, soon complicated by a parallel addiction to alcohol.

By 1890 Sasha, once the life and soul of the family, beloved by all, was seriously ill. She had developed epilepsy from continued morphine abuse, and was now an alcoholic. When Tchaikovsky was away in Paris in 1891, he learned by accident from reading a Russian newspaper that the sister of the famous composer had died. She was forty-nine.

Tchaikovsky's immediate concern was for Bob, above the other children and her husband. Bob was now nineteen, and Tchaikovsky wrote to Modest imploring him to look after their nephew.

In fact Bob reacted with some equanimity, to his own surprise, putting it down for the most part to his age: 'At *my age* grief is borne easily – if it really is my age which is to account for this, and not my particular character,' he wrote somewhat enigmatically to his uncle.[9]

Tchaikovsky, too, found himself more phlegmatic than he had expected, the trauma with Tanya's and Sasha's descent into addiction and alcoholism having prepared him for the worst.

Thus, at the beginning of the final decade of Tchaikovsky's life, we find him in vastly changed circumstances. The saga of his marriage is ended, even if not satisfactorily resolved by the divorce he so wanted. His relationship with his patron is over. His beloved sister Sasha is dead.

Yet at the same time a certain peace had entered Tchaikovsky's life. He was about to settle down for good, to find a home in which he wanted to remain for the rest of his life.

There was a new love in his life. And, most importantly for posterity, some of his greatest musical works were still to come.

Little could he, or anybody, know that this new-found state of happiness would last less than three years.

26

ON TOUR AND UNHAPPY

lesser musician might well have found his creativity stifled by the traumatic events of the previous five years, but during that period Tchaikovsky had written *Manfred* and the opera *The Enchantress*. He then went on to compose a new symphony, one of his finest, the Symphony No. 5; the Fantasy Overture: *Hamlet*; the ballet *Sleeping Beauty*, and an entirely new opera, second only to *Eugene Onegin*, *The Queen of Spades*. This was followed by the string sextet, *Souvenir de Florence*, his homage to one of his favourite European locations. Barely was the ink dry on this when, in February 1891, he began work on yet another ballet, *The Nutcracker*.

It was not as if he was idling his time away at Maidanovo, leading a placid life that afforded him plenty of time to compose. In December 1887, the end of the year following the death of his niece Tanya, he embarked on his first European conducting tour, which in the space of three months took him to Leipzig, Hamburg, Berlin, Prague, Paris and London.

It was on his return that he composed the Symphony No. 5 and *Hamlet*. He conducted the premiere of the new symphony in St Petersburg. Not for the first time in his career, the audience applauded loud and strong while the critics were less than impressed.

Tchaikovsky, however, agreed with the critics, describing it in a letter to von Meck as having 'something repulsive in it, a kind of excessive diversity

of colour and insincere artificiality'.[1] Posterity has seen fit to disagree. It remains to this day one of his best-loved and most performed works.

At the beginning of 1889 Tchaikovsky was off on his travels again for a second European tour, with concerts in Cologne, Frankfurt, Dresden, Berlin, Geneva, Hamburg and London.

One anecdote from this tour is particularly memorable. Johannes Brahms was not a composer Tchaikovsky had ever greatly admired, and the feeling was mutual. After an earlier meeting, he had described Brahms as a 'pot-bellied boozer' (in contrast to Edvard Grieg, whom he also met, and who impressed him as 'an extraordinarily charming man').[2]

The two met again, reluctantly, in Hamburg on Tchaikovsky's second European tour. They agreed to have lunch together. Both being more than partial to a glass of wine, several bottles were consumed. The two composers were soon laughing – unimpeded by their lack of fluency in each other's language – and behaving as though they were old friends.

There was a piano on the premises. They played excerpts of their works to each other, then played each other's, parodied passages, and generally had a convivial, and intoxicated, time. They parted the best of friends, praising each other – though they never met again – for the rest of their lives.

The new ballet, *Sleeping Beauty*, premiered in early January 1890. The final dress rehearsal had been performed in the presence of Tsar Alexander III, who damned with faint praise. 'Very nice,' he remarked before leaving.

Tchaikovsky, always notoriously thin-skinned, wrote in his diary: 'His Majesty treated me very condescendingly. So be it!'[3]

This from the same tsar who, a year previously, had granted Tchaikovsky a lifetime annuity of 3,000 roubles – something that would come in very useful indeed when, a year later, Nadezhda von Meck ended her patronage.

The premiere was an impressive production – extravagant set designs, opulent costumes, and remarkable dancing. Tchaikovsky's beautiful compositions were an instant success, resonating from that day to this. Even Tchaikovsky himself was pleased.

The news of Sasha's death reached him in Paris, shortly before he was due to embark on a tour of America, which if successful which would cement his reputation as one of the most popular living composers in the world. Despite the inevitability of his sister's death, he still found himself descending into grief, though true to character his immediate concern was for Bob. On the ship, as he later wrote to Modest, he craved the company of his brother and nephew Bob, already longing to be back home with them.

Events soon took over, however, and Tchaikovsky found himself fully occupied with his concert schedule. Arguably the most important concert on the tour was the very first one. It was the inaugural concert of the newly built Carnegie Hall, and he conducted his *Coronation March*, written eight years previously as part of the coronation celebrations for Tsar Alexander III.

He directed four concerts at Carnegie Hall, and at the fourth he conducted his Piano Concerto No. 1 with the young German pianist Adele aus der Ohe as soloist. It was a triumph, he wrote in his diary, earning more applause and enthusiasm than he had ever achieved in Russia.

He so admired aus der Ohe's playing that he invited her to come to Russia and perform the concerto with him again. Neither she nor he could have any inkling of how different things would be when that concert actually took place. She would barely be able to see the piano keys for the tears she shed. The concert would be a memorial to Tchaikovsky.

The normally shy, reserved, and home-loving Tchaikovsky found himself thoroughly taken with America and its people. He had met Andrew

Carnegie himself, who despite his riches he found 'simple, modest, and in no way arrogant'.

Carnegie was similarly charmed, showering Tchaikovsky with adulation and imitating Tchaikovsky's conducting, to the composer's amusement:

> He grasped my hands, crying that I am the uncrowned but veritable king of music, embraced me (without kissing; here men never kiss) and, exclaiming about my greatness, raised himself on tiptoe and held his arms high and finally delighted the entire company by imitating how I conduct. He did this so seriously, so well, so like me – that I myself was carried away.[4]

He was enthralled and bemused by how far ahead of Russia America was when it came to modern conveniences – electric lighting everywhere, a bathroom containing bath, basin *and* toilet, and a device that enabled him to speak to the front desk.

He found the people of New York friendly – straightforward, generous and sincere. And he was shocked and surprised – evidence of his genuine modesty – to discover how well known he was. He wrote home to Bob:

> I am petted, honoured, and entertained here in every way possible. It turns out that in America I am ten times more renowned than in Europe. At first when they told me this, I thought it was an exaggerated courtesy. Now I see that it is true . . . Here I am much more of a bigwig than in Russia. Isn't that curious?!![5]

He was equally pleased by critical reaction to his concerts, though confessed himself a little shocked at the personal nature of one particular review in the *New York Herald*:

> Tchaikovsky is a tall, grey, well-built, interesting man, well on sixty [he was actually just days short of his fifty-first birthday]. He seems a trifle embarrassed, and responds to the applause by a succession of brusque and jerky bows. But as soon as he grasps the baton his self-confidence returns. There is no sign of nervousness about him as he taps for silence. He conducts with the authoritative strength of a master and the band obeys his lead as one man.[6]

Apart from the (considerable) mistake over his age – a misjudgement Carnegie confessed to as well – the description seems to be accurate, capturing Tchaikovsky exactly: shy, modest and a little awkward – until he is making music.

Tchaikovsky went on to perform in Buffalo (visiting the Niagara Falls), Baltimore, Washington and Philadelphia, always receiving unrestrained adulation. After one concert, he noted in his diary, a lady tossed a splendid bouquet of red roses straight into his face.

In all Tchaikovsky was absent for nearly two months. More than anything he missed the company of his nephew Bob. His diary entries, not to mention his letters, suggest it is not an exaggeration to say he pined for the young man. Just before leaving New York, he wrote:

> *[Our meeting] seems to me an unattainable, fabulous happiness. I try to think of it as little as possible, so as to be able to endure a few more days of torment.*

Once back in Europe, homeward bound, he wrote of his

> *. . . terrible, inexpressible, maddeningly agonising homesickness . . . Most of all [while away] . . . I thought of you and so longed to see you, to hear your voice, and this appeared to me such unbelievable bliss, that, it seems, I would have given up ten years of my life (and, as you know, I value my life very much) to have you appear for even a second . . . Bob! I adore you.*

And in his joy at receiving a letter from Bob:

> *Like a youth having received a letter from the girl he loves, I kissed over and over again, mercilessly, the traces of your wretched, abominable hand. My dear, wonderful fellow, I adore you!*[7]

He arrived back in Mother Russia tired and worn out – although the *Herald* mistake over his age suggests he was exhausted before the tour had

hardly begun. Bob came to see him in Maidanovo, but we are left with no details of the reunion.

The summer of 1891, despite his obvious weariness, saw Tchaikovsky throwing himself back into composition. In his rented house outside Moscow he worked on his new ballet, *The Nutcracker* and, at the same time, a new one-act opera, *Iolanta*.

As autumn turned to winter he had to put aside work on both in order to supervise the Moscow premiere of the new opera, *The Queen of Spades*. This he had written to a commission from the Imperial Theatres, completing it in the extraordinarily short time of just forty-four days. The libretto was written by Modest.

The world premiere of *The Queen of Spades* the year before in St Petersburg had been a triumph, but Tchaikovsky knew how fickle audiences could be; a triumph in one city was no guarantee of a triumph in another. He need not have worried. Audiences in Moscow took it to their heart, as they also did shortly afterwards in Kiev, and it was to become his second most popular opera after *Eugene Onegin*.

That year there had been no summer sojourn in Kamenka. But bracing himself for what he knew was likely to be a final visit to his adored sister's estate, he spent Christmas and the New Year in Ukraine.

Writing to Bob, he described his 'painful feeling [as he] entered the courtyard, in the middle of which the empty, locked house produces a doleful impression'.[8] He was entertained to tea by an eighty-four-year-old cousin. Most of the residents in small cottages on the estate were members of Lev Davydov's family. Lev himself was away in St Petersburg.

Old age and death hung over the estate, where Tchaikovsky had once enjoyed so much fun and laughter with his nieces and nephews. He cheered himself up, though, by writing to Bob:

> *You ask, my inestimable one, what my mood's like. Bad! . . . You are constantly in my thoughts, for at every feeling of sadness, melancholy, at every clouding of the mental horizon – like a ray of light the thought appears that you exist, and that I shall see you in the not too distant future. On my word of honour, I do not exaggerate. Incessantly, of its own accord, this ray of comfort breaks through . . . : 'Yes, it's bad, but it's nothing – Bob is still in this world.'*[9]

Refusing to give in to the physical strain he was placing himself under, he was on the move again in early 1892, conducting a concert of his music in Warsaw, before travelling again to Hamburg, where he was impressed by Gustav Mahler's conducting of *Eugene Onegin*.

The travelling was taking a toll on his health. As people had in America, those close to him back home in Russia remarked on how he was ageing, and how much older he looked than his years. It also did not go unnoticed that he was drinking heavily.

Returning home, he threw himself into completing *The Nutcracker* and *Iolanta*. He knew he had written some exceptionally good music in the former, and extracted from it the suite of pieces that evoke *The Land of Sweets* in Act II.

This he conducted as a separate composition called *The Nutcracker Suite*, before the ballet itself opened, and it became instantly popular. The little dances, perhaps the best known being *The Dance of the Sugar Plum Fairy*, along with *The Waltz of the Flowers*, remain a fixture in concert halls around the world.

The instant popularity of *The Nutcracker Suite* possibly worked against the success of the full ballet. The premiere on 6 December 1892 at the Mariinsky Theatre in St Petersburg received a lukewarm welcome.

It did not help that the dancers and the choreography were not exactly ideal. The Sugar Plum Fairy was described as 'corpulent' and 'podgy', the Columbine doll as 'completely insipid'. The battle scene was 'disorderly, pushing about from corner to corner and running backwards and forwards – quite amateurish'.

One critic praised Tchaikovsky's music as 'astonishingly rich, beautiful, melodious and original'. But another castigated it as 'ponderous' and the *Grand Pas de Deux* 'insipid' (a favourite word of the critics).[10]

As for the accompanying one-act opera *Iolanta*, which premiered with *The Nutcracker* as a double bill, it was largely ignored then and thus it has remained.

This time, Tchaikovsky was in a better frame of mind to deal with the comparative failure of *The Nutcracker*. Just a few months before the premiere, he had taken a dramatic step to improve the quality of his life. Now certain that the area around Maidanovo was perfect for him, he found a comfortable house with a sizeable garden in the nearby village of Klin, which he had often admired from afar and that had now come on the market.

He bought the house, the first time he had purchased a property in his life. At last he had a place he could call his own. Sadly for him, he would have less than year and a half in which to enjoy it.

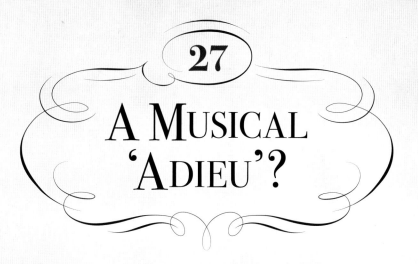

27

A MUSICAL 'ADIEU'?

The world-famous composer who at the end of 1892 stood nervously on the threshold of the small cottage in Montbéliard waiting for his governess of long ago to open the door, could ill afford the time for an unplanned detour to France.

Two weeks earlier he had staged the premieres of his ballet *The Nut-cracker* and its companion piece *Iolanta* in St Petersburg. In less than a fortnight he was due to conduct a concert of his music in Brussels. Ten days after that he was he was scheduled to arrive in Odessa on the Black Sea to conduct a series of concerts of his own works, including a production of *The Queen of Spades*.

Perhaps it was just as well Tchaikovsky extended his visit to Fanny Dür-bach. He needed some time to relax ahead of what awaited him in Odessa, where his welcome would exceed even that in America.

As his train pulled into the main station, he was greeted by the local branch of the Russian Musical Society. An exhausting round of engagements followed, both formal receptions and social events. He simply could not believe how popular he had become. He wrote to a cousin, 'They honour me here like some great man, almost like the saviour of my fatherland.'[1]

On arrival for the first rehearsal he was greeted with pomp, ceremony and boundless applause. At the first concert, several pieces were encored

no fewer than four times – people got out of their seats, shouting, crying; handkerchiefs and hats were waved in the air.

At the second concert, the *1812 Overture* had to be repeated. At the third, which took place in the morning, *The Tempest*, the *Andante cantabile,* and *The Nutcracker Suite* all had to be repeated.

Local newspapers reported on his every move. Such was his fame that a Ukrainian artist, Nikolay Kuznetsov, begged Tchaikovsky to allow him to paint his portrait. This went against all Tchaikovsky's instincts of modesty and self-deprecation. But he agreed, for which we have reason to be grateful.

The painting is the only one Tchaikovsky ever sat for. It shows a sensitive, artistic face, imbued with determination. Modest would later praise it for capturing the 'tragic' side of his brother's character. He also said it was a truthful likeness of him.

Surprisingly Tchaikovsky too liked the portrait. He said of it, 'In terms of its expression, lifelikeness, and authenticity it really is remarkable.'[2]

It has to be said that the forcefulness and determination Kuznetsov found in his sitter are not revealed in any surviving photographs of Tchaikovsky, of which there are many. The painting remains the best-known image of the composer, and perhaps it shows us the man Tchaikovsky wished himself to be.[*]

Proof of Tchaikovsky's worldwide fame – if such were still needed – came the following summer when Tchaikovsky was awarded an honorary degree by the University of Cambridge.

His visit to England began with a performance of his Symphony No. 4 at a Royal Philharmonic Society concert in London, with the composer conducting. He then conducted his *Francesca da Rimini* at a concert in Cambridge, before receiving his honorary degree there on 1 June.

Receiving a similar honour alongside him – to mark the fiftieth anniversary of the Cambridge University Musical Society – were Max Bruch, Edvard Grieg (though he was too unwell to attend), and Camille Saint-Saëns. This was the first meeting between Tchaikovsky and Saint-Saëns since they had danced that impromptu ballet together at the Moscow Conservatory twenty years earlier.[†]

Weeks before the trip to England, Tchaikovsky had begun work on a new composition. At home in Klin he put it aside to work on a Third Piano Concerto, which would ultimately become a concert piece for piano and orchestra.

---

[*] The painting hangs in the Tretyakov State Gallery in Moscow. In 2016 it was loaned to the National Portrait Gallery in London.

[†] See p. 115.

That completed, he worked intensively on the new composition, which would become his Symphony No. 6, the *Pathétique*. He wrote to Modest:

> *I am now wholly occupied with the new work . . . and it is hard for me to tear myself away from it. I believe it comes into being as the best of my works. I must finish it as soon as possible, for I have to wind up a lot of affairs and I must soon go to London.*[3]

The work Tchaikovsky produced stands alone among his symphonies, in that it begins quietly and ends quietly. A low bassoon opens the first movement; the final movement ends with low notes on cellos and bassoons descending into the depths. It is the only symphony that ends in the minor key.

The second movement is ostensibly a waltz, but it is in 5/4 time, which is not the time signature for a waltz. It has been described as a 'limping waltz'. Optimism and buoyancy return in the third movement, ending in the kind of triumphant tones in which Tchaikovsky would normally end the complete work. But the sense of gloom returns in the fourth and final movement, and it never lifts.

From Tchaikovsky's day to our own – and no doubt beyond – theories abound as to what Tchaikovsky was saying with his Sixth Symphony. The speculation started after the very first performance, when Nikolay Rimsky-Korsakov, who attended the concert, asked Tchaikovsky whether there was a 'programme' to the new work, in other words whether it told a particular story. Tchaikovsky responded that there was, but he refused to divulge it.

The title *Pathétique* has been taken to reflect the mood that Tchaikovsky was in when he composed it. Whether we believe Modest that it was he who suggested it, or whether it was Tchaikovsky himself, the fact remains that the word can be used to mean either 'deserving of pity' or 'passionate'.* Whatever the theory, the facts of the music can be moulded to fit it.

We can be certain of the following. In the period that Tchaikovsky was composing his Symphony No. 6, which he dedicated to his nephew Bob Davydov, he was established in a house he loved. There was domestic stability in his life for the first time.

He had achieved more success than any Russian composer in history. He had equalled, and then surpassed, every name that he had been compared to in his earlier years.

He had plans for the future – concerts in St Petersburg and Moscow, followed by a European tour taking in Amsterdam, Helsinki and London.

---

* As it can with Beethoven's Piano Sonata No. 8, also labelled *Pathétique*.

He was also considering invitations from Odessa, Kharkov, Warsaw, Frankfurt and others.

We also know that he was prone to regular bouts of depression. He had lost his beloved sister and her daughter, and several close friends had died in the preceding months, including Apukhtin. It is also true that he continued to mourn the loss of his mother throughout his life, as we know from his annual diary entries on the anniversary of her death.

His general health was not good. In letters he complained continuously about headaches and poor digestion. In recent years he had taken to drinking heavily. His friends and family remarked on it, and tried to persuade him to reduce his intake, but to no avail. He was also a chain smoker of strong cigarettes.

Always a hard worker, over the previous decade he had driven himself to the point of exhaustion. He kept late hours and when he was working he ate irregularly, despite the best efforts of loyal Aleksey.

People as far afield as New York, and as close to home as his own family, had remarked on how prematurely he had aged.

There is one more thing we know. On the evening of 9 October 1893, when Tchaikovsky, at the age of fifty-three years and a little over five months, boarded a train in Moscow for the familiar journey to St Petersburg to conduct the premiere of his Symphony No. 6, it was the last journey he would take.

Above
Tchaikovsky's draft of the Sixth Symphony.

Postscript

As news spread that Tchaikovsky had died, streams of people came to Modest's apartment in St Petersburg to pay their respects. Soon there were two lines of mourners on the staircase to the top floor, one ascending, one descending.

Tchaikovsky lay in an open coffin. No fewer than four requiems were sung, those who could not get into the apartment listening on the landing and staircase outside. A death mask was made. A portrait of the composer was placed in the foyer of the Mariinsky Theatre, wreathed in black and garlanded in flowers.

The funeral was set for 28 October, three days after his death, and was to take place in the Kazan Cathedral in St Petersburg, the first time such an honour had been granted to a commoner. The building could hold six thousand, and admission would be by ticket only. More than sixty thousand applied. In the end eight thousand mourners crammed in.

By the time of the funeral, more than three hundred wreaths had arrived, not only from within Russia but from across Europe.[1] The coffin was borne by members of Tchaikovsky's family alongside two singers who had performed in his operas, one nearly thirty years previously, the other more recently: two different generations chosen to personify the length of his career.

After the service in the cathedral, the cortège made its way to the Alexander Nevsky Cemetery. There was total silence from the crowds lining both sides of the route. The royal family watched the procession, and the tsar was heard to say, 'We have many dukes and barons, but only one Tchaikovsky.'[*2]

---

[*] Reminiscent of Beethoven's barb to his patron Prince Lichnowsky: 'There are many princes and noblemen; there is only one Beethoven.'

Above

Tchaikovsky's funeral
procession, 1893.

Traffic had been diverted, but it still took four hours for the cortège to reach the cemetery. There, people crowded in to watch as Tchaikovsky was buried alongside Glinka, Borodin and Mussorgsky.

In 1897 a monument with a bust of Tchaikovsky was erected on a pedestal over his grave, surrounded by a weeping Muse and an angel with outstretched wings bearing a cross. The following year a seated statue of the composer was placed in the St Petersburg Conservatory, where he had spent so many years.

At a memorial concert Adele aus der Ohe – the German pianist who had so impressed Tchaikovsky in New York – performed. She later wrote:

> It was difficult to play, I could hardly see the keys for tears. People felt that a great and noble man was gone and that the hope of musical Russia had found a fast utterance in that Sixth Symphony, which they called his song.[3]

Nadezhda von Meck was too ill to attend the funeral of the man she so admired, although she sent an expensive funeral wreath. She was by this time largely incapacitated and found it difficult to move.

Her daughter-in-law Anna, daughter of Sasha and Lev Davydov, was asked how her mother-in-law had endured Tchaikovsky's death. She replied: 'She did not endure it.'[4] Nadezhda von Meck died three months after Tchaikovsky.

The union of the two families ended unhappily. Nadezhda von Meck's son Nikolay was executed in the first wave of the Stalinist Terror in 1929 under a false charge of sabotage. Anna Davydova lived into the Second World War and died during the German occupation of 1942. They had no children.

In the year after Tchaikovsky's death, Modest visited Fanny Dürbach, governess to the young Tchaikovsky in Votkinsk. He noted down her recollections of his famous brother for the biography he intended to write. He also took back several of the composer's exercise books and childhood letters, which she had kept for half a century and had shown to Tchaikovsky when he visited her. She died in 1901 at the age of seventy-nine.

To his family's chagrin, Tchaikovsky had bequeathed his house to his servant and companion Aleksey. Modest bought the house back from Aleksey and turned it into a museum to the composer, which it remains to this day. He also produced a massive three-volume biography of his brother, which eschewed total honesty in favour of portraying Tchaikovsky in the best possible light. It was nonetheless heavily censored during the Soviet regime. Modest failed to find fame as a dramatist and opera librettist, and died in 1916 at the age of fifty-six.

Like Nadezhda von Meck, Antonina Tchaikovskaya sent a large wreath to sit alongside her husband's coffin. She chose forget-me-nots, tied with blue ribbon.

Antonina continued to live an unhappy life. Tchaikovsky – his feelings of guilt and obligation persisting to the end – left her a monthly pension of 100 roubles in his will. She moved from Moscow to St Petersburg to be near him, taking up residence close to the Alexander Nevsky Cemetery.

Soon after his death, however, she began to display signs of an emotional disorder that was diagnosed as persecution mania. In October 1896 she was admitted to the St Petersburg Hospital of St Nicholas the Wonderworker for the emotionally disturbed. In February 1900 she was released, but was returned there eighteen months later with a diagnosis of chronic paranoia.

A month later, thanks to the intervention of Tchaikovsky's brother Anatoly, she was transferred to a more comfortable psychiatric hospital outside the city. There she spent the last ten years of her life.

In later life she wrote or dictated her memoirs, which have been described as 'naive, superficial and not very intelligent'. They do, however, reveal a woman devoted to honouring the memory of her husband, and her belief in his greatness. She puts down the failure of their marriage to an enormous misunderstanding between them. She goes into no further intimate detail.[5]

Antonina died of pneumonia on 16 February 1917, aged sixty-eight, and was buried at the Uspensky Cemetery in St Petersburg. Her grave has not survived.

Tchaikovsky had high hopes for Bob Davydov. When Bob was just eight years of age, his uncle spotted in him a remarkable aptitude for music as well as for drawing. He also wrote poetry. He was convinced Bob would grow up to be an artist – either a painter or poet.

There is evidence that Tchaikovsky's deepening devotion to his nephew, which amounted to infatuation, was not reciprocated. Bob clearly found it difficult to accept his uncle's unconditional love. In a letter of 25 January 1890, he wrote:

> I just can't reconcile myself to the fact that you love me, not because I am good but because I am who I am, and that if I turn out to be bad (as is actually the case), then you'll still not stop loving me, since I won't have stopped being myself.[6]

Bob Davydov, like his uncle, was homosexual. At the School of Jurisprudence he formed a lasting relationship with his classmate Baron Rudolph Buchshoevden, to Tchaikovsky's distress.

Bob did not pursue either the musical or the literary talent his uncle had spotted in him. At the age of twenty-two he joined the army, but frequently took sick leave and resigned from active military service in 1900.

He moved into the house at Klin, occupying the rooms that Modest had added to the house five years after his brother's death, preserving the original part as a museum. He was comfortably off, his uncle having left all royalties from his works to him, with instructions to divide them among relatives, as well as all copyrights.

As his mother and sister had done before him, he turned increasingly to morphine and alcohol, soon becoming addicted to both. He began to suffer nervous breakdowns, as well as hallucinations and bouts of delirium tremens.

In December 1906 Modest was in Moscow; he was planning to return to Klin but was delayed by having to attend a performance of one of Tchaikovsky's string quartets. When he finally reached Klin, it was to discover that Bob had shot himself. He had just turned thirty-five years of age.

AFTERWORD

The town of Votkinsk, where Russia's most famous composer was born on 25 April 1840, sits on the banks of a picturesque lake in the Urals. Yet all is not as it seems. The lake is not a lake but a huge reservoir, 11 kilometres wide and 15 kilometres long, dug by a labour force of more than a thousand people in the mid-eighteenth century, and held by a dam built for the town's ironworks.

The town of Votkinsk was not a town when Tchaikovsky was born there. It was a settlement created entirely for employees of the state-run ironworks, who numbered as many as ten thousand. The house occupied by the Tchaikovsky family was one of the largest and best furnished of any in the area, sitting on the banks of the reservoir. It came with the job of ironworks manager.

After he was appointed to the position, Ilya Tchaikovsky moved to Votkinsk on his own. He made some renovations and wrote endearingly to his wife:

> *The house we are going to live in is very good and spacious . . . The furniture has been placed, the pictures have been hung, the house has become really nice and I think you will kiss me when you come, and your kiss is better than any medal or a rank for me.*[1]

Ilya's position brought him both status and respect. There were not many who could boast, as Ilya could and most certainly did, that a future tsar had stayed under his roof.

The bedroom that the infant Pyotr shared with his elder brother Nikolay looked out over the reservoir, on which swans were said to swim in the nineteenth century. Fanny Dürbach recalled that Pyotr would kneel at the window gazing out over the water. Could it have been an early inspiration for the future much loved ballet? Perhaps.

What most certainly did begin on the banks of the reservoir was Tchaikovsky's lifelong love of Russian folk music. Fishermen would pass the hours in song, before they – and the Tchaikovsky family – enjoyed what Fanny described as the best sunset she had ever seen, the dying rays spreading across the water from the opposite bank.

The house in which Tchaikovsky spent the happiest years of his life – a sentiment echoed by Fanny – fell into disrepair in the early twentieth century, housing different government organisations that paid scant attention to its musical heritage, bar a memorial plaque that hung outside between 1909 and 1917.

It was renovated in 1940, five years after Votkinsk was granted the status of a town, and opened as a museum commemorating its famous resident with the title 'Museum of Happy Recollections'. The rooms and outbuildings have been restored, and a visitor today can feel the comfort, almost opulence, of the surroundings in which Pyotr spent his idyllic childhood.

The children's room on the mezzanine still has a beautiful view from the window, although there are now more trees along the bank than there were nearly two hundred years ago, and the town clearly visible on the opposite side of the reservoir did not exist in his day.

On the right-hand side of the room is a small platform covered in green velvet and surrounded by a frame. It was on this mini 'stage' that Pyotr and Nikolay would create 'living pictures' – moving to music until mother or father called out 'Stop!' and they would assume a theatrical pose.

Standing against the wall in the reconstructed study where Ilya ran the ironworks is a firescreen showing the delightful image of a family enjoying the countryside. The father is entertaining the family on a guitar. This was embroidered by Alexandra for her husband while she was pregnant with Pyotr.

Above

Tchaikovsky's birthplace is now a museum.

Left The room in which he was born.

Right The Tchaikovsky children's play room.

The actual room in which Pyotr was born has been lovingly reconstructed. The furniture is all reproduction, but high on the wall above the crib is an icon of the Virgin Mary said to have witnessed Pyotr's birth. On the reverse side is the inscription: 'To the God-loving head of the Votkinsk Plant Ilya Tchaikovsky'.

Without doubt the most valuable item in the house (dating from a few years after the family left) is a grand piano by the Viennese piano maker Franz Wirth, with the name 'Wirth' ornately inscribed on the upright board above the keys. It was purchased by Alexandra Tchaikovsky when the family lived in St Petersburg in 1852.

It was only when the piano was renovated in 2006 that an inscription was found on the reverse side of a small panel in childish handwriting: *Pyotr dorachina* ('Pyotr is a little fool'). The likelihood is it was written by Pyotr's brother Nikolay, but knowing his intolerance of his own mistakes, it is quite possible Pyotr wrote the words himself.

Our delightful guide, Maria Svetlakova, allowed my wife Nula and me to touch the keys that the fingers of the great composer once touched – as she put it. Also on display is the large wooden flute that Ilya enjoyed playing but struggled to master.

Remember the time a frustrated Pyotr drummed his fingers so hard on the window that he broke the pane? That pane today appears cracked, the jagged lines helpfully painted onto the glass by an artist.

Also in the house is the desk that Tchaikovsky owned in his postgraduate years in Moscow, on which he wrote many early works, including the Fantasy Overture: *Romeo and Juliet*, and the Piano Concerto No. 1.

Musical recitals are routinely held inside the house in the summer months, and in an ornate pergola outside in summer. Since 1958 there has been an annual music festival devoted to the composer in his birthday week in the nearby state capital of Izhevsk, and a mile or so along the reservoir bank from Votkinsk lies the small town of Chaykovsky.

Votkinsk itself, lying west of the Urals in the Udmurt Republic, and then as now rich in iron ore deposits, was founded purely for the manufacture of iron. Its main product was anchors for the Russian navy. To this day an anchor is emblazoned on Votkinsk's coat of arms and town flag.

Many English engineers came to Votkinsk to help with the extraction of iron ore, using skills acquired during the boom years of the Industrial Revolution. There are residents today proud of their English heritage.

Ilya Tchaikovsky greatly expanded production at the ironworks and in 1848, his final year in Votkinsk, he began the building of steamships. The more one learns of the Tchaikovskys' time in Votkinsk, the harder it becomes to understand why Ilya gave it all up for what turned out to be

"The more one learns of the Tchaikovskys' time in Votkinsk, the harder it becomes to understand why Ilya gave it all up."

a non-existent job in Moscow. The 'small town' life of the provinces must really have got him down.

When I suggested to Maria that it was sad for Pyotr that his idyllic childhood came to such a sudden and unwelcome end, and that he might have been much more content had he remained in Votkinsk, she smiled ruefully and said that had he stayed in the Urals he might never have received the stimulation that led him to create the masterpieces he went on to produce.

There is an irony in the fact that the two museums in Russia devoted to its most famous musical son are the house in which he was born, and the last house he occupied. So peripatetic was Tchaikovsky that it is easy to lose track of his numerous addresses in between, in Moscow and particularly St Petersburg. But few remain, and in any case none held any significance for him.

It was only at the age of fifty-two that he finally found the house of his dreams, the only one he actually owned in his lifetime, and it was a tragedy that he was able to enjoy it for less than two years before his early and untimely death.

Klin is today an unprepossessing town situated about fifty miles north-west of Moscow, reached in around three hours by road, heavy traffic all the way, via the unprepossessing north-west suburbs of Moscow, through unprepossessing industrial areas outside the city.

When Tchaikovsky knew Klin, it was a very different place indeed. First mentioned in 1317, it was celebrating its 700th anniversary when Nula and I visited.[*] Klin was one of several attractive small towns and villages in a rural setting a full day's carriage ride from the big city, and it still sits on the main railway route from Moscow to St Petersburg, though the high-speed train no longer stops there.

Tchaikovsky spent eight years living in the area, particularly during warm summers, relishing the outdoors and fresh air. He enjoyed long walks, notebook in hand to jot down musical ideas.[†] Of the various towns and villages in the region, Klin in particular appealed to him. It had a small station, and was on the direct rail route from Moscow to St Petersburg. The

---

[*] In October 2017, to the consternation of musicians, the statue of Tchaikovsky that stood in the central square was moved to the outskirts of the town, as residents said they wanted a different monument for the town's 700th anniversary.

[†] Reminiscent of Beethoven in the Austrian countryside around Vienna.

Above

Tchaikovsky's
house in Klin.

house he eventually bought in 1892 was one of the last on the outskirts travelling north to St Petersburg.

In his will Tchaikovsky left the house to his faithful servant Aleksey Sofronov. He in turn sold it – for a considerable sum of money, causing deep resentment in the Tchaikovsky family – to Modest Tchaikovsky.

The sale took place in 1897, four years after Tchaikovsky's death, during which time the Sofronov family had continued to live in the house. Bob Davydov sold the Davydov estate at Kamenka, which Tchaikovsky knew and loved so well, partly to help finance the purchase. He also planted many hundreds of Tchaikovsky's favourite flower, lily of the valley, a tradition that is continued to this day.

Modest added a wing to the house and restored the rooms to the condition they were in when his brother lived there. He opened it as a museum and memorial to Pyotr Tchaikovsky, which it remains to this day.

In his turn, Modest left the house not to the Tchaikovsky family but to the Russian Musical Society to be preserved as a museum, no doubt feeling that was the best way to secure his brother's legacy. The house survived the 1917 Revolution, and remained a museum by order of the Soviet authorities.

The only time the house has been threatened was when the German army of the Third Reich reached the outskirts of Moscow in 1941.

German soldiers requisitioned the house and billeted themselves in it for three short weeks in December. Before that, all the contents were safely evacuated to Votkinsk, from where they were returned after the war. Fortunately for posterity the Germans left the house intact.

Before Modest Tchaikovsky added the extension, the house was fairly small and compact. Tchaikovsky, his tastes as frugal as ever, occupied just two rooms upstairs and a kitchen and dining room downstairs.

When we visited in October 2017, our guide – as she took us up the staircase – told us to imagine we were going up the stairs with Tchaikovsky himself. It is easy to do. The house looks and feels much as Tchaikovsky knew it.

If there is a certain darkness, even oppressiveness, to the house – in contrast to the lightness and happiness that imbues the house at Votkinsk – it is due largely to the hundreds of trees that surround it, blocking out the light in summer and resembling stark skeletons in winter.[*]

The music room contains a grand piano, on which recitals are played today, and portraits of Mozart and Beethoven. While Tchaikovsky admired Beethoven, he simply adored Mozart, whom he called 'the Christ of music'.

Also on the wall is a portrait of Désirée Artôt, the singer Tchaikovsky came so close to marrying. A recording of the Romance Tchaikovsky dedicated to her is played in the room today. It is a melancholy piece of music.[†]

On the first floor is Tchaikovsky's favourite room, a light and airy breakfast room. It was here that he would take morning tea each day, read the newspapers and go through his mail. At the height of his fame, he would receive laudatory letters from around the world.

It has been estimated that in his lifetime Tchaikovsky received at least seven thousand letters from over one thousand correspondents, and wrote five thousand letters in reply! Work is continuing on a definitive edition of the entire correspondence. Fifteen volumes have so far been published (in Russian only). It is not even certain all the letters have yet been uncovered.

Tchaikovsky was an avid reader. All his life there would be a pile of books on his bedside table, and he read every night to help settle himself to sleep. The huge library he assembled at Klin included books on Russian history, novels and poetry by his great heroes Pushkin, Chekhov and Tolstoy, as well as philosophy by the likes of Descartes and Spinoza. There is also a full-length book on ants – testimony to Tchaikovsky's love of nature!

---

[*] Which is exactly how Giuseppina Verdi described the Villa Sant'Agatha, which her husband Giuseppe loved so much.

[†] See p. 86.

His favourite English authors were Dickens and Thackeray. He was competent enough in the English language to be able to read them, though he did not trust himself to speak English in conversation.

In a large ground-floor room today given over to photographs and mementoes of Tchaikovsky's life, there is one truly extraordinary exhibit. It purports to be a recording of Tchaikovsky's voice, among others.

The recording was made by Julius Block, a Russian of German descent who was fascinated by the phonograph, newly invented by Thomas Edison. Block managed to gather together a number of prominent musicians and persuaded them to talk into a phonograph. Among them were Anton Rubinstein and Pyotr Tchaikovsky.

The recording is just 1 minute and 21 seconds long. Several voices are heard, including, according to the label, that of Tchaikovsky. He speaks three times, saying in Russian: 'This trill could be better'; 'Block is good but Edison is better'; 'Who just spoke? It seems to have been Safonov.' (Vassily Safonov, pianist and conductor, was also present.) Tchaikovsky then whistles.

His voice is surprisingly high-pitched and shrill, which could of course be explained by the excitement of knowing he was about to hear his own recorded voice. But that contrasts with contemporary descriptions of him having a pleasing baritone voice. This has led some to doubt the veracity of the recording, which came to light only in 1997. Further doubt is cast by the fact that, although Rubinstein is labelled as speaking, one of those present said Rubinstein flatly refused to speak into the machine.

Nevertheless, visitors to the house at Klin are left in no doubt that this is the sole recording (so far discovered) of Tchaikovsky's voice.

There are two aspects of Tchaikovsky's life that are not routinely mentioned in tours of either his birthplace in Votkinsk or his final residence in Klin. These are his homosexuality and the manner of his death.

In both locations, at the end of our private tour in English, I felt obliged to raise both subjects. How could I claim to present 'the man revealed' without doing so? Since both topics had been conspicuous by their absence, I felt some trepidation when I said, 'There are just a couple of other points I wonder if I could discuss . . .'

In Votkinsk our guide smiled when she heard the word 'homosexuality'. I had the impression she was used to being asked about it. She said that it was well known that Tchaikovsky was homosexual, but that to this day Russian people do not like to speak of it. In fact, she said, many refuse even now to accept it.

She was herself reluctant to discuss it further. She quoted Tchaikovsky as saying that after his death, 'I fear people will look into my correspondence and discover things I do not want them to know.' 'We respect that,' she told us. 'We do not want to intrude into someone's private life.'

On the vexed, and disputed, matter of how Tchaikovsky died, she was quite clear. Cholera, she said, had been established as the cause of death. There was no question of suicide, since he had immediate plans for the future.

In Klin we had a similar reaction to both questions. On the subject of homosexuality, our guide said, 'It is true. He was homosexual. Russian people dislike talking about homosexuality. Now we may talk about it, but we still dislike it.'

Regarding the manner of Tchaikovsky's death, for her it was cut and dried. Cholera has been documented. There is no evidence to suggest suicide.

The house in Klin, as well as being a museum, is now the most important research centre into Tchaikovsky's life and works in the world. It is here that the thousands of letters are being edited and published, and here that scholarship into his works and life continues.

I was fortunate to secure a meeting with Ada Aynbinder, Head of the Department of Manuscripts and Printed Sources at Klin.

She confirmed to me that there was no doubt about Tchaikovsky's homosexuality. Just as our two guides had done, she acknowledged the widespread reluctance to speak about it. In fact, she claimed, 'We are more reluctant to speak about it today than they were in his own time.'

It was Ada who gave me statistics about the number of letters Tchaikovsky received and wrote. She told me that many were censored during the Soviet era, and that sometime soon these letters would be republished with the redacted passages restored.

Above Tchaikovsky's house in Klin.

Left The desk at which Tchaikovsky composed his final works, including the Symphony No. 6, the *Pathétique*.

Right The music room. Note the portrait of Beethoven on the far wall.

In particular, she said, several new volumes of letters both to and from Nadezhda von Meck would be published. She assured me that nothing currently planned for publication would throw any light on his homosexuality.

On the subject of Tchaikovsky's death, she was forthcoming – and adamant. There was no question but that Tchaikovsky contracted cholera, as his mother had done before him, and that he died as a result.

She reminded me that Tchaikovsky's father at one stage had contracted the disease, but recovered from it. Cholera was prevalent and almost constant in the city of St Petersburg. Tchaikovsky contracted cholera in a mild form in early 1893. He took medicines for it, but they were ineffective.

With the premiere of his *Pathétique* Symphony attracting hostile reviews, his mood was low. As always he took criticism deeply to heart. In fact, said Ada, he was devastated that such a personal work had been attacked so vociferously.

Still suffering mild symptoms of cholera, in late 1893 he became depressed and rundown. Plenty of restaurants in St Petersburg, Ada Aynbinder told me, were casual about serving boiled water. Tchaikovsky, perhaps himself careless in his despondent state, drank contaminated water that proved fatal.

What about Modest's description of him deliberately drinking unboiled water in his apartment, or Yuri Davydov's more melodramatic account of Tchaikovsky demanding unboiled water in Leiner's restaurant and drinking it before anyone could stop him? 'You will have to ask them,' she said, smiling facetiously. She discounted all such claims.

I raised the question of Tchaikovsky lying in an open coffin in Modest's apartment, and indeed his forehead being kissed. Was not the argument for suicide reinforced by this, since coffins of cholera victims were always sealed?

Not so, she countered immediately, clearly familiar with the claim. It was not true that cholera victims were always placed in sealed coffins, and Tchaikovsky's own mother was the proof. It is documented that she lay in an open coffin, and her children were brought into the room to kiss her forehead. None of them contracted cholera as a result.

The custom in Tchaikovsky's day, she told me, was for the coffin to be open for family and friends to pay respects, then sealed for the funeral.

As if to clinch the argument, she told me Tchaikovsky's death had been certified as being caused by cholera by several doctors, all experts in their field. The death certificate, and other necessary paperwork, was signed and countersigned in accordance with procedure. Furthermore, since cholera was so endemic in St Petersburg, the newspapers carried a daily list of victims in its pages. Tchaikovsky's name had appeared, along with others. A cover-up would have been impossible.

The conversation was informative and friendly, as it was with our two guides in Votkinsk and Klin. None was reluctant to address the issue of either Tchaikovsky's homosexuality or his cause of death.

I confess that after voluminous reading, but before my research trip to Russia, I was inclined to subscribe to the theory that Tchaikovsky committed suicide. Given the sensitive nature of the man, the ease with which he was wounded, it would not have been out of character.

I returned from Russia fairly certain that the official account, that he had accidentally drunk contaminated water and contracted cholera, which proved fatal, was correct. Modest's and Yuri's accounts, I believe, were deliberately dramatised for effect. There was, after all, a Tchaikovsky 'industry' within days of his death. They had a story to tell, and we know that many 'facts' presented by Modest in his voluminous biography of his brother are either exaggerated or might be incorrect.

There is yet another theory that gained a certain amount of currency in the second half of the twentieth century: that Tchaikovsky had been conducting a homosexual relationship with the nephew of the tsar – as some versions have it, even his son.

Ordered by Tsar Alexander III – or, in other versions, by a 'court of honour' – to stand trial for sodomy, with suicide the only alternative, Tchaikovsky chose suicide. The tsar – or the court – gave him a revolver, as well as a ring filled with arsenic. He could choose his method, and – ruefully comparing himself with Socrates – chose to empty the poison into a glass of wine.[2]

Of the three most comprehensive biographies in English, Anthony Holden regards suicide, as ordered by the court of honour, as proved beyond doubt. David Brown cites the source material, stating that it deserves study but cannot be considered conclusive. Alexander Poznansky dismisses it entirely. All three rely on the same sources; each draws a different conclusion.

I was keen to know what opinion today's leading Russian musicians hold, and I am enormously grateful to two of the busiest maestros on the planet for taking time to talk to me.

Both were born in St Petersburg/Leningrad and, like Tchaikovsky, attended the St Petersburg/Leningrad Conservatory where they both shared the same teachers. Both have recorded, or are in the process of recording, the complete cycle of Tchaikovsky symphonies and other works.

Semyon Bychkov, current Music Director of the Czech Philharmonic, is in no doubt about the cause of Tchaikovsky's death. It was suicide, he told me, brought about by shame over his homosexuality. Tchaikovsky had

"Given the sensitive nature of the man, the ease with which he was wounded, suicide would not have been out of character."

become involved with a young man who was the son of one of the tsar's closest confidants, and that simply could not be tolerated.

He said that, growing up in Leningrad in the Soviet era, it was accepted totally that Tchaikovsky took his own life. There had never been any uncertainty; it was local legend.

As to the question of how Tchaikovsky took his life, Maestro Bychkov shrugged. 'We will never know,' he said. He was adamant that cholera could not have been the cause of death. Had it been, Tchaikovsky would never have lain in an open coffin, and no one would have kissed him for fear of contracting the disease.

I put the counter argument to him, as presented to me by Ada Aynbinder. Again he shrugged. They have always tried to hide the truth, he said. They do not want to admit that this great Russian hero took his own life.

What, then, are we to make of the Symphony No. 6, the *Pathétique*? I asked him. Does the darkness in it lend weight to the theory of suicide, pointing to his resignation to death?

'It has nothing to do with resignation!' Bychkov said vehemently. 'If you study the score,' he said, 'you will find how utterly radical it is. There is syncopation where you do not expect it, harmonies that clash with the key signatures, even the waltz in the second movement is not in triple time – I know of no other waltz like it in music,' he said. 'The symphony is not resignation, it is defiance. This symphony is Tchaikovsky's defiance in the face of death. Listen to my recording of it, and you will see what I mean.'

Vasily Petrenko, Chief Conductor of the Royal Liverpool Philharmonic Orchestra, takes a slightly more nuanced view. He told me that Tchaikovsky believed all his life in fate: 'What is to be will be.'

At the age of fifty-three Tchaikovsky was approaching old age. He was drinking regularly; he had stomach problems. He had no desire to be remembered as an old man. The depression from which he habitually suffered was stronger than ever, made worse by Bob's evident difficulty in accepting his uncle's unconditional love.

Vasily Petrenko told me he could not imagine that Tchaikovsky had drunk contaminated water by accident. It was totally credible that Tchaikovsky, in Leiner's restaurant, probably a little bit drunk, ordered water, was told that there was only unboiled water, but insisted on it being brought. He probably said something along the lines of 'I'll drink it anyway. Fate will determine if I develop cholera. If my time has come, it has come.'

It was a form of Russian roulette, Petrenko said, which accords with Tchaikovsky's character and state of mind. His music backs this up. The last four symphonies – the Fourth, Fifth, *Manfred* and Sixth – all deal with fate. What is mortality? How can we overcome it?

Petrenko agrees with Bychkov that the Sixth Symphony, the *Pathétique*, is deeply significant. The second movement is a waltz, but a corrupted waltz. The third movement, loud and triumphant, provokes the audience to applaud.* This should be the climax of the symphony, the final movement, which would accord with the structure of the Fourth and Fifth. But Tchaikovsky subverts this scheme. He writes a fourth and final movement that descends into the depths. It is there to shock us.

'Definitely not resignation,' Petrenko told me, 'but an acknowledgement that everything must come to an end, and we are powerless to change that.'

Whatever the cause of death, and putting all controversy aside, we do know where Tchaikovsky died, and where he lies now. In both cases the answer is in the city he loved most, or disliked least, St Petersburg.

The 'Venice of the North', with over 60 rivers and canals, nearly 350 bridges, more than 30 islands, is as elegant today as it was when Tchaikovsky knew it. If Moscow is the ancient capital of Russia, it has little to show for it – the walled Kremlin and St Basil's Cathedral in Red Square being the main exceptions.

After the 1917 Revolution, Joseph Stalin ordered much of Moscow's old imperial past to be destroyed. So for evidence of Russia under tsarist rule, it is to St Petersburg that we must turn, with the Hermitage, the Winter Palace, and more than 300 palaces of the nobility.

Our guide, Olga Miheyeva, spoke with pride of the fact that St Petersburg is culturally, and historically, the most important city in Russia. She also told me, somewhat to my surprise, that in many years of conducting guided tours, she had never before been asked to locate sites connected to Tchaikovsky.

In the composer's day as in ours, the main thoroughfare is Nevsky Prospekt, which runs right through the city from north to south, with its restaurants and shops crowded by night as well as by day. Tchaikovsky was a regular at various eating and drinking establishments. He liked nothing more than to take long walks to and from the Conservatory, stopping for refreshment on the way.

As if to contradict everything I have said about the splendour of St Petersburg, Leiner's restaurant, where Tchaikovsky might well have drunk

---

*Which in performance it often does.

Above

Tchaikovsky's
tomb at Tikhvin
Cemetery.

contaminated water, is today an unprepossessing Burger King.* That aside, walking along Nevsky Prospekt it is easy to feel a kinship with Tchaikovsky.

Modest's apartment block is little changed on the outside from Tchaikovsky's day. The building is an old one situated on a street corner. Modest's apartment was on the fourth floor at the top of the building, the windows stretching round on both sides of the corner.

Today it is in private hands and request for entry is declined. On the first floor of the block, however, there is a small hotel named 'Old Vienna'. One of the rooms is dedicated to Tchaikovsky, his image gazing from pictures, newspaper reports, even the wallpaper.

The hotel has a restaurant, which in Tchaikovsky's day was a café. The proprietor told us proudly it is beyond doubt that Tchaikovsky and his brother frequently stopped for a coffee there, if only to fortify themselves before climbing the stairs to the top floor.

It was in this apartment that Tchaikovsky died, and where he lay in an open coffin for friends and family to bid him farewell.

Tchaikovsky was buried in the Tikhvin Cemetery, which belongs to the Alexander Nevsky Monastery, in the centre of the city. Of the nearly two

---

* It is situated next to the Literary Café, which is often mistakenly described as the establishment where Tchaikovsky dined. It is certainly where Pushkin ate for the last time before taking part in a fatal duel in 1837.

hundred graves, many belong to artists – musicians, actors, writers, painters – as well as statesmen, military leaders and scientists.

Along the path at the northern end of the cemetery lie, in order, Russia's great composers: Glinka, Balakirev, Rimsky-Korsakov, Mussorgsky, Borodin, Glazunov. At the top of the path lies Peter Ilyich Tchaikovsky, his monument larger and grander than any of his contemporaries.

The bust of the composer is held in place by the hands of an angel, her wings spread high on either side of a large cross. A larger angel is seated at the base of the pedestal, singing from a manuscript. On the day we visited, there were fresh flowers on his grave.

Across the path, directly opposite, is the grave of Anton Rubinstein. A bust of the founder of the St Petersburg Conservatory sits atop a pillar. His stern gaze is directed straight at Tchaikovsky.

Even in death, the composer is unable to escape the man who was so mercilessly critical of his early works.

A final word on the vexed question of the cause of Tchaikovsky's death. Only one course of action is likely to settle the matter beyond doubt – exhuming his remains and subjecting them to scientific analysis. There is no appetite, either in Russia or elsewhere in the world, to have this done.[*]

We are therefore left with several conflicting sets of facts and theories. We have academic opinion on the one hand, local legend on the other. Which carries more weight?

It would be folly to say the book is closed on the issue of how Tchaikovsky died. A lock of Beethoven's hair, and fragments of his skull, have told us much about his health, details that only a few years ago would have been considered impossible.

Who knows what new evidence might yet come to light in letters still to be discovered? Who knows what precious information might be held in private hands somewhere in the world?

For the present, though, the case is unresolved. The cause of death of Russia's greatest composer, the most natural melodist who ever lived, remains a mystery.

---

[*] Unlike in Poland, where applications to allow examination of Chopin's heart, which is preserved in a jar of cognac in the Holy Cross Church in Warsaw, are repeatedly refused by both government and church. In the most recent investigation, in 2017, the first since 1945, the jar remained sealed.

TIMELINE

1840
25 APRIL[*] Pyotr Ilyich Tchaikovsky is born in Votkinsk.

1841
28 DECEMBER Birth of sister Alexandra (Sasha).

1843
10 APRIL Birth of brother Ippolit (Polya).

1844
NOVEMBER Fanny Dürbach becomes governess to the Tchaikovsky family in Votkinsk.

1845
Takes piano lessons with Mariya Palchikova.

1848
SEPTEMBER The family moves to Moscow, leaving Fanny Dürbach behind in Votkinsk.
NOVEMBER The family moves to St Petersburg, and Pyotr is sent to boarding school.
DECEMBER Pyotr suffers a serious bout of measles, leaving him debilitated.

1849
MAY The family moves to Alapayevsk in the Ural mountains.

1850
1 MAY The birth of twin brothers Anatoly and Modest.
22 AUGUST Sees a production of Glinka's *A Life for the Tsar*, which makes a lasting impression.
SEPTEMBER Enrols in the Imperial School of Jurisprudence in St Petersburg.

1852
MAY The family leaves Alapayevsk and joins Pyotr in St Petersburg.

1854
13 JUNE Alexandra Tchaikovskaya, Pyotr's mother, dies from cholera.

1859
13 MAY Graduates from the Imperial School of Jurisprudence.
JUNE Begins work as a civil servant in the Ministry of Justice.

1861
JULY–AUGUST Travels outside Russia for the first time, across Europe, with Pisarev, a friend of his father.

1862
SEPTEMBER Enrols as a student in the newly opened St Petersburg Conservatory.

1863
11 APRIL Resigns from the Ministry of Justice.

1864
SUMMER Composes his first orchestral piece, Overture: *The Storm*.

1865
30 AUGUST The first public performance of a work by Tchaikovsky: *Characteristic Dances* conducted by Johann Strauss II in Pavlovsk.
27 NOVEMBER Conducts the premiere of his Overture in F.

---

[*] All dates are given in the Julian calendar; see p. ix (footnote).

29 December Premiere of the cantata *Ode to Joy* at the St Petersburg Conservatory graduation ceremony.

1866

January Leaves St Petersburg for Moscow, becomes a teacher of musical theory at the Russian Musical Society under Nikolay Rubinstein.

4 March Nikolay Rubinstein conducts Overture in F.

Summer Begins work on Symphony No. 1, 'Winter Daydreams'.

1 September Employed at the newly opened Moscow Conservatory.

1867

March Begins work on his first opera, *The Voyevoda*.

June–August Spends the summer at Hapsal (Haapsalu), Estonia, where he composes three piano pieces, *Souvenir de Hapsal*.

1868

3 February Premiere of Symphony No. 1, Nikolay Rubinstein conducting.

29 July Completes work on *The Voyevoda*.

Summer Travels to Berlin and Paris with his friend Vladimir Shilovsky.

September Becomes romantically involved with the opera singer Désirée Artôt.

September–December Composes the symphonic fantasia *Fatum*.

1869

January–July Writes his second opera, *Undine*.

30 January Premiere of *The Voyevoda* at the Bolshoy Theatre in Moscow.

15 February Premiere of the symphonic fantasia *Fatum* in Moscow.

October Meeting with Balakirev in Moscow, following which he begins composition of the Fantasy Overture: *Romeo and Juliet*.

1870

February Starts work on his third opera, *The Oprichnik*.

1871

16 March The newly composed String Quartet No. 1 is performed at an all-Tchaikovsky concert in Moscow. The second movement, *Andante cantabile*, becomes instantly popular.

2 December Nephew Vladimir (Bob) Davydov is born.

1872

5 February Premiere of the revised *Romeo and Juliet* is a success.

20 March Completes work on *The Oprichnik*.

June–September Composes Symphony No. 2, 'Little Russian'.

1873

26 January Premiere of Symphony No. 2 in Moscow.

March–April Composes incidental music for Ostrovsky's play *The Snow Maiden*.

August–October Composes Symphonic Fantasia: *The Tempest*.

2 November Eduard Zak commits suicide.

7 December Premiere of Symphonic Fantasia: *The Tempest* in Moscow.

1874

10 March Premiere of String Quartet No. 2 in Moscow.

April Travels to Italy, visiting Venice, Rome, Naples and Florence.

12 April Premiere of *The Oprichnik* at the Mariinsky Theatre, St Petersburg.

June–August Composes the opera *Vakula the Smith*.

November Starts work on Piano Concerto No. 1.

24 December Plays Piano Concerto No. 1 for Nikolay Rubinstein, who delivers a scathing verdict.

1875

June–August Writes Symphony No. 3.

August Begins work on his first ballet, *Swan Lake*.

13 October Hans von Bülow gives the premiere of Piano Concerto No. 1 in Boston, USA.

November Meets Saint-Saëns in Moscow.

1 November Russian premiere of Piano Concerto No. 1 in St Petersburg.

7 November Premiere of Symphony No. 3 in Moscow.

1876

January Sees and is greatly impressed by a performance of Bizet's *Carmen* in Paris.

18 March Premiere of String Quartet No. 3 in Moscow.

April Completes work on *Swan Lake*.

July Travels to Vichy, France, to take the waters. Holidays with Modest and his deaf-mute pupil in Palavas-les-flots in southern France.

August Attends the premiere of Wagner's *Ring* cycle

in Bayreuth. Meets Franz Liszt but fails to meet Wagner.

19 August Tells Modest of his decision to marry.

September Composes *Marche slave* in aid of victims of war between Serbia and Turkey.

November Writes the symphonic fantasia *Francesca da Rimini*.

24 November Premiere of *Vakula the Smith* in St Petersburg.

December Composes *Rococo Variations* for cello and orchestra. First exchange of letters with Nadezhda von Meck, who becomes his patroness.

1877

January Forms close relationship with violinist Iosif Kotek.

March–May Makes sketches for his Symphony No. 4.

26 March Receives first letter from Antonina Milyukova declaring her love for him.

May Begins work on the opera *Eugene Onegin*.

20 May Meets Antonina for the first time in Moscow.

23 May Proposes marriage to Antonina.

6 July Marries Antonina at St George's Church in Moscow.

7–13 July The couple spend a disastrous honeymoon in St Petersburg.

27 July Travels to Kamenka on his own.

24 September Travels to Switzerland with his brother Anatoly.

October Nadezhda von Meck offers him a regular allowance.

1878

January Completes the Symphony No. 4 and *Eugene Onegin*.

10 February Premiere of Symphony No. 4 in Moscow with Nikolay Rubinstein conducting.

March Composes the Violin Concerto while staying in Clarens, Switzerland, with Iosif Kotek.

May Stays at Nadezhda von Meck's estate at Brailov, where he writes *Souvenir d'un lieu cher*.

November Resigns from the Moscow Conservatory.

December Settles in Florence, where he begins work on the opera *The Maid of Orleans*.

1879

17 March Premiere of *Eugene Onegin* in Moscow.

October Begins work on the Piano Concerto No. 2.

November Leaves for four-month trip to France and Italy.

1880

January Writes *Italian Capriccio* in Rome.

9 January His father Ilya dies at the age of eighty-four.

September–October Composes the Serenade for Strings.

October–November Composes the *1812 Overture*.

1881

14 February Leaves for trip to Vienna, Florence, Rome and Naples.

13 March Attends Nikolay Rubinstein's funeral in Paris.

June Begins work on the opera *Mazeppa*.

31 October Premiere of Piano Concerto No. 2 in New York.

22 November Premiere of Violin Concerto in Vienna with Adolph Brodsky as soloist.

1882

21 May Russian premiere of Piano Concerto No. 2 in Moscow by Sergey Taneyev.

8 August Premiere of *1812 Overture* in Moscow.

1883

January–May Stays in Paris, caring for his niece Tatyana, who is expecting an illegitimate child.

1884

3 February Premiere of *Mazeppa* in Moscow.

7 March Summoned to St Petersburg to have the Order of Saint Vladimir conferred on him by Tsar Alexander III.

19 October Premiere of *Eugene Onegin* in St Petersburg, an overwhelming success.

November Visits his dying friend Iosif Kotek in Switzerland.

1885

14 February Settles into a house of his own for the first time, which he rents in the country at Maidanovo near Klin outside Moscow.

April–September Composes the *Manfred Symphony*.

September Starts work on the opera *The Enchantress*.

1886

31 March Arrives in Tiflis, Georgia, where he spends a month with his brother Anatoly.

May–June Travels to Paris, where he meets Gabriel Fauré and Édouard Lalo.

1887

19 JANUARY Conducts the premiere of *Cherevichki* at the Bolshoy Theatre in Moscow.

MAY Completes the opera *The Enchantress*.

JUNE Second visit to Tiflis to see his brother Anatoly.

JULY–AUGUST Travels to Aachen to see his friend Nikolay Kondratyev, who is critically ill.

20 OCTOBER Conducts the premiere of *The Enchantress* at the Mariinsky Theatre in St Petersburg.

24 DECEMBER Embarks on his first conducting tour of Europe, during which he meets Brahms, Grieg, Mahler, Dvorak, Gounod and Delibes.

1888

24 APRIL Moves into a new house at Frolovskoye, near Klin.

MAY–OCTOBER Writes Symphony No. 5 and the Fantasy Overture: *Hamlet*.

OCTOBER Makes first sketches for the ballet *Sleeping Beauty*.

5 NOVEMBER Conducts the premiere of Symphony No. 5 in St Petersburg.

12 NOVEMBER Conducts the premiere of the Fantasy Overture: *Hamlet* in St Petersburg.

NOVEMBER–DECEMBER In Prague, where he conducts Symphony No. 5 and *Eugene Onegin*.

10 DECEMBER Conducts the Moscow premiere of Symphony No. 5.

1889

JANUARY Embarks on second European tour as conductor.

APRIL–MAY Visits Tiflis again to see his brother Anatoly.

AUGUST Completes work on *The Sleeping Beauty*.

1890

3 JANUARY Premiere of *Sleeping Beauty* at the Mariinsky Theatre in St Petersburg.

JANUARY–MARCH Stays in Florence, where he begins work on the opera *The Queen of Spades*.

JUNE–JULY Writes the string sextet *Souvenir de Florence*.

22 SEPTEMBER Nadezhda von Meck writes her last letter to Tchaikovsky, ending her patronage.

28 NOVEMBER Premiere of *Souvenir de Florence* in St Petersburg.

7 DECEMBER Premiere of *The Queen of Spades* in St Petersburg.

1891

FEBRUARY Starts work on the ballet *The Nutcracker*.

14 APRIL Arrives in New York at the start of his American tour.

23 APRIL Conducts his *Coronation March* at the opening concert of Carnegie Hall.

1892

FEBRUARY Completes work on *The Nutcracker*.

7 MARCH Conducts the premiere of *The Nutcracker Suite* in St Petersburg.

29 APRIL Moves into a house in Klin, the first home he has ever owned.

JUNE Visits Vichy with his nephew Bob.

6 DECEMBER Premiere of *The Nutcracker* at the Mariinsky Theatre in St Petersburg.

20 DECEMBER Visits the former family governess Fanny Dürbach in Montbéliard, France.

1893

12 JANUARY Arrives in Odessa to conduct a series of concerts of his own works; has his portrait painted by Nikolay Kuznetsov.

3 FEBRUARY Back at home in Klin, where he starts to sketch Symphony No. 6.

20 MAY Conducts Symphony No. 4 at a Royal Philharmonic Society concert in London.

31 MAY Conducts *Francesca da Rimini* at a concert in Cambridge.

1 JUNE Cambridge University awards him an Honorary Doctorate of Music.

18 JULY Back home in Klin he works on the Piano Concerto No. 3.

9 OCTOBER Travels to St Petersburg to conduct the premiere of Symphony No. 6.

16 OCTOBER Conducts the premiere of Symphony No. 6 in St Petersburg.

20 OCTOBER Dines out with friends at Leiner's restaurant on the Nevsky Prospekt.

21 OCTOBER Falls ill and a doctor is called, who diagnoses cholera.

25 OCTOBER Tchaikovsky dies at around 3 a.m.

26–27 OCTOBER Requiem services and tributes are held throughout Russia.

28 OCTOBER Tchaikovsky's funeral takes place in the Kazan Cathedral in St Petersburg. He is buried in the Alexander Nevsky Monastery in St Petersburg.

Adapted from en.tchaikovsky-research.net/pages/Chronology, and David Brown, Tchaikovsky Remembered.

SELECT BIBLIOGRAPHY

A note on sources

As will be evident from even a cursory reading of this book, it is not easy to get at the true facts behind Tchaikovsky's life. Censorship has reared its ugly head from all directions – from Tchaikovsky's formative adult years through to the present, and no doubt beyond.

In the first place, there is – understandably – self-censorship. From his earliest correspondence, Tchaikovsky rarely used direct language about his private life. Euphemisms, metaphors, vagueness and even deliberate misdirection abound, and given the risks involved, who can blame him? Similarly with his brother Modest, who was unable to be as candid as he wanted and he knew his brother deserved.

Then we have the heavy hand of Soviet censorship in the twentieth century to contend with. The voluminous correspondence between Tchaikovsky and Nadezhda von Meck is still being edited, and it is possible that the letters could be sanitised, to a greater or lesser degree, given the homophobic prejudice that still exists.

Unquestionably the most comprehensive biographer of Tchaikovsky, who has had more access to original source material than any other, is Alexander Poznansky. Born in the Soviet Union, he emigrated to the United States in 1977, where he is currently Slavic & East European Languages librarian at Yale University. No writer on Tchaikovsky can afford to ignore any of the many volumes Poznansky has himself written, or edited, on the composer, and he is one of the few, along with David Brown and Anthony Holden, to accord the life as much weight as the music. I am enormously grateful to him for permission to quote extensively from his publications and translations.

David Brown (1929–2014), a British musicologist, published the first of his four-volume account of Tchaikovsky's life and works in 1978. What began as a 20,000-word entry in the *New Grove Dictionary of Music and Musicians* became a single volume. That single volume became four, as 'Tchaikovsky himself took over', in Brown's own words. Recognising that this magisterial work was directed more at fellow professionals than amateur music lovers, in 2006 he published a single volume work, *Tchaikovsky: The Man and his Music*. This highly readable account, with more accessible description and musical analysis, achieves Brown's aim totally: to bring the life and music of Russia's greatest composer to a much wider audience of music lovers. By 2006 previously unseen archive material was in the public domain following the fall of the Soviet Union and he was able to cover the new theories on Tchaikovsky's demise. He reaches the conclusion, as did I, that we shall probably never know the true cause of death.

Anthony Holden's biography is a highly readable account of the composer's life, made all the more accessible in my view by the fact that he does not interrupt the narrative to analyse the music, weaving it instead into the story. Holden recounts the suicide theory in great detail, coming to the firm conclusion that Tchaikovsky took his own life. Holden's book was published in 1995, and the scholarship has moved on considerably since then. More archive material has been released, more books published – most notably by Poznansky, who disagrees with Holden's analysis. Agree or disagree, Holden's account is a thoroughly good read, as one would expect from an author, broadcaster and critic, rather than musicologist.

There follows a selected list of the works I have consulted:

Bagar, Robert, *Peter Ilyich Tchaikovsky, The Concert Companion: A Comprehensive Guide to Symphonic Music* (New York: McGraw-Hill Book Company, 1947)

Bowen, Catherine Drinker, *Free Artist* (Boston: Little Brown & Co., 1939)

Brown, David, *Tchaikovsky: A Biographical and Critical Study*; vol. 1: *The Early Years (1840–1874)* (London: Victor Gollancz, 1978) [Brown *EY*]; vol. 2: *The Crisis Years 1874–1878* (New York: Norton, 1983) [Brown *CY*]; vol. 3: The Years of Wandering 1878–1885 (New York: Norton, 1986) [Brown *YW*]; vol. 4: *The Final Years 1885–1893* (London: Victor Gollancz, 1991) [Brown *FY*]

Brown, David, *Tchaikovsky Remembered* (London: Faber and Faber, 1993) [Brown *TR*]

Brown, David, *Tchaikovsky: The Man And His Music* (London: Faber and Faber, 2006) [Brown *MHM*]

Fisher, Jennifer, *Nutcracker Nation: How an Old World Ballet Became a Christmas Tradition in the New World* (New Haven: Yale University Press, 2003)

Holden, Anthony, *Tchaikovsky: A Biography* (London: Bantam Press, 1995) [Holden]

Poznansky, Alexander, *Tchaikovsky: The Quest for the Inner Man* (London: Lime Tree, 1993) [Poznansky]

Poznansky, Alexander, *Tchaikovsky's Last Days* (Oxford: Oxford University Press, 1996) [Poznansky *TLD*]

Poznansky, Alexander, *Tchaikovsky Through Others' Eyes* (Bloomington: Indiana University Press, 1999) [Poznansky *TTOE*]

Rimsky-Korsakov, Nikolay, *My Musical Life* (Leipzig: Eulenburg Books, 1974)

Schonberg, Harold C., *The Great Pianists* (New York: Simon & Schuster, 1963)

Suchet, John, *Beethoven: The Man Revealed* (London: Elliott & Thompson 2012)

Suchet, John, *Mozart: The Man Revealed* (London: Elliott & Thompson, 2016)

Suchet, John, *Verdi: The Man Revealed* (London: Elliott & Thompson, 2017)

Tchaikovsky, Modest, *The Life and Letters of Peter Ilyich Tchaikovsky*, ed. with an introduction by Rosa Newmarch (John Lane The Bodley Head, 1906) [*MTLL*]

Tchaikovsky, Peter Ilich, *The Life and Letters of Peter Ilich Tchaikovsky*, trans. Rosa Newmarch (London: John Lane, 1906)

REFERENCES

Abbreviations used in references

Brown *CY*   David Brown, *Tchaikovsky: The Crisis Years, 1874–1878*

Brown *EY*   David Brown, *Tchaikovsky: The Early Years, 1840–1874*

Brown *FY*   David Brown, *Tchaikovsky: The Final Years, 1885–1893*

Brown *MHM*   David Brown, *Tchaikovsky: The Man and His Music*

Brown *TR*   David Brown, *Tchaikovsky Remembered*

Brown *YW*   David Brown, *Tchaikovsky: The Years of Wandering, 1878–1885*

CAM   Pyotr Ilyich Tchaikovsky, *Critical Articles on Music*

CCW   Pyotr Ilyich Tchaikovsky, *Complete Collected Works*

CNvM   Pyotr Ilyich Tchaikovsky, *Correspondence with Nadezhda von Meck (ed. Vladimir Zhdanov and Nikolai Zhegin)*

D   Pyotr Ilyich Tchaikovsky, *Diaries* (ed. P. I. Chaikovskii)

Holden   Anthony Holden, *Tchaikovsky: A Biography*

LHF   Pyotr Ilyich Tchaikovsky, *Letters to His Family*

LHR   Pyotr Ilyich Tchaikovsky, *Letters to His Relatives* (ed. Vladimir Zhdanov)

MTLL   Modest Tchaikovsky, *The Life and Letters of Peter Ilyich Tchaikovsky*

MTTL   Modest Tchaikovsky, *Tchaikovsky's Life*

Poznansky   Alexander Poznansky, *Tchaikovsky: The Quest for the Inner Man*

Poznansky *TLD*   Alexander Poznansky, *Tchaikovsky's Last Days*

Poznansky *TTOE*   Alexander Poznansky, *Tchaikovsky Through Others' Eyes*

RT   *Reminiscences of Tchaikovsky*

Quote p. iii

1   David Brown, *Tchaikovsky: The Man and His Music*, p. 209.

Prologue

1   Alexander Poznansky, *Tchaikovsky: The Quest for the Inner Man*, hereafter Poznansky, p. 573.

2   Ibid., p. 579.

3   Modest Tchaikovsky, *The Life and Letters of Peter Ilich Tchaikovsky*, trans. Rosa Newmarch, hereafter *MTLL*, p. 722.

4   Anthony Holden, *Tchaikovsky: A Biography*, hereafter Holden,

p. 356.

5   Ibid.

6   Ibid.; Yuri Davidov, *Tchaikovsky's Last Days*.

7   *MTLL*, p. 723.

8   Ibid., pp. 723–5.

1 • Pyotr, the Fledgling Seagull

1   Poznansky, p. 554; Pyotr Ilyich Tchaikovsky, *Complete Collected Works*, hereafter *CCW*.

2   David Brown, *Tchaikovsky: The Final Years 1885–1893*, hereafter Brown *FY*, p. 399; *CCW*; Modest Tchaikovsky, *Tchaikovsky's Life*, hereafter

MTTL; Pyotr Ilyich Tchaikovsky, *Letters to His Family*, hereafter *LHF*.

3   David Brown, *Tchaikovsky: The Man and His Music*, hereafter Brown *MHM*, p. 3.

4   *MTLL*, p. 6.

5   Ibid., p. 7.

6   Ibid.

7   Ibid.

8   Ibid., p. 8; Holden, p. 9; *MTTL*.

9   *MTLL*, pp. 8–9.

10   Holden, pp. 4–5; letter to Nadezhda von Meck, 21 February 1878.

11   *MTLL*, p. 12.

12 Ibid., pp.12–13.
13 Brown *MHM*, p. 7.
14 *MTLL*, p. 13.
15 Ibid., p. 14.
16 Holden, p. 6.
17 *MTLL*, p. 4.
18 Ibid.
19 Poznansky, p. 5; *MTTL*.
20 Ibid., p. 6; *MTTL*.
21 Brown *MHM*, p. 13.
22 Ibid., p. 212.
23 Ibid., p. 318.

2 • Upheavals and Loss
1 Poznansky, p. 8; *CCW*.
2 Ibid.; *MTTL*.
3 *MTLL*, p. 16.
4 Poznansky, p. 9; *MTTL*.
5 Ibid., p. 10; *MTTL*.
6 Holden, p. 13.

3 • An Unbearable Farewell
1 *MTLL*, p. 20.
2 Poznansky, p. 11; CCW.
3 *MTLL*, p. 20.
4 Ibid.
5 Poznansky, p. 12; *LHR*.
6 Ibid., pp. 12–13; *LHR*.
7 Ibid., p. 13; *MTTL*.
8 *MTLL*, p. 21.
9 Poznansky, p. 16; *MTTL*.
10 Holden, p. 20.
11 Poznansky, p. 57.
12 Ibid., p. 31.
13 Ibid., p. 32; Taneev, *Detstvo*, p. 148.

4 • Guilt and the Cruellest Loss
1 Tchaikovsky Research website, 'Modest Tchaikovsky', (en. tchaikovsky-research.net/pages/ Modest_Tchaikovsky#The_ Biographer).
2 Poznansky, p. 47; *MTLL*.
3 For this and the following quotations from Modest's autobiography relating to the relationship with Kireyev, see the Tchaikovsky Research website, 'Sergey Kireyev',

Alexander Poznansky (en. tchaikovsky-research.net/pages/ Sergey_Kireyev).
4 Poznansky, p. 47; Apukhtin, *Stikhotvoreniia*.
5 Ibid., p. 44.
6 Ibid., p. 45.
7 Holden, p. 199.
8 Poznansky, p. 46.
9 Holden, *Tchaikovsky*, p. 27, citing a Russian scholar who had seen the letter in which this appeared in the Tchaikovsky Archive at Klin, and who wished to remain anonymous.

5 • A Difficult Journey
1 Holden, p. 30; *MTTL*.
2 Poznansky, p. 53; *RT* (1962.
3 Poznansky, pp. 55–6; *MTTL*.
4 Ibid., p. 56, quoting Konstantin de Lazari.
5 Ibid.; citing *RT* (1962)..
6 Alexander Poznansky, *Tchaikovsky's Last Days*, hereafter Poznansky *TLD*, p. 10.
7 Ibid.
8 Poznansky, p. 57.
9 Poznansky, *TLD*, p. 10.
10 David Brown, *Tchaikovsky: The Early Years*, hereafter Brown *EY*, p. 54; *CCW*.
11 *MTLL*, p. 36.
12 Brown *EY*, p. 55; *CCW*.
13 *MTLL*, p. 37.
14 Brown *EY*, p. 55,; *CCW*.
15 Ibid.; *CCW*.
16 Ibid.; *CCW*.
17 Ibid.; *CCW*.
18 Ibid.; *CCW*.
19 Ibid.; *CCW*.
20 Brown *MHM*, p. 18.
21 Holden, p. 35.
22 Brown *EY*, p. 57; *CWW*.
23 Ibid.
24 Ibid.
25 Ibid., p. 57; *CWW*.

6 • Pyotr Chooses Music
1 *MTLL*, pp. 44–5.
2 Harold C. Schonberg, *The Great Pianists*
3 Catherine Drinker Bowen, *Free Artist*
4 Schonberg
5 Poznansky, pp. 63–4.
6 Ibid., p. 66.
7 Ibid., p. 67; *MTTL*.
8 Holden, p. 45.
9 Ibid., p. 46; *MTTL*.
10 Poznansky, p. 75; *LHR*.
11 Ibid., pp. 76–7; *LHR*.

7 • Tchaikovsky, Music Teacher
1 Holden, p. 52.
2 Ibid.
3 Ibid., p. 53.
4 *MTLL*, p. 64.
5 Ibid., p. 65.
6 Ibid., p. 70.
7 Poznansky, p. 89.
8 *MTLL*, p. 71.
9 Poznansky, p. 88; *LHR*.
10 Ibid.; *LHF*.
11 Ibid.; *LHR*.
12 Ibid., p. 86.
13 *MTLL*, p. 72.
14 Ibid., p. 73.
15 Holden, p. 57.

8 • The Ladies' Man
1 Poznansky, p. 97; *LHR*.
2 Ibid.; *LHR*.
3 Ibid., *LHR*.
4 Ibid., p. 102; *LHR*.
5 Brown *EY*, p. 122; *CCW*.
6 Holden, p. 61.

9 • A Most Unlikely Affair
1 Brown *MHM*, pp. 38–9.
2 Poznansky, p. 95; *MTTL*.
3 *MTLL*, p. 96.
4 Poznansky, p. 110; *MTTL*.
5 Ibid.; *LHR*.
6 Ibid.; *LHR*.
7 Ibid., p. 112; *LHR*.
8 Ibid.; *LHR*.
9 Ibid, p. 114; *LHR*.

10 Ibid., pp. 113–14; *LHR*.
11 Ibid., p. 116.
12 Ibid.; *LHR*.

10 • A Tragic Love
1 Holden, p. 74.
2 *MTLL*, p. 107.
3 Brown *EY*, p. 180; *CCW*.
4 Ibid., p. 181; Balakirev, *Perepiska*.
5 Ibid., p. 182; *CCW*.
6 Ibid., p. 184; Balakirev.
7 Nikolay Rimsky-Korsakov, *My Musical Life*.
8 Poznansky, p. 120.
9 Ibid.; *CCW*.
10 Ibid.; *CCW*.
11 Ibid.; *D*.

11 • The Lake of the Swans
1 Brown *MHM*, p. 59.
2 Holden, p. 81.
3 Poznansky, p. 139; Klimenko, *Moi vospominaniia*.
4 Ibid., p. 134; *MTTL*.
5 Holden, pp. 80–81.
6 Poznansky, p. 141; *LHR*.
7 Ibid., p. 131.
8 Ibid., p. 132.
9 Holden, p. 80.
10 Poznansky, p. 132; *CCW*.
11 Ibid., p. 133; *LHR*.
12 Ibid., p. 151.
13 Poznansky *TTOE*, p. 57.
14 David Brown, *Tchaikovsky Remembered*, hereafter Brown *TR*, pp. 31–3.
15 Holden, p. 83.
16 Ibid., pp. 83–4.
17 Poznansky, p. 156.

12 • Unexpected Inspiration
1 Holden, p. 88.
2 Poznansky, p. 155; Klimenko, *Moi vospominaniia*.
3 Ibid., p. 156; *LHR*.
4 Ibid.
5 Ibid.; *LHR*.
6 Holden, p. 89.
7 Ibid., p. 90.

8 Ibid., p. 91; letter to Nadezhda von Meck, 4 May 1878.
9 Ibid.
10 Ibid.
11 Ibid.
12 Brown *EY*, p. 305.
13 Poznansky, p. 159; *LHR*.

13 • Bending the Rules
1 *MTLL*, p. 176.
2 Ibid.
3 Poznansky, p. 161; *LHR*.
4 Holden, p. 96.
5 Brown *EY*, p. 310; *CCW*.
6 Ibid., p. 311.
7 Ibid.
8 Ibid., p. 313; *CCW*.

14 • Misery and Defiance
1 *MTLL*, p. 165.
2 Ibid., pp. 165–6.
3 Ibid., pp. 166.
4 Ibid.
5 Ibid., p. 167.
6 David Brown, *Tchaikovsky: The Crisis Years 1874–1878*, hereafter Brown *CR*, p. 19; *CCW*.
7 Steven Ledbetter, notes for Colorado Symphony Orchestra, www.coloradosymphony.org.
8 Brown CR, p. 19; *CAM*.
9 Ibid., p. 27; *LHR*.
10 Ibid., pp. 27–8; *LHR*.

15 • Swan Lake – and Failure
1 Brown *CR*, p. 42; *CCW*.
2 Ibid., p. 61; *CCW*.
3 Ibid., p. 58; *MTTL*.
4 Poznansky, p. 167; *LHR*.
5 *MTLL*, p. 382.
6 Brown *CY*, p. 42; *CCW*.
7 Ibid., p. 54.
8 Poznansky, p. 175; *LHR*.
9 *MTLL*, p. 201.
10 Brown *CY*, p. 70.

16 • In Love – and Alone
1 Poznansky, pp. 176–7; *LHR*.

2 J. P. E. Harper-Scott, 'Myths and Legends of Chopin and Tchaikovsky', *The Sunday Times*, 7 July 2010.
3 Brown *CY*, p. 90; *CCW*.
4 Ibid., pp. 92–3; *MTTL*.
5 Poznansky, p. 179; *LHR*.
6 Alexander Poznansky, 'Tchaikovsky: A Life', Tchaikovsky Research website (http://en.tchaikovsky-research.net/pages/Tchaikovsky:_A_Life).
7 Ibid.

17 • A Woman Enters His Life
1 Brown *MHM*, pp. 121–2.
2 Ibid., pp. 122–3.
3 Ibid., p. 123.
4 Poznansky, p. 197; *CNvM*.
5 Ibid., p. 198; *CNvM*.
6 Ibid., p. 198; *CNvM*.
7 Brown *CY*, p. 130; *CNvM*.
8 Ibid., pp. 130–31; *CNvM*.
9 Ibid., p. 134; *CNvM*.
10 Holden, p. 137.
11 Ibid., p. 138.
12 Ibid.
13 Ibid.
14 Ibid., p. 139.
15 Ibid., p. 140.
16 Ibid.

18 • 'She Is Repulsive to Me'
1 Brown *CY*, p. 139; *CNvM*.
2 Ibid., pp. 139–40; *CNvM*.
3 Ibid., p. 141; *CCW*.
4 Ibid., pp. 141–2; *CCW*.
5 Ibid, pp. 145–6; *CCW*.
6 Ibid., p. 146; *CCW*.
7 Ibid., p. 147; *LHR*.
8 Poznansky, p. 222; *LHR*.
9 Ibid.; *LHR*.
10 Holden, p. 148.
11 Ibid.
12 Ibid.
13 Brown, p. 147; *LHR*.
14 Ibid., p. 149; *CCW*.
15 Ibid., p. 150; *CCW*.
16 Holden, p. 149.

17 Ibid., pp. 149–50.
18 Ibid., p. 150.
19 'Antonina Tchaikovskaya',
   Tchaikovsky Research website
   (http://en.tchaikovsky-research.
   net/pages/Antonina_
   Tchaikovskaya).

19 • Fate
1 Poznansky *TLD*, p. 13.
2 Ibid., p. 16.
3 Ibid., p. 21.
4 Poznansky, p. 243; *CNvM*.
5 Ibid., p. 248; *CNvM*.
6 Ibid., p. 249; *CNvM*.
7 Brown *CY*, p. 143.
8 Ibid., p. 167.
9 Ibid., p. 165.
10 Ibid.; *CCW*.
11 Ibid, p. 166; *CCW*.
12 Ibid.; *CCW*.
13 Ibid., pp. 166–7; *CNvM*.
14 Ibid., p. 160; *CNvM*.

20 • 'It Stinks to the Ear'
1 Brown *CY*, p. 244; *CCW*.
2 Brown *MHM,* p. 175.
3 Poznansky, p. 265; *LHR*.
4 Brown *MHM*, p. 176.
5 Poznansky, p. 267.
6 Brown *MHM*, p. 172.
7 Holden, p. 173.
8 Poznansky, p. 297.
9 Poznansky, p. 253; *LHR*.
10 Ibid.
11 Ibid., pp. 296–7; *LHR*.
12 Brown *CY*, p. 261; *CCW*.
13 Eduard Hanslick, *Music
   Criticism 1846–99*, trans. and
   ed. Henry Pleasants, pp.302–3.

21 • A Sort of Freedom
1 Brown *CY*, p. 271; *CNvM*.
2 Ibid., p. 272; *CNvM*.
3 Ibid., p. 274.
4 Poznansky, p. 298; *LHR*.
5 Ibid. p. 299; *CNvM*.
6 Ibid., p. 300; *CNvM*.
7 Ibid., p. 301; *LHR*.
8 Ibid., p. 305; *CNvM*.

9 Ibid.; *LHR*.
10 Brown *CY*, p. 295; *CCW*.
11 Poznansky, p. 307; *LHR*.
12 Ibid., p. 318; *LHR*.
13 Brown *CY*, pp. 297–8; *CNvM*.
14 Ibid., p. 298; *CNvM*.

22 • The Boulevardier
1 Poznansky, pp. 314–15;
   CNvM.
2 Ibid., p. 316; *LHR*.
3 Holden, pp. 184–5.
4 Poznansky, p. 325; *LHR*.
5 Holden, p. 186.
6 Poznansky, p. 325.
7 Brown *MHM*, pp. 194–5.
8 Poznansky, p. 329; *CNvM*.
9 Holden, pp. 188–9.
10 Ibid., p. 189.
11 Ibid.
12 Poznansky, pp. 344–5; *LHR*.
13 Ibid., p. 345; *CNvM*.

23 • An Impenetrable Secret
1 Brown *MHM*, p. 207.
2 Ibid.
3 Ibid., p. 209.
4 Ibid., p. 210.
5 Ibid., p. 209.
6 Poznansky, p. 359; *CCW*.
7 Poznansky, pp. 259–60; *CCW*.
8 Ibid., p. 380; *CNvM*.
9 David Brown, *Tchaikovsky: The
   Years of Wandering 1878–1885*,
   hereafter Brown *YW*, p. 120;
   CCW.

24 • A Family Crisis
1 Poznansky, p. 414; *CCW*.
2 Ibid.; *CCW*.
3 Ibid. p. 422; *CCW*.
4 Holden, p. 227.
5 Poznansky.; *CNvM*.

25 • A Benefactor Bids 'Adieu'
1 Poznansky, pp. 432–3; *CnvM*.
2 Ibid., p. 451; *CNvM*.
3 Ibid.
4 Ibid., p. 462; *CCW*
5 Ibid., p. 461; *D*.

6 Ibid p. 462; *CCW*.
7 Ibid., p. 512; *CNvM*.
8 Ibid., p. 515; *CNvM*.
9 'Vladimir Davydov',
   Tchaikovsky Research website
   (http://en.tchaikovsky-research.
   net/pages/Vladimir_Davydov).

26 • On Tour and Unhappy
1 Poznansky, p. 495; *CNvM*.
2 Ibid., p. 485; *CCW*.
3 Ibid., p. 505; *D*.
4 Ibid., p. 533; *D*.
5 Ibid., p. 532; *CCW*.
6 Ibid., p. 533.
7 Ibid., p. 534; *CCW*.
8 Brown *FY*, p. 383; *CCW*.
9 Ibid., p. 384; *CCW*.
10 Jennifer Fisher, *Nutcracker
   Nation*, p. 17.

27 • A Musical 'Adieu'?
1 Brown *FY*, p. 402; *CCW*.
2 'Nikolay Kuznetsov',
   Tchaikovsky Research website
   (http://en.tchaikovsky-research.
   net/pages/Nikolay_Kuznetsov).
3 Robert Bagar, *Peter Ilyich
   Tchaikovsky, The Concert
   Companion*, p. 754.

Postscript
1 Brown *FY*, p. 486.
2 Brown *MHM*, p. 435.
3 'Adele aus der Ohe',
   Tchaikovsky Research (http://
   en.tchaikovsky-research.net/
   pages/Adele_aus_der_Ohe).
4 Poznansky, p. 611; *RT*.
5 Ibid., p. 205.
6 'Vladimir Davydov',
   Tchaikovsky Research (http://
   en.tchaikovsky-research.net/
   pages/Vladimir_Davydov).

Afterword
1 Museum-estate of P.I.
   Tchaikovsky, Votkinsk, *A
   Journal of Happy Memories*.
2 Holden, pp. 374–5.

INDEX

Acknowledgements

When I began presenting the flagship morning programme on Classic FM back in 2011, I intended to write a single composer biography, 'Beethoven: The Man Revealed'. That was published in 2012. In the intervening years I have published four more, on Johann Strauss II, Mozart, Verdi, and now Tchaikovsky, thanks to the encouragement of the former Managing Director of Classic FM Darren Henley, and his successor, Managing Editor Sam Jackson.

It is my good fortune that Classic FM's publisher of choice during this whole period has been Elliott & Thompson. A small independent publisher, they pride themselves on producing books that look good, feel good, and above all are a good read. This means editors and designers at the top of their game, and I am indebted to each of them, all names familiar from my previous books. This consistency has led to a collection of books that complement each other, that stand as a set.

Director and commissioning editor has been Olivia Bays, whose advice has been offered – and accepted – at every stage. Pippa Crane, senior editor, was also involved in editing, and once again sourced all the illustrations. Jill Burrows was copy editor and Anna Herve proofread the finished product. I never cease to marvel at how no inconsistency, however small, escapes unnoticed. The finished product is incomparably better than it would have been without the careful attention of each of them.

This book looks as handsome as it does, and matches the others so well, thanks to Tash Webber, who again designed the cover, and James Collins, who again designed the pages.

My gratitude to 'my team' is boundless, and I hope I may be forgiven for feeling a considerable amount of pride in seeing the five books alongside each other on my shelf.

Picture Credits

CLASSIC *f*M

Classic FM is the UK's most popular classical music brand, reaching 5.6 million listeners every week. Classic FM's programmes are hosted by a mix of classical music experts and household names including John Suchet, Alexander Armstrong, Myleene Klass, Bill Turnbull, Alan Titchmarsh, Charlotte Hawkins, Aled Jones, Margherita Taylor and Nicholas Owen. Since its launch in 1992, Classic FM has aimed to make classical music accessible and relevant to everyone and in doing so, introduce an entirely new audience to the genre. ClassicFM.com is the UK's biggest classical music website and has 1.8 million unique monthly web and app users. Owned by Global, the media and entertainment group, Classic FM is available across the UK on 100-102 FM, DAB digital radio and TV, the Classic FM app, at ClassicFM.com and on the Global Player.

Source: RAJAR/Ipsos-MORI/RSMB, period ending 1 April 2018.